Tom Weaver presents the SCRIPTS FROM THE CRYPT collection

No. 7

BORIS KARLOFF'S

The Veil

FRANK P. BIBAS'
TALES of the
UNEXPLAINABLE

by **Barbara Bibas Montero, Tom Weaver** and **Dr. Robert J. Kiss**

The Veil
© 2017 Tom Weaver. All Rights Reserved.
No part of this book may be reproduced in any form or by any means, electronic, mechanical, digital, photocopying or recording, except for the inclusion in a review, without permission in writing from the publisher.

Published in the USA by:
BearManor Media
P. O. Box 71426
Albany, GA 31708
www.bearmanormedia.com

ISBN 978-1-62933-166-9

Printed in the United States of America.
Book design by Robbie Adkins, www.adkinsconsult.com
Front cover design by Marty Baumann
Back cover design by Bunky Runser

Dedicated to Frank P. Bibas (1917-1997), creator of *The Veil*

... and to Ned Comstock.

Table of Contents

Introduction by Boris Karloff 1

"Behind the Veil" by Barbara Bibas Montero 3

***The Veil*: Production History and Episode Guide** by Tom Weaver 13

***Veil* Scripts:** "A Chapter of Genesis," "No Food on the Table" and 61
"The Return of Mme. Vernoy"

Appendix 1: Additional Scripts Un*Veil*ed! by Tom Weaver 181

Appendix 2: "The Monster Was Very, Very Good to Me" by Martin Varno . 189

Appendix 3: "The Downs and Ups of Boris Karloff as 193
Television Series Host" by Dr. Robert J. Kiss

Appendix 4: "I Wish He Were My Grandfather" 225
by Tom Weaver

Appendix 5: Karloff and the Kritters 239

Appendix 6: The Niece of Frankenstein 245

Appendix 7: "The Vestris" by Robert Dale Owen 249

Appendix 8: A Karloff Kavalcade 253

Endnotes 262

Acknowledgments

Many sincere thanks to John Antosiewicz, Marty Baumann, Frank Bibas Jr., Ronald V. Borst, Ryan Brennan, John Brunas, Mike Brunas, Keith Call, Jim Clatterbaugh, Ned Comstock, the Classic Horror Film Board's "Dugan," Patrick Gatov, Ron Hagerthy, Boyd Magers, Leonard Maltin, Mark Martucci, Dave McDonnell, Mike Nevins, Jennifer Nichols, Maurice Daniel Pinkey, Rick Pruitt, Chris Ed Rock, Alan K. Rode, Mary Runser, David Schecter, Rich Scrivani, Scott Skelton, Jo Swerling Jr., Tony Travis, HL Tyler, Laura Wagner, Lucy Chase Williams and Wade Williams.

And, now behind the Veil, Eve Brent, Booth Colman, Arthur Hiller, Paul Landres, Tom Neal Jr., Aubrey Schenck, Herbert L. Strock, Martin Varno and Mike Vraney.

Extra-special thanks to Frederick Rappaport, who did an above-and-beyond job of providing frame grabs from episodes of *The Veil*. Surely stills were taken on the *Veil* sets – in fact, I *know* they were, because a still photographer named Stax Graves is listed in some of the production paperwork. But I've never seen a *Veil* still in my life. Since the Hal Roach Studios went kaput when *The Veil* was in midstream, perhaps not one was ever printed.

Introduction
By Boris Karloff

> In November 1958, while "Inside Television" columnist Eve Starr vacationed, a variety of celebrities pinch-hit for her: from Jackie Gleason, Mickey Rooney and Red Buttons to Tristram Coffin, Barbara Billingsley and Ann B. Davis. Some (most?) just touted their own TV shows. Boris Karloff tried to fire-up his base for *The Veil* on November 24:

During the past few weeks I have renewed proof that nothing is more challenging to human curiosity than the veiled revelation of truths beyond tangibility.

Since starting my new television series, *The Veil*, for Hal Roach Jr., I've been asked countless times what kind of shockers these are that I'm coming up with this time.

Until the series is released, probably this spring, when the public will be able to see for itself, I can only say *The Veil* is an anthology of authenticated true stories that couldn't have happened—yet they did!

All the stories are vouched for in every respect by the highest, most reliable authorities, but we don't attempt any explanation of the bizarre, offbeat facts they bring to light.

Of course, I find myself constantly having to point out that they're not "horror" stories. I object to that word "horror" in connection with any of the plays, films or television shows I've done in my long career.

Horror suggests repugnance … disgust … revulsion. The idea back of my portrayals has often been to make your hair stand on end — but never to make you lose your dinner!

Many years ago, after I played the Frankenstein Monster (and I did that in only three pictures), my fan mail justified my insistence that these were not horror pictures. Even when children wrote to me – as they did in droves – they all express great compassion for the Monster.

The sympathetic reaction has always been a source of much satisfaction to me, and I got it by following a cardinal rule of the theater.

If you want to get sympathy in a part—play against it. Don't ask for it. Self-pity begets no sympathy in the theater any more than it does in real life.

The stories we're doing for TV are in themselves exciting, unusual and sometimes hair-raising, but never horrifying. For the first time in my life I'm acting as narrator and host of an entire series, and I find that along with appearing in most of the stories, this entails an astonishing amount of hard work. But then, we actors carry on so about how hard we work. With all my narrating, hosting and acting, I don't actually have to work as hard as the director and cameraman. After all, they are, in a manner of speaking, in every scene. No actor gets very far without the director's guiding hand. A performer must yield final authority to someone outside himself, and that someone is the director, whose perspective isn't impaired by the kind of personal involvement which affects the actor.

A coincidence almost weird enough to rate a place of its own in our series came up the other day when I learned that one of the stories we're going to do for *The Veil* is a tale I first heard when I was a lad of 19 in London.

An 80-year-old family friend who had lived in Jamaica told it as a true story, which I immediately rejected on the grounds that it was utterly incredible. He sent me to the British Museum to do some research on it, and there I found complete documentation with testimony from the Governor of Jamaica on down, verifying every impossible happening that could only be recorded, but never explained.

I remember wishing at the time that I could bring this fascinating story to the attention of the world. Now — more than a half a century later, I shall be doing just that in *The Veil*.

Behind the Veil
By Barbara Bibas Montero

> *Good evening, I am going to tell you another strange and unusual story of the unexplainable, which lies behind the veil...*
> – Boris Karloff

My father Frank P. Bibas, who by profession was a film director and producer, always had an interest in the paranormal. When I was young, he used to tell stories about Houdini, another paranormal enthusiast. Houdini made a pact with his wife that whoever should die first would come back and make contact through a secret code. His wife never was able to connect with Houdini's spirit after he died even though she tried for a decade.

Frank P. Bibas (right) behind a camera.

Because of Dad's interest, he created, wrote, produced and directed a television series in 1958 entitled *The Veil*. It was based on actual case studies of paranormal occurrences: people being contacted by ghosts from the other side, etc. Boris Karloff hosted and starred in each episode, which was presented in a mysterious, chilling manner with eerie music.

Unfortunately, Hal Roach Studios, where Dad produced eight episodes of this TV series, got into financial trouble at a point when only ten episodes of *The Veil* had been made. Once the studio went under, Dad could never claim his work since he had been an employee of the studio with no ownership rights. The series remained in receivership for years. I recall family stories about how, after making his last *Veil*, my now unemployed father had to pack up and drive across country from California with my mother Susan, infant brother Frank Jr., family dog Jocko and three-year-old me in tow because he couldn't even afford plane tickets back to New York.

Dad's attraction to paranormal stories seemed to be the start of a trend for TV. Shortly after *The Veil* was produced, other series such as *One Step Beyond* and *The Twilight Zone* popped up and remained successful for a long time. *The Twilight Zone*, of course, were fictional stories, unlike my father's tales which were true and authenticated.

Even though Dad was frustrated with the loss of *The Veil*, he did lead a full life and had an exciting career making films and videos. His career started in advertising working for McCann Erickson (he was a true Mad Man). He produced over 3000 commercials for television and radio, for products including Ajax, Ford, Nabisco and Hertz Rent a Car. His greatest achievement was winning the Academy Award for best documentary short subject. His film *Project Hope* (1961) was initially commissioned by the Kennedy administration and is available for viewing on the Project Hope website.[1]

Even with all the successes he had in his career and personal life, I know *The Veil* was unfinished business for him. He tried to resuscitate it several times since he had access to a few episodes, but to no a-*veil*. While I

An airplane view of the Hal Roach Studios in Culver City. According to the original caption, "The thoroughfare in the foreground is famous Washington Blvd. ...At the extreme right of the picture is 'Our Gang Inn,' the studio commissary which is also popular with the public. In the center foreground is the administration building, housing the general offices and the writing department. In the extreme background is a street scene which has been used in many Hal Roach-MGM comedies. To the left is seen one of the largest sound stages in the film capital. It was on this stage that *Babes in Toyland* and many other lavish feature spectacles were filmed. Outlying buildings to the rear include the mill, carpenter shop, painting shop, film vaults, blacksmithing shop, garages and other mechanical departments." (Photo courtesy Leonard Maltin)

The day was glorious and the water crystal clear. A man, perhaps in his late seventies, began conversing with the girls while they were splashing around. He showed them some live conch shells and took an interest in them even though he was there with his wife and his own grandson.

While I was basking in the sun watching from afar, it dawned on me that this was the first Father's Day without him and I was on his favorite beach. Suddenly, I felt his presence.

Then the elderly gentleman approached me to say how proud I should be of my two girls. He said they were delightful and beautiful, and while one was very smart, the other had a devilish twinkle in her eyes. I knew he meant these comments endearingly and I was impressed that he had captured their essences in such a short time. I asked him if he was vacationing, and he said that he lived full-time in a gated community two towns away. It happened to be the same place where my father had lived, but they had never known each other. There was an energy about him that reminded me of my father, particularly his voice and demeanor, and also his grandfatherly connection to the girls.

was living in Spain, I tried to help him and pitched it to a few Spanish TV stations. At the time, there was a need for more programming because more stations were being added. However, the Ministry of Culture was only interested in increasing national programming in an attempt to control the oversaturation of American-made films.

In October 1997, Dad succumbed to prostate cancer. What a year - both my husband and I lost the last of two generations in our families. No more grandparents and no more parents. We were now middle-aged orphans.

But what was to follow was something out of *The Veil*. A few months after his death, Dad began to make himself known from the other side. Houdini had promised to come back, which never transpired, but now Dad seemed to be creating his own *Veil* episode!

It started on Father's Day, eight months after my father's departure. I was at Barefoot Beach in Bonita Springs, Florida, with my daughters Jenna and Kylie.

A few weeks later, a front-page article in a local newspaper caught my eye on the rack at the supermarket. It was about a local video producer who had had an unusual experience with a well-known psychic medium from New York. This medium, John Edwards, could communicate with people on the other side and pass helpful messages to their living loved ones. My initial interest in the article was to connect with the video producer to collaborate on a few of my marketing projects. However, I have to admit, the "other side" part of it was intriguing, since I had been thinking a lot about my father. The girls and I had started dreaming about him with more frequency. In these unusually vivid dreams, he looked much younger and did amusing, playful things.

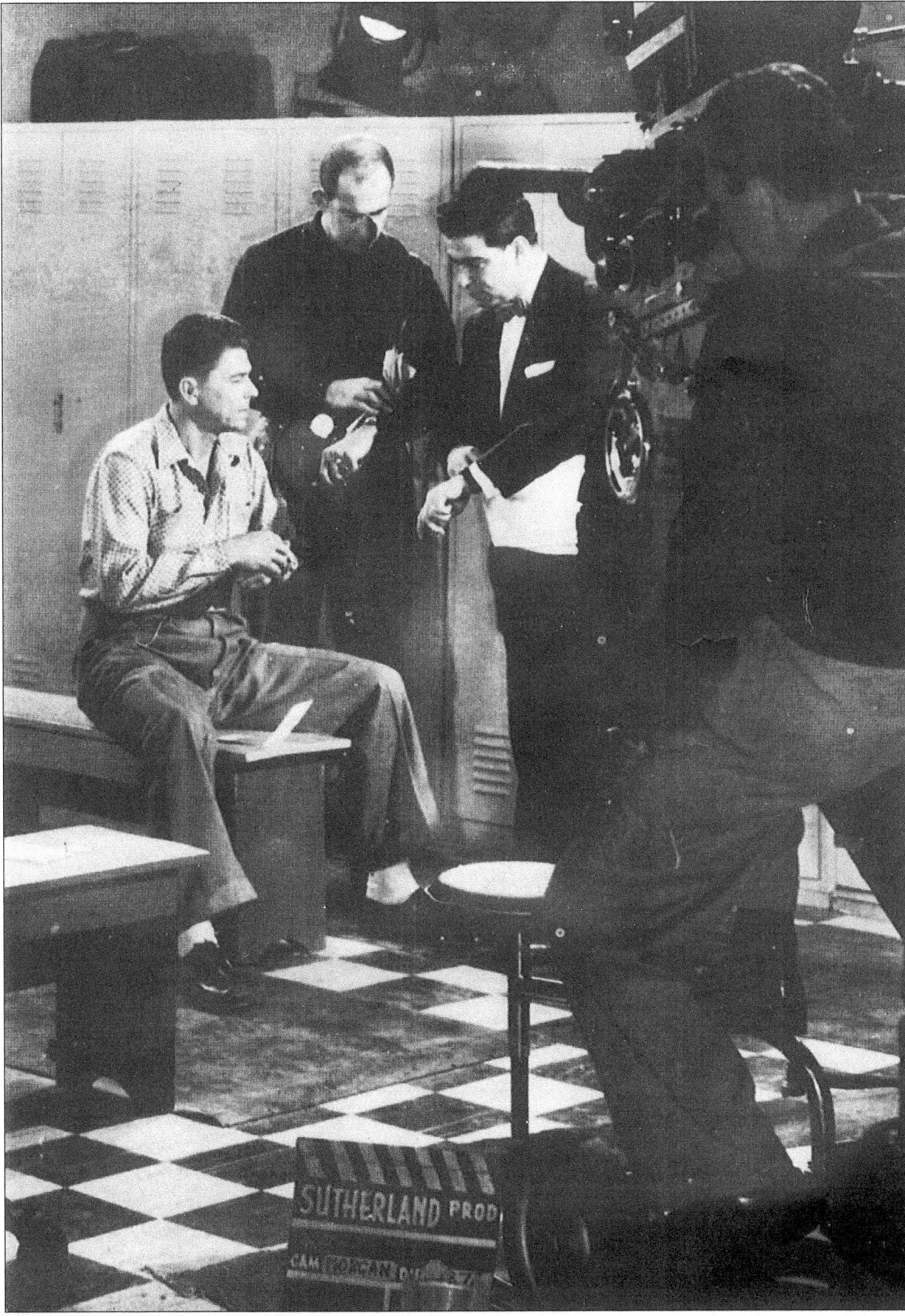
Ronald Reagan is directed by Bibas in a watch commercial.

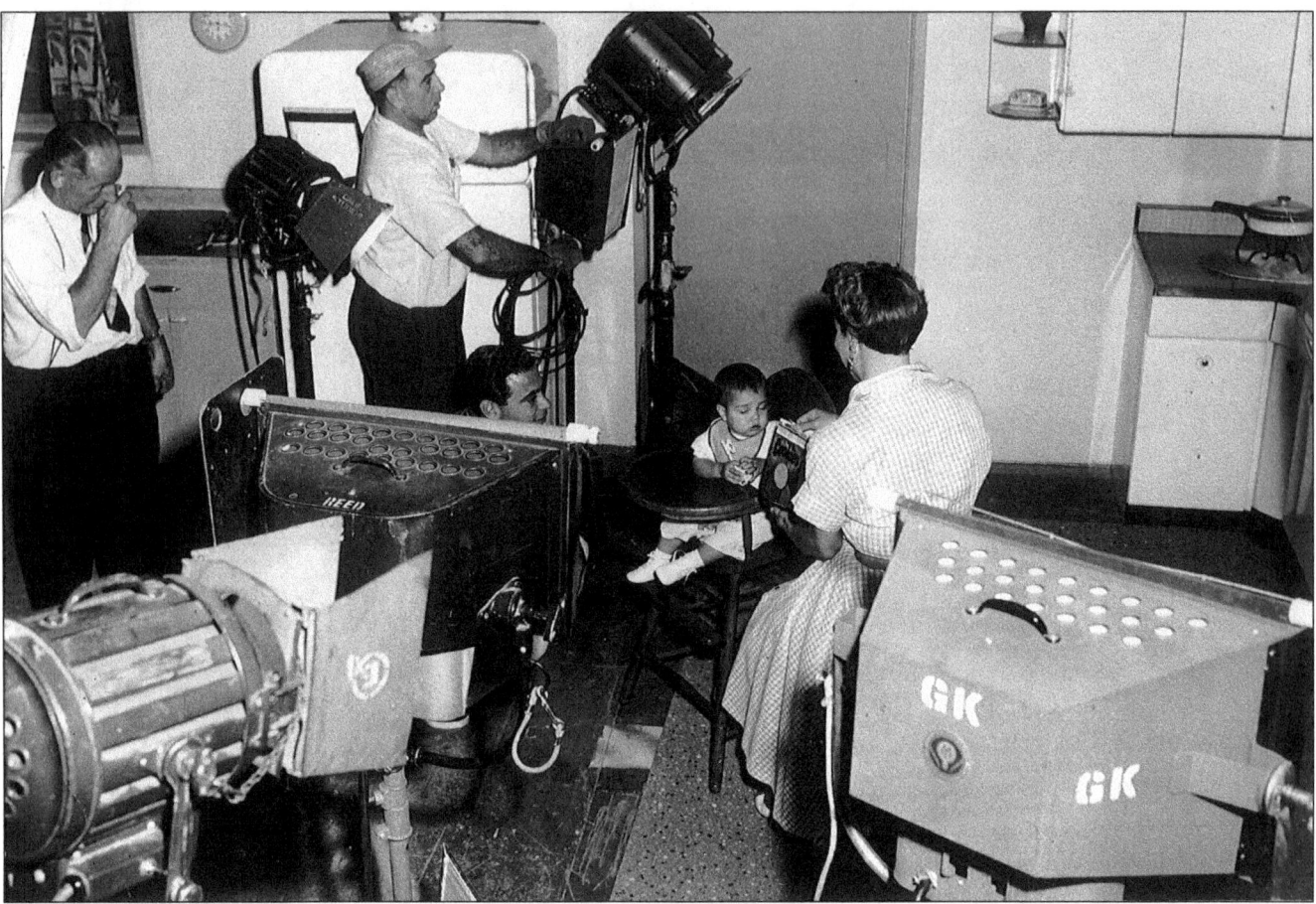
Bibas directs daughter Barbara in a cookie commercial.

I met with the video producer, who told me the story of how strange and coincidental his project was with John Edwards. He said he didn't believe in this sort of thing, but felt compelled to approach Edwards at a seminar to offer his services. Edwards psychically knew they would be working together even though they had never met. The two spent the next six months producing a set of videos showing how to connect with people on the other side and receive messages. They sent the videos to Larry King and, shortly thereafter, Edwards was invited to be a guest on King's show. It was a major success. The show was inundated with callers asking questions of Edwards, and as a result, he was asked back on the show many times.

The videotapes they produced consisted of footage of Edwards' workshops and showed him providing incredibly accurate information about people whom he couldn't possibly have known. One tape was an instructional video on how to read the symbols and signals that your loved ones send from the other side. Apparently they hide things or play around with electronics, light bulbs, machinery and telephones. Ever notice how, without warning, a radio, television or telephone goes haywire and then for no apparent reason starts to work again? According to Edwards, it could be a relative fooling around or trying to get your attention. Our loved ones also come to us vividly in our dreams. Well, this seemed to be happening with my father. His contact with me started to intensify and those vivid dreams with meaningful messages increased.

One night, my sister Bonnie called me around midnight to share an unusual experience she'd just had. Bonnie was seeking some advice concerning her personal life and an employee from her office, who was also a professional intuitive, offered to give her an afterhours psychic reading at her (the psychic's) home. In the middle of the reading, Dad's spirit barged in to make his presence known. He was accompanied by my mother and my uncle, but his energy was so strong, he overpowered the other two. Apparently Bonnie and the psychic had quite an evening with Dad's antics: He sent airplanes and helicopters over the house to insure that everyone knew he was there. The psychic's home was never on any flight paths. The woman's dog barked hysterically and ran around the room chasing *some*thing throughout the reading. The psychic was becoming more and more agitated because Dad was interrupting with comments and instructions on how she

Director and producer of the 1961 documentary short subject *Project Hope,* Bibas received an Academy Award. By his side is his wife Susan, eight months pregnant with their son John.

Frank P. Bibas at work on various projects.

should wear her hair and what to say and do. He told her that Bonnie needed to tell me to call the psychic in the morning so that I could hear what he wanted to say. Dad was determined to get messages to me even though he was rudely invading Bonnie's reading and the psychic's personal space.

As instructed, I called the psychic the next morning. She was exhausted, and asked if I could hear the commotion. And yes indeed, I could. The dog was still barking, and I could hear what sounded like low-flying airplanes and helicopters around her house. All night long, she had been kept awake by this noise. Dad had essentially moved in with her and instructed her to watch a Danish movie on television at two a.m., *Smilla's Sense of Snow* (1997). She didn't understand the film. His message to me was that it was imperative that I watch that same movie.

The thoroughly exhausted psychic had to get ready for work and asked me to call her at lunchtime to continue the conversation. Unfortunately, it was the last time I ever talked with her. She quit her job that day and never returned my sister's numerous phone calls.

My connection with Dad was now left in limbo and I could feel he was frustrated (he wasn't the most patient man in real life) because he still had more to tell me. I decided to call a woman known in town as an intuitive past life reader and ask her for help. As we were scheduling an appointment, the phone line started crackling loudly. She said, yes indeed, my father was a strong-willed soul and that the crackling was him barging in on our conversation. She decided to teach him some patience and made him wait a week for the reading. She also explained that the previous psychic had not learned to establish her boundaries, so Dad essentially took over her house and yes, she had flipped out. That explains why she quit her job and wouldn't return calls.

After the call, I was amazed at how crazy this all was – I found myself talking to Dad (actually to the air) and laughing at him and his antics. First, I berated him for bothering the poor woman and messing with her. Then I assured him that one way or another, I would make sure his message to me was heard. Immediately following that thought, something on the living room floor caught my eye. It was a small "Happy Face" sticker. I burst out laughing. You see, the Happy Face was Dad's hallmark. He signed every letter and greeting card with a happy face next to his name. He stuck it on all fan switches in his house to differentiate them from regular

light switches. And here it was, on my living room floor, as if he were signaling to me that he was relieved and happy about my promise.

To this day, when I see a Happy Face, I think of him. Sometimes it's the other way around – I think of him and then immediately I find a Happy Face sticker on the floor.

Throughout the week to follow, as my dad and I waited patiently for the appointment, airplanes and helicopters circled the house. One helicopter hovered outside my large living room window for about three minutes – I could see the pilot's face! Mind you, my house was not on any flight path, and helicopters had never flown over our house so frequently before. This is exactly what happened to the other psychic when my father "moved in" with her. Here he was again. Dad had been a pilot during the Second World War. He flew 106 missions, including D-Day, so flying was a passion for him and a meaningful symbol from the other side.

According to bestselling author James Van Praagh, the clairvoyant and spiritual medium, departed loved

During World War II, Bibas' cocker spaniel General Hap accompanied him on every flight mission.

ones often try to connect with us; we only have to be open and aware of the signs. He wrote that one way they communicate is via butterflies, dragonflies and birds: "Your loved one may have sent a winged messenger from the other side as a sign that they are always by your side." Dad sent planes and helicopters! Other ways mentioned in Van Praagh's inspirational 2015 article

"10 Signs the Dead Are Communicating with You":

- rainbows that appear after you have asked for a sign from your loved one;
- meaningful numbers (your loved one's birth date or date of passing) on sales receipts, food checks, etc.;
- unexplained aromas that you connect with the departed (their favorite flower, perfume, even cigar or pipe smoke);
- seeing someone who looks like your loved one when you've been thinking about them.

Yet more signs listed in the Van Praagh article appear in the sidebar below.

Common Ways the Spirit World Connects with You

Dream Visits: The dead often speak to us, clearly and vividly, in our dreams. There is nothing frightening about these visits—they are a wonderful way for the departed to spend time with you, providing guidance and support.

Visions: You might see a loved one or pet in the room, or in your mind's eye, when you are fully awake. They may look transparent, semi-transparent, whitish or in full color. A vision might come in the form of a loved one's face in the mirror, a window, or even briefly superimposed on another person's face!

Sounds and Music: A sure sign from beyond is hearing your loved one's voice calling your name either "internally" inside of your head or "externally." You might even hear a voice warning you of something. Music is a sign, too. Musical signs can come in the form of a meaningful song being played in your head or a song being played on the radio at an opportune time that is very meaningful to you.

Sensing a Presence: Sensing a strong or heavy energy presence in the room or a breeze going by you can be a sign that a spirit is reaching out to you. Some people feel a sensation of love and peace, a sudden weight on the bed, or wake up at the exact time that a loved one has passed.

– from James Van Praagh's 2015 article "10 Signs the Dead Are Communicating with You." Google and read the full article on the website healyourlife.com

Another Dad symbol was frogs. They frequently appeared on our windows or on my car after my father's passing. One in particular liked to hang out by our front door looking through the window at us. He was a big fellow and liked to be there on special occasions like birthdays and Christmas Day, or when there was an upset in the house, as if he was there to comfort us.

One time toward the end of Dad's life, he was at a doctor's office and he noticed on the wall a framed picture of a crane trying to swallow a frog. The frog, in the meantime, is clutching the bird's throat, choking it, and thus preventing himself from being swallowed. The caption read **NEVER GIVE UP!** Dad was moved by this picture since he had his own health issues; he made a photocopy of the picture and asked me to make a painting of it for him. It was the last painting I painted for him after many I had given to him throughout the years. The frog in the picture was his symbol of survival: He never gave up. I suppose that by Dad sending in the frogs, I would know that I shouldn't either.

Finally the day for the psychic reading arrived. The hour-long session was conducted by telephone and the line didn't crackle once. Essentially, Dad was excited about showing me what it was like on the other side. He was having fun exhibiting his new talents. The movie he wanted me to watch, *Smilla's Sense of Snow*, would show me that I should be aware of my own intuitive-psychic self. He said that I should develop this and be discerning as I discover more about the true reality and, like the frog, I should never give up. In the movie, a father helps his highly intuitive daughter uncover a mystery to help the planet.

The psychic suggested I pace myself with all this information – it would be spiritual aerobics. I was amazed how strongly Dad was coming through to tell me all this. Even my dreams were reflecting these messages. For instance, I dreamt he (a much younger version of himself) and I would be accomplishing missions and helping people together. It was as if he were on the sidelines doing jumping jacks to get my attention and rooting me on. He really made me laugh.

From time to time, I was approached on the street by other psychics, unsolicited, and they would say things like, "Your father wanted me to tell you…," and the message would be so personal that the person couldn't possibly have known the information on their own.

A few months later, my husband Manuel and I were watching *Larry King Live*. Again John Edwards was the guest and he was taking calls from viewers. We thought it would be a kick to phone in to see if Dad would come through. I put out a cosmic message to him and then phoned. Unfortunately, we couldn't get through, but we continued watching. Edwards was connecting with each caller with amazing accuracy. Then a caller from Denmark asked about his relative and Edwards said that he was getting pilot symbols. Edwards asked if his relative was a pilot. The man paused and said no, that he had no pilots in his family. Edwards insisted that a pilot was coming through and apologized to the caller. Manuel and I looked at each other and laughed. We both felt that Dad had once again barged his way through.

At the end of October 1998, my brother Frank Jr. called from California to tell me that a writer from New York had emailed him. This writer wanted to do an article on our father and the television series he had created in 1958: *The Veil*.

Since I was the keeper of the family records, and had some information on the series in Dad's files, Frank Jr. gave the writer my number. Tom Weaver called and informed me that a company called Something Weird Video had discovered prints of the original *Veil* episodes in a going-out-of-business warehouse and had put them on video and was selling them as a three-tape (VHS) set. Tom had seen it advertised in a magazine and wanted to write about the series, and asked to interview me. He was a wealth of information about the series and knew many details I had no idea about, since I was so young when it was happening.

After the interview, I called Something Weird and had a pleasant conversation with one of the employees. Upon hearing that I was the daughter of the creator of *The Veil*, she kindly sent me the video set at no charge. When they arrived, I watched all of them. Some of the stories were tucked away in my early childhood memory banks, others I didn't remember at all. Dad was the producer of all but one of the episodes in this set, and he directed one.

When Tom was finishing up his article, he asked me to help him write the closing paragraph. This is what we came up with:

> Barbara Bibas believes her father would be pleased to know that *The Veil* has resurfaced. "It must have been frustrating for him to work hard on the series only to have it never get farther than a dusty old basement at Movielab," Barbara said. "Where it ended up certainly wasn't intended, but at least something good came out of it – a three-tape video set and this very informative article. He's probably smiling about this up in Heaven…or, who knows, behind that veil!"

Incidentally, upon learning the date of Dad's death (October 16, 1997), Tom pointed out to me that it was exactly one year to the day later (October 16, 1998) that he had gotten the idea to write an article on *The Veil* and began to search for my father. Did Dad strike again?

Again, all the *Veil* episodes were true stories about people having paranormal experiences. The veil is thin and this was exactly what Dad was trying to show me. It seemed as though he wanted me to peek through this veil and share the truths he had found and I had forgotten. I came to the realization that he was actually creating his own episode of *The Veil* … the eleventh one, where he is the protagonist. *The Veil* continues.

Now, 20 years later, oddly enough, Tom and I have reconnected and the saga of *The Veil* continues. I happened to acquire some of the original *Veil* scripts from an Amazon book dealer and reached out to Tom to see if there was anything we could do with them. It so happened that Tom was in the midst of putting out a series of books called "Scripts from the Crypt" and was trying to decide what movie or TV series to spotlight as the seventh in this series. So when I called him out of the blue and told him I had these scripts, he told me that between my scripts and material that he could provide, we could make *The Veil* the seventh "Scripts from the Crypt." The timing was uncanny. *The Veil* strikes again.

So what's next? Maybe remakes of the original scripts? Maybe new episodes? Or even a new story based on the chains of events described in this intro? Whatever the future holds … as Mr. Karloff ends each episode, it will be "another journey into the world of the unexplainable, which lies somewhere behind the veil."

This one's for you, Dad!

The chapter's writer, Barbara Bibas Montero.

Barbara Bibas Montero lives in Miami Beach, Florida. She is the eldest of Frank and Susan Bibas' four children. Even though the stories her father collected for the *Veil* series were mysterious and unexplainable, she hopes her story will give solace to those who have lost their loved ones, to know that they are still close to us, separated only by a thin veil.

"The Veil": Production History and Episode Guide

By Tom Weaver

Horror and sci-fi-themed theatrical features and television series were so popular in the late 1950s and early '60s that it's difficult to imagine any one of them not standing a fighting chance in the marketplace. And a TV series toplined by the horror genre's greatest star would naturally be a shoo-in, one of the most memorable (and perhaps profitable) of the lot...wouldn't it?

Strangely enough, no. In 1958-59, Boris Karloff starred in the Hal Roach Studios' anthology series *The Veil*, eerie tales purportedly based on real-life psychic phenomena. Ten episodes were shot, and then the plug was pulled — not just on the series, but on the entire studio. No other company stepped forward to continue producing the series, despite the current popularity of chillers *and* blue-chip horror star Karloff.

In fact, the episodes that *were* made ... were never aired.

The Beginnings

Hal Roach Studios, located on Washington Blvd. in Culver City, probably seems like a strange spot for a Boris Karloff supernatural TV series to take root. Established during the silent era, it was famous as the lot where legendary producer Hal Roach and some of Hollywood's earliest comedy greats, up to and including Laurel and Hardy, made their famous features and shorts. Its nickname was "The Lot of Fun." But by the late 1940s and the '50s, the days of Stan and Babe, Charlie Chase, Our Gang shorts, etc., were in the ancient past. The lot was now advertising itself as the first and only major motion picture studio devoted exclusively to television films. (And, on an incidental note, a number of indie sci-fi and horror flicks were also shot there, among them *The Flying Saucer*, *The Man from Planet X*, *Gog*, *Riders to the Stars*, *The Monster That Challenged the World*, *The Vampire*, *The Return of Dracula*, *The Flame Barrier*, *Tormented* and *The Angry Red Planet*.)

On February 28, 1955, after well over a year of negotiations, Hal Roach Jr. acquired ownership of the studio from his father. Born into the movie business, Jr. was 21 when he and his father co-directed the Roach Studios' *One Million B.C.* in 1939. (To get a behind-the-scenes look at a bit of the Hal Roach Studios, watch the *Gale Storm Show* episode "It's Murder, My Dear" with Boris Karloff, described on pages 45 through 47. To see Hal Roach Jr. in the flesh, catch the end of the 1954 *This Is Your Life* episode honoring Laurel and Hardy.)

The first Hollywood trade paper to mention *The Veil* may have been *Variety*, which in its March 26, 1958, edition ran the blurb "Karloff Pilot Winds": "*The Veil*, pilot film starring Boris Karloff as host, narrator and star, has been completed by producer Jerry Stagg for Hal Roach Productions." In truth, no pilot was shot. What served as a *Veil* pilot was actually an eerie episode of the Roach Studios' series *Telephone Time*, "The Vestris," that had aired on February 25; Karloff was a "Special Guest Star" in it. In order for it to serve as the *Veil* pilot, at some point he also did a *Veil* intro and outro, i.e., hosted the episode. (In its original form as a *Telephone Time*, the host was Dr. Frank Baxter.) Another Roach pilot then making the rounds, *Cavalry Surgeon* with John Hudson, set in 1845 during the Mexican War, was also a recent *Telephone Time* episode. My synopsis and review of "The Vestris" starts on page 17.

For Hal Roach Productions, 1958 was a busy time, if by "busy" you mean wishin' and hopin' and plannin' and dreamin' but not often shootin'. By late April, they were crowing that they'd already shot nine pilots for projected 1958-59 TV series and had another eight on the drawing boards. Did nine pilots actually get shot, or were a lot of them re-purposed *Telephone Time*s like "The Vestris" and "Cavalry Surgeon"? Who knows. My research leads me to believe that there was more big talk than action at Hal Roach Studios.

Variety announced on April 23 that pilots currently in New York City for presentation to network and Madison Avenue agency executives included *Cindy*; *The Tall Man* with Michael Rennie as a post-Civil

Hal Roach Sr. and Jr. in an undated shot. Jr. died young in 1973 while his dad soldiered on for almost two more decades. In 1992, at the age of 100 years and seven days, Sr. got wild applause on *The Tonight Show with Jay Leno* when he tossed aside his cane, removed his jacket and danced "The Old Man's Hula." (Photo courtesy Leonard Maltin)

In late May, it was announced that, in a deal said to be in excess of $12,500,000, the Scranton Corp. of Scranton, Pennsylvania, a lace manufacturing firm, bought out Hal Roach Studios. Included in the sale was the Culver City studio plant and the entire Roach film library. Roach Jr. was retained as head of studio operations. In August, when Roach Jr. held a press conference at the Hollywood Brown Derby, it was covered by columnist Starr, who noted that this was the first time the "tall and stoutish ... still boyish-looking" Jr. had faced the press "since he up and sold the old family homestead to a bunch of Easterners." She continued:

> Just why young Hal sold the studio to the Scranton Corporation of Pennsylvania is quite apparent. He needed fresh capital for expansion.
>
> That the capital has been forthcoming, and in no niggardly amounts, is indicated by the ambitious production schedule Roach has been able to line up for himself.
>
> He will start immediate production of 39 episodes of *The Veil*, a mystery-ghost series with Boris Karloff as the host and star.

Starr went on to mention other series in the offing, and concluded with, "That's quite a lineup for a studio which only a few short weeks ago had only ... *Oh Susanna!* [aka *The Gale Storm Show*] on its production

War investigator; and *The Veil*. Some of the other pilots Roach said would soon be available for screening were the waterfront adventure *Mann of Action* with John Ireland, the comedy-adventure *McGarry and Me* with Virginia Mayo and her real-life hubby Michael O'Shea, and *The Fabulous Oliver Chantry* with George Sanders. In her newspaper column "Inside Television," Eve Starr described *The Veil* as "stories of weird and inexplicable happenings, all of them true. Karloff will host, narrate and appear in every show, some of them for the full 24 minutes, some of them merely as a bit player. But he's very much enthused over the project."

Prior to *Telephone Time* and *The Veil*, Boris Karloff hadn't worked for the Hal Roach Studios since their "Golden Age," when he played a convict in the French-language version of Laurel and Hardy's *Pardon Us* (1931). (Photo courtesy John Antosiewicz)

tion schedule." Columnist Philip K. Scheuer also wrote about Roach Jr.'s future plans, revealing that among the 20 feature films Jr. had in the works were the sci-fi *It Lived a Million Years Ago* and a musical remake of the studio's 1939 comedy *The Housekeeper's Daughter*.

The year 1958 should have been a good time for TV series like *The Veil*, at least according to *The Hollywood Reporter*. A July 18, 1958, article predicted that the next big video trend might possibly be set by the first invasion into TV prime time of horror and/or SF filmed series that coming fall:

> Obviously cueing the TV industry's move is the fact horror-scientification theatrical films are, with the roadshow type blockbusters, bellwethering the box office all over this country. TV is well aware that much of the youthful (15-27) American generation is veering more and more rapidly from video fare in favor of theatrical pictures; and that this same age bracket comprises a good 90 percent of the audiences, thronging horror-sci-fi product theatrically exhibited.
>
> CBS [already planning on running *The Invisible Man* and *World of Giants*] also has another science-fictioner, Rod Serling's *Twilight Zone*, on the planning boards and is reportedly giving special attention to other fantasy submissions, as are the other webs. Revue already reports increased submissions of format ideas and, in varying degrees, so do Desilu and Screen Gems ….
>
> Although ABC has only one horror series penciled in for fall [*Tales of Frankenstein*], it, too, would be wide open for others of the same genre. NBC is not slotting any horror or science fiction series for fall, preferring to sit things out till next year. However, NBC's subsid, Cal National, is kicking around the possibility of a horror series or two to be filmed on foreign locale.
>
> Meanwhile, Kirk Douglas' Bryna Productions yesterday set for immediate production a space science series, *Report from Space*, based on two best-sellers by Ray Bradbury, *The Illustrated Man* and *The Martian Chronicles*. John Fulton will produce.
>
> That there is a heavy TV audience potential for the horror and fantasy themers is evidenced by the fact that Screen Gems' "Shock" ("Nightmare" on the West Coast), comprised of 52 old Universal and Columbia horror pics, has broken all ratings records from coast to coast, with most stations going to two and three times weekly on the package. Screen Gems' second package of 52, "Son of Shock," is being snapped up so readily in all markets that the Columbia subsid is currently putting together a third package of the old chillers.

Also in pre-production during 1958 was ABC's *Alcoa Presents* – better known today by its syndication title, *One Step Beyond*. John Newland hosted the weekly series, which premiered January 20, 1959, and presented actual case histories of supernatural occurrences.

On August 19, 1958, the trades announced that *The Veil*'s producer Frank P. Bibas had hired 11 writers to script the initial group of segments. The roster of names included Laslo Vadnay (*Tales of Manhattan*, *Flesh and Fantasy*) and Jack Laird. The New York-born Bibas (1917-1997) had served in the Air Force during World War II (over 100 missions) and began laboring in the film industry in 1950. Throughout his career, he worked extensively in TV commercials, including such memorable spots as the Hertz Rent-a-Car commercials (a man flies through the air into the driver's seat of a convertible as the announcer intones "Let Hertz put you in the driver's seat!") and the Ajax "White Knight" commercials. Bibas' daughter Barbara was knee-high at the time, but still recalls the filming of a White Knight commercial in the parking lot of City Hall in Rye, New York. "We had the white horse and the White Knight and everything!" she laughs.

Barbara also remembers that her father "*always* had an interest in the paranormal – he used to tell us stories about Houdini's interest in the paranormal. He *studied* it, sort of. For instance, voodoo interested him – he just wanted to pick it apart and take its 'mystery' out of it. Then, in a library, or wherever, he came across some files of actual case studies of the paranormal. And he decided that that would be a great series. That's how *The Veil* came about."

The Veil began production on October 13. Episodes open in a castle as the camera moves toward an ornate archway into a medieval-looking room with a bookcase and a huge fireplace with a nicely banked-up fire. (According to *Veil* director Herbert L. Strock, this impressive set was left over from some past Roach production. It gives the first impression of an expensive show, when *The Veil*'s production values were actually rather meager.) Musicologist David Schecter tells me that an electro-Theremin contributes to the eerie music we hear. Karloff, clad in suit and polka dot tie, is seated in

"Is it hot in here, or is it me?": *Veil* host Karloff always looked as though his back was on fire.

a chair, reading a book. Boris rises to greet us and now, in a close-up, intones:

"Good evening. Tonight I'm going to tell you another strange and unusual story of the unexplainable which lies behind the Veil." (These two shots open all but a few episodes.) After a Sponsor's Message, Karloff, still standing in the library-fireplace room, talks about characters in the story which is about to begin. As host of *The Veil*, he avoids the hamminess that afflicted his later *Thriller* intros; here he very placidly and matter-of-factly lays the groundwork for the coming story, the fireplace flames behind him creating a Hell connotation.

What follows is an episode guide to *The Veil*. It begins with a cursory look at *Telephone Time*'s "The Vestris," because of its *Veil* connection.

Episode Guide

"The Vestris" (a 1958 *Telephone Time* episode passed off as the pilot for *The Veil*)

Production No. 9067, Shot on January 2, 3, 6 and 7, 1958; Broadcast on ABC on February 25, 1958; Directed by Arthur Hiller; Produced by Jerry Stagg; Executive Producer: Hal Roach Jr.; Teleplay: David Evans; Story: Robert Dale Owen; Production Supervisor: Sidney Van Keuren; Photography: Paul Ivano; Production Coordinator: E.H. Goldstein; Production Manager: James W. Lane; Assistant Director: Bruce Fowler Jr.; Editor: Charles L. Freeman; Art Director: William Ferrari; Photographic Effects: Jack R. Glass; Set Decorator: Rudy Butler; Sound: Jack Goodrich and Frank Moran; Casting: Ruth Burch; Costumer: Ed Lassmann; Makeup: Sid Perell; Hair Stylist: Carmen Dirigo; **Uncredited**: Director of Dr. Frank Baxter Intro and Outro: J. Stagg (Jerry Stagg?); Second Assistant Directors: Thomas F. Kelly and B. Templeton; Script Supervisor: S. Scheuer [Stanley Scheuer?]; Stand-ins: M. Olson (Mildred Jean Olsen?) and J. Garcio

Cast: "Special Guest Star" Boris Karloff (*Dr. Pierre*), Torin Thatcher (*Capt. Robert Norrich*), Rita Lynn (*Mary Norrich*), Thomas G. Duggan (*William Lloyd*), Ben Wright (*Robbins*), Ashley Cowan (*First Seaman*), Patrick O'Moore (*Second Seaman*), Dr. Frank Baxter (*Host*)

A write-up on this Karloff-starring episode of the ABC-TV series *Telephone Time* appears here because it was reworked to serve as the pilot episode of *The Veil*. If *The Veil* had come to TV as a series, it would not have been possible for Roach to make "The Vestris" one of the episodes.

The *Telephone Time* episode was shot early in 1958 and telecast on February 25. In its original version, series host Dr. Frank Baxter opens the episode, standing on a set that looks like part of an old sailing ship's deck and telling us a bit about the spooky story ahead. He begins by defining *déjà vu* and then tells us that the upcoming, supposedly true tale "was first written down by a distinguished American of the nineteenth century, Robert Dale Owen. He was a writer, a political thinker, a Congressman, and served as United States minister abroad." (Karloff's *Veil* intros could have done with some of this kind of name-dropping, to add verisimilitude. Even when Baxter introduced *The Mole People* in 1956, he made that story sound more legit and plausible than Karloff makes his *Veil* yarns.)

On the *Vestris*, a bark sailing from Plymouth, England, to Boston in the spring of 1828, a mystery man in a hooded jacket (Karloff) makes a supernatural appearance in the chart room, staggering mutely toward the captain's frightened wife and showing her a slate on which he has written "Steer North West." The wind begins blowing the ship northwest, into the ice floes. On one of the floes, a wrecked lifeboat and three people are spotted; one is the mysterious stranger, who has no idea how his apparition appeared on the *Vestris*. Neither do the other characters, or the audience. (This supernatural plot wrinkle is similar to the one in *The Veil*'s "The Doctor.") According to the *Telephone Time* episode's end credits, "The Vestris" was directed by Arthur Hiller, but he watched the copy I sent him and swore to me that he didn't direct it. I have to believe that Hiller simply forgot "The Vestris" because his name is not only on-screen as director but also in all the daily production reports. (Hiller did direct three early episodes of Karloff's later teleseries *Thriller*.) The episode's d.p. Paul Ivano famously (among Monster Kids, anyway) photographed Bela Lugosi's *Frankenstein* screen test. Karloff gets "Special Guest Star" billing in the end credits.

Variety liked "The Vestris": In a February 27 review, they called it "an eerie we-don't-ask-you-to-believe-it-but-it-happened plot which sustains interest with its overtones of fantasy. David Evans' teleplay is penned with simplicity and directness, and Arthur Hiller's direction is keyed to the somber mood of the 19th century story." As mentioned above, the story of the *Vestris* was first put on paper by Robert Dale Owen (1801-77), a believer in spiritualism who wrote a couple books on the subject. One of them, the evocatively titled *Footfalls on the Boundary of Another World*, included the story on which "The Vestris" was based. Just for fun, it's been included in the back of this book (starting on page 249).

Veil episodes were shot in two and a half days each but "The Vestris," which doesn't strike me as one bit better production-wise, took four. Karloff worked three of the four days, January 2, 6 and 7. He was staying at the Chateau Marmont in L.A. while it was shot, and probably during the shooting of the *Veil*s also. According to the production paperwork, J. Stagg (presumably episode producer Jerry Stagg) directed the Baxter footage at the end of the fourth day.

To turn "The Vestris" into a *Veil*, Dr. Baxter's footage got tossed overboard and a new opening was shot. A voice intones "Presenting *The Veil* and Boris Karloff" as we see weird lights and what looks like out-of-focus, rippling satin. Next we see (out of focus) Karloff stood up against a white wall, his head hanging; he looks like the guilty guy in a police lineup. When he raises his head and faces the camera, he comes into focus and goes into his spiel:

> How do you do? The story you are about to see actually happened and is completely documented. It's one of those strange events that seem to defy alllll explanation. They lie behind the veil of human knowledge and yet they happened. Science has many terms or labels for these strange occurrences, but no explanation ... as yet. But then, not too long ago, they had no explanation for a bolt of lightning, or a falling star. [*He goes back out of focus.*] They too seemed to come from ... behind *The Veil*." [The title *The Veil* now appears on screen.]

In this opener, Karloff is *very* obviously reading from cue cards or a teleprompter.

The Veil Episode 1: "Summer Heat"

Paige (Harry Bartell) takes detectives (Paul Bryar and Ray Montgomery) to the scene of the crime. Except that there was no crime (yet) and there's barely a scene!

Production No. 9204, Shot on October 13, 14 and 15, 1958; Directed by george waGGner; Produced by Frank P. Bibas; Executive Producer: Hal Roach Jr.; Teleplay: Rik Vollaerts; Production Supervisor: E.H. Goldstein; Photography: Howard Schwartz; Production Coordinator: William Sterling; Production Manager: D'Estell Iszard; Assistant Director: James W. Lane; Editor: Otho Lovering; Art Director: McClure Capps; Photographic Effects: Jack R. Glass; Set Decorator: Rudy Butler; Music: Leon Klatzkin; Sound: William Russell and Joel Moss; Casting: Ruth Burch; Costumer: John Zacha; Makeup: Sid Perell; Hair Stylist: Margit McEllroy; *The Veil* Created by Frank P. Bibas; **Uncredited**: Script Clerk: Verna Moran; Second Assistant Director: Miles Middough; Gaffer: Paul Grancell; Best Boy: Gordon Wells; First Grip: Larry Milton; Second Grip: Jerry Walton; First Prop Man: Mitch Grimes; Second Prop Man: Don Sandstrom; Laborer: Robert Steinman; Camera Operator: Cy Hofberg; First Assistant Cameraman: Dick Johnson; Second Assistant Cameraman: Palmer Belmont; Sound Recorder: Tom Rennings; Boom Man: John McDonald; Cable Man: Malcolm Rennings; Grip: Dean Rose; Stand-ins: Mildred Jean Olsen and Ralph Stein; **Second Unit (Boris Karloff's Opening and Closing, shot on October 28, 1958):** Directed by Frank P. Bibas; Photography: Jack Glass; Assistant Director: William Forsyth; Makeup: Sid Perell; Gaffer: James Ferguson; Best Boy: A.H. McPhearson; First Grip: T. Joiner; Second Grip: Bill Forcade; First Prop Man: E. Trickle (Eddie Trickle?); Laborer: Bert Steinman;

Camera Operator: Hugh Wade; First Assistant Cameraman: Al Colombo; Sound: Jack Goodrich; Sound Recordist: Ben Remington; Boom Man: Orrick Barrett; Cable Man: Earl Winegarden; Special Effects: Bob Overbeck; Electricians: Bill Robinson and Jack Barbee; Stand-in: Ralph Stein

Cast: Boris Karloff (*Host/Dr. Francis Mason*), Harry Bartell *(Edward Paige)*, Paul Bryar (*Police Lt. Davis*), Ray Montgomery (*Police Sgt. Fenton*), Gene Collins (*Ralph Kerwin*), Vici Raaf (*Blonde Woman*), Gretchen Thomas (*Elizabeth Foley*), Connie Van (*Mrs. Rebus*), Robert Griffin (*Dr. Dragstedt*)

Synopsis: One night during a New York heat wave, shipping clerk Edward Paige (Harry Bartell) looks out a window of his small midtown boarding house and sees, through the window of a third-floor apartment across the way, a burglar (Gene Collins) enter. When the night-clad blonde tenant (Vici Raaf) walks in from another room, the burglar grabs and chokes her until she bites his arm; he fatally clubs her with his flashlight. Paige instantly notifies the police, who accompany him to the scene of the crime — which turns out to be an unoccupied, unfurnished apartment. Paige is so insistent about what he saw that two suit-and-tie cops (Paul Bryar, Ray Montgomery) take him into custody.

Paige ends up at Bellevue, where police psychiatrist Dr. Mason (Karloff) listens patiently to his account and becomes convinced that Paige isn't crazy. Meanwhile, a blonde does move into the empty apartment and is killed by the burglar exactly as witnessed by Paige. The police suspect Paige until, going by the description he provided, they haul in Ralph Kerwin (Gene Collins). In an interrogation room, Kerwin is unfazed by rugged police persuasion. When the cops bring Paige and Kerwin together, the killer tries to brazen it out, but the bite mark on his arm cinches the case against him.

In his outro, Karloff tells us, "Paige's experience was an example of what is defined as precognition — the ability to foresee the future. Throughout history, there have been many such instances, reported *and* documented. How does it happen? Why?"

The kickoff *Veil* has a clever story that combines elements from *Rear Window* with *Dragnet*-like qualities and, of course, a supernatural twist.

Karloff-wise, however, the series got off to an inauspicious start. In "Summer Heat," he plays one of his less interesting *Veil* roles, a Sherlock Holmes of the couch (police psychiatrist) who lends Paige a sympathetic ear. It isn't much of a part, and the scripter doesn't even bother to keep him around for the wrap-up.

Paige is played by Harry Bartell, one of those actors you've seen a thousand times, and will see a thousand more times, without remembering his name. He plays his part with the proper combination of confusion and angry frustration. Bartell was even busier in radio than in movies and TV. Maybe he got the role in this *Dragnet*-flavored *Veil* because he regularly appeared on the *Dragnet* radio show and TV series and even the 1954 *Dragnet* movie. Also seen at his wit's end is the reliable Paul Bryar as Police Lt. Davis, who is convinced that Paige described to the police a crime he intended to later commit himself — at least until the case goes around several unexpected bends.

The blonde's murder is shown twice, once as Paige is getting his advance peek and a second time when it really happens. Therefore, a continuity gaffe – the blonde's purse moves from one position to another on the couch – is also seen twice. Even funnier is a flub in the closing scene: In one shot, Lt. Davis angrily tells burglar Kerwin to sit back down, but it's not until the next shot that the seated Kerwin *begins to get up*. Lt. Davis is positioned right next to Paige when he tells the about-to-stand Kerwin to sit down;

Paige (Harry Bartell) fingers the punk (Gene Collins) he saw in his vision. Former kid actor Collins is easy to hate because he has a face only a fist could love.

Harry Bartell, a veteran of *Dragnet*'s radio, TV and movie incarnations, played this "Summer Heat" tape-recording scene the way a *Dragnet* actor would.

maybe this precognition thing is contagious.

Like all the *Veil* episodes, "Summer Heat" was made in two and a half days. It began shooting at 9:05 a.m. on the morning of Monday, October 13, 1958. There was no Karloff that first day, as scenes set in Paige's apartment and the blonde's apartment were photographed. Karloff made a none-too-bright-and-early appearance on the set at 10:30 the next morning and worked until 4:45. October 15 was the half-day: There was an 8 a.m. company call with Karloff again on hand to shoot

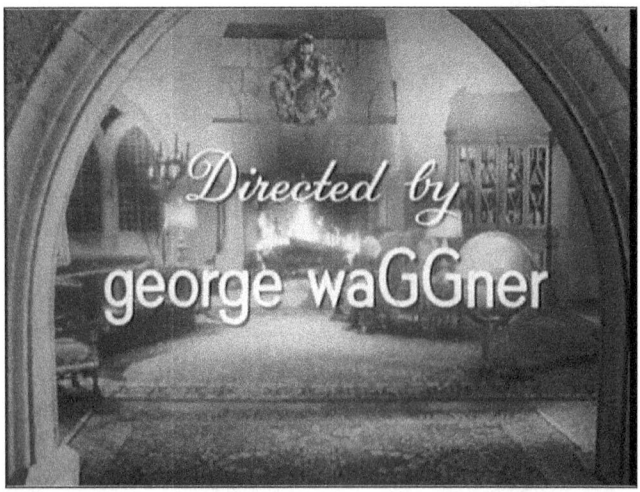

Starting in the '50s, this is how the director's name would appear on screen ... and in the Hollywood trade papers ... and, believe it or not, even on behind-the-scenes Hal Roach production paperwork. It's probably safe to assume that for some screwy reason, he must have insisted on it.

scenes set in Dr. Mason's office, and a 12:30 p.m. wrap, with *Veil* Episode 2, "A Chapter of Genesis," rolling a short time later. Both episodes had the same director, george waGGner. Monster Kids will recall that in the 1940s, when his name would appear on screen conventionally, George Waggner permitted Karloff to give one of his worst performances in one of his worst pictures, Universal's *The Climax*. But Waggner also made good movies at Universal, among them Lon Chaney Jr.'s first two horror vehicles *Man Made Monster* and *The Wolf Man* (both 1941).

In every Karloff intro and outro, he wears the same polka dot tie – and in "Summer Heat," he also wears it as the doctor in the story itself. Maybe, like a lot of low-budget shows, *The Veil* had its actors wearing their own clothes, and this was one of Boris' few ties. Aubrey Schenck, who produced the Karloff vehicles *Voodoo Island* (1957) and *Frankenstein 1970* (1958), described Karloff to me as "a very fine fellow, a gentleman, very nice ... [but] he was the *stingiest* guy who ever lived!"

The "Summer Heat" script calls Mason a man of 40; this is one of *several Veil* scripts where the characters Karloff would play are described as much younger than the actor. Some script-to-screen differences: Paige and Dr. Mason have a longer talk in Mason's office. Just before the doomed blonde stops at the stoop of Mrs. Foley's rooming house to ask directions, the script calls for distant thunder. (Mrs. Foley: "It'll rain up in Westchester for the rich people. We poor slobs here in town can just sweat.") By the time the blonde gets directions and walks away, there's thunder and lightning.

In the script's Act Two, we see the blonde come home from work, we even see through a partially open bathroom door her shadow as she disrobes and steps into the shower, but the script doesn't call for us to see the murder a second time. While the police are looking for Paige, we see him wandering down a street, "without purpose, without direction. Bumps into pedestrian." Finally, the script calls for a daytime shot of a police car pulling up to a hard stop in front of a police station, the two detectives getting out with the cuffed killer between them.

An almost identical tale was spun in *One Step Beyond*'s second-season episode "The Open Window."

There it was a Greenwich Village artist (Michael Higgins) who through his window hears a woman (Lori March) move into a hotel room across the way (almost close enough to reach out and touch her!), listens as she makes a distraught phone call and then watches as she turns on the gas. He rushes to the hotel and gets the manager to let him into the room – which is unoccupied. The manager thinks the artist is a nut ("Ya know, runnin' a hotel in Greenwich Village is sometimes better'n watchin' TV…"). Later, the woman does move into that room and does turn on the gas, but the artist is again watching, this time with his model (Louise Fletcher), and tragedy is averted. The hotel manager, staring at the artist, murmurs to himself, "How did he *know*? How in God's name did he *know*?" The Manhattan setting and a hot summer night also link the two episodes. In *One Step Beyond* host John Newland's "Open Window" outro, he talks about time, scientific theories, even Albert Einstein but, like Karloff, fails to say a word about the true-life event (if there really *was* one) that inspired the story.

New York's Finest played by two Hollywood dependables, Ray Montgomery (co-star of TV's *Ramar of the Jungle*) and Paul Bryar.

The Veil Episode 2: "A Chapter of Genesis"

Haney's ghost (Charles Meredith) looks as elderly and pain-riddled as *he* was on his deathbed; do we get to Heaven in the shape we were in when we left this Earth? Perhaps John Derek was correct when he said in *Knock on Any Door* (1949), "I'll live fast, die young and leave a good-looking corpse!"

(Modern sources refer to this episode as "Genesis.") Production No. 9210, Shot on October 15, 16 and 17, 1958; Directed by george waGGner; Produced by Frank P. Bibas; Executive Producer: Hal Roach Jr.; Teleplay: Sidney Morse; Production Supervisor: E.H. Goldstein; Photography: Howard Schwartz; Production Coordinator: William Sterling; Production Manager: D'Estell Iszard; Assistant Director: James W. Lane; Editor: Otho Lovering; Art Director: McClure Capps; Photographic Effects: Jack R. Glass; Set Decorator: Rudy Butler; Music: Leon Klatzkin; Sound: William Russell and Joel Moss; Casting: Ruth Burch; Costumer: John Zacha; Makeup: Sid Perell; Hair Stylist: Margit McEllroy; *The Veil* Created by Frank P. Bibas; **Uncredited**: Script Clerk: Verna Moran; Second Assistant Director: Miles Middough; Gaffer: Paul Grancell; Best Boy: Gordon Wells; First Grip: Larry Milton; Second Grip: Jerry Walton; First Prop Man: Mitch Grimes; Second Prop Man: Don Sandstrom; Laborer: Robert Steinman; Camera Operator: Cy Hofberg; First Assistant Cameraman: Dick Johnson; Second Assistant Cameraman: Palmer Belmont; Sound Recorder: Tom Rennings; Boom Man: John McDonald; Cable Man: Malcolm Rennings; Grip: Dean Rose; Stand-ins: Mildred Jean Olsen and Ralph Stein;

Second Unit (Boris Karloff's Opening and Closing, shot on October 28, 1958): Directed by Frank P. Bibas; Photography: Jack Glass; Assistant Director: William Forsyth; Makeup: Sid Perell; Gaffer: James Ferguson; Best Boy: A.H. McPhearson; First Grip: T. Joiner; Second Grip: Bill Forcade; First Prop Man: E. Trickle (Eddie Trickle?); Laborer: Bert Steinman; Camera Operator: Hugh Wade; First Assistant Cameraman: Al Colombo; Sound: Jack Goodrich; Sound Recordist: Ben Remington; Boom Man: Orrick Barrett; Cable Man: Earl Winegarden; Special Effects: Bob Overbeck; Electricians: Bill Robinson and Jack Barbee; Stand-in: Ralph Stein

Cast: Boris Karloff (*Host/Jonas Atterbury*), Katherine Squire (*Emma Haney*), Peter Miller (*James "Jamie" Haney*), Lee Far [Farr] (*John Haney Jr.*), Charles Meredith (*John T. Haney*), Morris Ankrum (*Judge Davis*), Thomas B. Henry (*Mr. Blue*)

Synopsis: In this story from the horse-and-plow era, farmer John Haney (Charles Meredith) lies dying in an upstairs bedroom of his farmhouse while, downstairs, Jamie (Peter Miller), the black sheep of the family, returns for the first time since he stole every cent in the house and cleared out ten years earlier. (The script describes Jamie as "a 1920s sharpie.") The slick, citified Jamie gets a cool reception from his careworn younger brother John Jr. (Lee Farr), who picked up all the slack in his brother's absence.

After Farmer Haney's death, lawyer Jonas Atterbury (Karloff) is officiating at the reading of Haney's will when Jamie presents him with a different, more recent will in which Haney leaves everything to Jamie. (This new will was written at a time when Haney and his son John were on the outs.) Scoundrel Jamie intends to sell the farm, send John away and put his mother Emma (Katherine Squire) in an old folks home. But the late Haney makes a supernatural reappearance: John sees his dead father in his rocking chair, intoning, "Look in Genesis 27." Momentarily distracted, Jamie looks away; when he looks again, the chair is still rocking but Dad is gone.

Genesis 27, a reference to the Biblical story of Jacob and Esau, gives John the idea that in the family Bible, yet another will may be hidden. In the attic, Jamie finds the Bible just as John arrives; the two fight, John gets knocked out, and Atterbury appears just in time to stop Jamie from bashing his brother with a statuette. In the family Bible is a third will bequeathing everything to John. According to host Karloff's wrap-up speech, Haney's Will Version 3.0 was presented in court and accepted as valid. He adds: "Over the years, many such instances [ghosts helping relatives find missing items] have been reported—*and* documented." Statements like this make you wonder if *The Veil* got its stories out of historical records or *The National Enquirer*.

A mundane story, "A Chapter of Genesis" slips a ghost into the proceedings for all of about 30 seconds, then goes right back to the business of telling a dull yarn about an unpleasant farm family. If there's any resemblance between the people in this story and anyone living or dead, they're better off dead.

"A Chapter of Genesis" is dragged down by its irritating characters, particularly the mother, a craven little lady who prefers to see her family pulled apart than to stand up for herself or for anybody else. The father runs a close second, *his* ability to irritate extending beyond the grave. In life, he wrote one will and gave it to his lawyer (Karloff), then wrote *another* will which somehow found its way into the hands of his long-missing, footloose son (Peter Miller); then wrote a *third* and fi-

Gall in the Family: Ne'er-do-well Jamie, inheritor of the family farm, intends to throw Momma from the terrain, along with brother John, and long-simmering resentments boil over into rage. Left to right, Lee Farr, Katherine Squire, Peter Miller.

nal one which he hid in a Bible which he hid in a desk which he hid in the attic! This mood-swinging dotard has to come back from the dead to rectify this fine mess, and even *then* the only clue he offers as to the location of the valid will is "Genesis 27." The Bible chapter in question describes how Jacob stole his brother's birthright — but why did Haney put the will there? Ne'er-do-well Jamie didn't try to steal John Jr.'s birthright until after Haney was dead. It would have made more sense for Haney to look for a Bible chapter about crazy old dirt farmers who write multiple wills and strew them all over Creation.

But perhaps all the Haneys have their little mental quirks: Many scenes are set in the farmhouse kitchen, where characters react to every upstairs noise (and every reference to the upstairs area) by looking straight up. But above their heads is the underside of a steep pitched roof—there *is* no upstairs, at least not over the kitchen.

Again as with "Summer Heat," the biggest and best role went to an actor who, in 1958, no one particularly cared to see, Lee Farr (his name misspelled Lee Far in the credits). A relative newcomer to TV, Farr had a Penn State master's degree in geology and had worked as a geologist before he began his acting career. In 1957, talent scouts noticed him in a local stage production of *A Hatful of Rain*, as the dope addict's (Brian Hutton) brother, with *Variety* saying he'd given "the outstanding performance of the night." After a shaky start, TV stardom came his way in 1959 with a co-starring role as a member of Robert Taylor's police squad on *The Detectives*. (Apparently not popular enough with the show's teenage viewers, Farr was gone a year later, replaced by Mark Goddard.) He was briefly married to glamorous Felicia Farr; after their split, she kept his last name. In the 1970s, their daughter Denise walked down the aisle with veteran TV-movie tough guy Don Gordon. Lee and Felicia hadn't lost a daughter, they'd gained a son … a son who was older than *both* of them! Days after I dialed Farr's number and introduced myself on his answering machine, asking if I could talk to him about *The Veil* and Karloff for this book, he died of cancer. There are better ways to avoid speaking with me.

Dressing up the supporting cast are Morris Ankrum as the judge (shades of *Perry Mason*) and Thomas B.

"Where there's a will … I want to be *in* it!": Peter Miller answers questions from his own lawyer Thomas B. Henry as Judge Morris Ankrum attends. Who's keeping the world safe from flying saucers and monsters with Hollywood brass hats Henry and Ankrum occupied here?

Henry as Jamie's attorney. Both got paid $150, as did Charles Meredith who played the father. The episode began shooting on the afternoon of Wednesday, October 15, 1958, after the morning was spent finishing "Summer Heat." Karloff worked on the second and third days.

"A Chapter of Genesis" is nothing to write home about, but the script (included in this book, starting on page 62) is worse. The first half is very much like the first act of the episode. In the opening scene (Jamie's homecoming), the script calls for thunder, lightning and very hard rain; in the reading-of-the-will scene, there's not two but *three* wills, Mrs. Haney tossing yet another one into the pot. Hers is from 1890, written the day after she and John married, John Jr.'s is from 1911 and Jamie's from 1917.

In Act Two, things start getting annoying with the appearance of John Sr.'s ghost, who wants John Jr. to find his final will. It's hidden in a rolltop desk, but instead of telling Jr. "rolltop desk," Sr. repeatedly says "overcoat." This necessitates a time-consuming search for his overcoat, which contains a folded piece of paper which says "Genesis 27," the *next* clue in this multi-step, scavenger hunt-like ordeal.

The episode provides some late-inning excitement, the attic confrontation and fight between John Jr. and Jamie, the latter ready to kill in order to hold onto his will-gotten gains. (A fight in a *Veil* is actually kinda surprising as it's a series where action is practically nil.) But there's no fight in this draft of the script: On page 33, lawyer Atterbury learns that Jr. intends to sneak back into the house and search the attic for the Bible, and he has a very definite reaction: "I will *not* break into that house with you, and I forbid *you* to do it!" The script then calls for a slow dissolve from a shot of Atterbury and Jr. staring at each other to a shot of the two men coming up through the attic trap door to search for the Bible. A quick "barn doors" transition from the first scene to the second, a few notes of funny music and a few laugh track guffaws would have made it worthy of a sitcom. With Jamie nowhere in sight, John and Atterbury find the Bible in a rolltop desk and extract the will, Atterbury looking at the date and happily announcing that it will supersede the others.

The Veil Episode 3: "Girl on the Road"

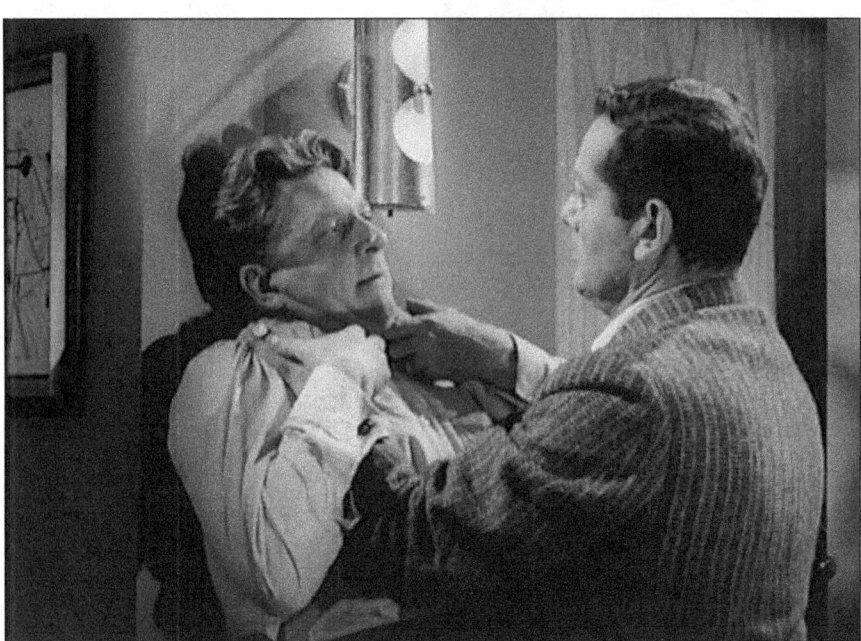

Prescott (Tod Andrews) gets tough with the bartender (Jack Lomas) in a scene that almost plays comically because the latter makes zero attempt to defend himself.

Production No. 9212, Shot on October 27, 28 and 29, 1958; Teleplay and Directed by george waGGner; Produced by Frank P. Bibas; Executive Producer: Hal Roach Jr.; Production Supervisor: E.H. Goldstein; Photography: Howard Schwartz; Production Coordinator: William Sterling; Production Manager: D'Estell Iszard; Assistant Director: James W. Lane; Editor: Otho Lovering; Art Director: McClure Capps; Photographic Effects: Jack R. Glass; Set Decorator: Rudy Butler; Music: Leon Klatzkin; Sound: William Russell and Joel Moss; Casting: Ruth Burch; Costumer: John Zacha; Makeup: Sid Perell; Hair Stylist: Margit McEllroy; *The Veil* Created by Frank P. Bibas; **Uncredited:** Script Clerk: Verna Moran; Second Assistant Director: Miles Middough; Makeup: Carl Russell; Gaffer: Paul Grancell; Best Boy: Gordon Wells; First Grip: Larry Milton; Second Grips: Jerry Walton and T.D. Fullerton; First Prop Man: Mitch Grimes; Second Prop Man: Ray Pedigo; Laborer: Bob Brian; Camera Operator: Cy Hofberg; First Assistant Cameraman: Ed Wade; Second Assistant Cameraman: Palmer Belmont; Sound Recorders: Ben Remington and Tom Rennings; Boom Man: John McDonald; Cable Man: Malcolm Rennings; Grip: Dean Rose; Greensman: Hank Ford; Special Effects: Bob Overbeck; Still Photographer: Stax Graves; Stand-ins: Mildred Jean Olsen and Ralph Stein; **Second Unit (Boris Karloff's Opening and Closing, shot on October 28, 1958):** Directed by Frank P. Bibas; Photography: Jack Glass; Assistant Director: William Forsyth; Makeup: Sid Perell; Gaffer: James Ferguson; Best Boy: A.H. McPhearson; First Grip: T. Joiner; Second Grip: Bill Forcade; First Prop Man: E. Trickle (Eddie Trickle?); Laborer: Bert Steinman; Camera Operator: Hugh Wade; First Assistant Cameraman: Al Colombo; Sound: Jack Goodrich; Sound Recordist: Ben Remington; Boom Man: Orrick Barrett; Cable Man: Earl Winegarden; Special Effects: Bob Overbeck; Electricians: Bill Robinson and Jack Barbee; Stand-in: Ralph Stein

Cast: Boris Karloff (*Host/Morgan Debs*), Tod Andrews (*John Prescott*), Eve Brent (*Lila Kirby*), Jack Lomas (*Bartender*), Kelly Thordsen (*Charles—Chauffeur*), Rusty Lane (*Sheriff*), Pitt Herbert (*Garage Attendant*), Claudia Bryar (*Mrs. Kirby*)

Synopsis: Making a fast turn onto a side road in his convertible, John Prescott (Tod Andrews) nearly sideswipes pretty blonde Lila (Eve Brent) and her disabled

Tod Andrews as Prescott. The actor's genre past included hero roles in two of Bela Lugosi's "Monogram Nine," *Return of the Ape Man* and *Voodoo Man* (1944), plus the "walking tree" cult classic *From Hell It Came* (1957).

Before she put on weight and starting playing roles like the grotesque Aunt Stella in the horror flick *Fade to Black* (1980), Eve Brent was quite the '50s glamourpuss. She was Jane to Gordon Scott's Tarzan on TV and in a feature.

sports car. Prescott apologizes to her, determines that her car is out of gas and offers her a ride to a gas station. First he stops at an inn and buys her a cocktail. When the bartender (Jack Lomas) goes to a pay phone and asks to be connected to Morgan Debs, Lila becomes frightened and flees with Prescott in tow. Prescott is concerned for the girl and, as he drops her at the gas station, he presses her to tell him her troubles. She promises to meet him at nine that night at Lookout Point.

Lila arrives at the clifftop site on foot, sits in Prescott's car and is about to tell her story when a chauffeur-driven car transporting Morgan Debs (Karloff) arrives. Lila vanishes while Prescott talks to the enigmatic Debs. Reporting Lila's disappearance to the local sheriff (Rusty Lane), Prescott learns that Debs is a big man in these parts. He goes to the gas station and talks to the attendant (Pitt Herbert), who says no pretty girl bought gas from him today. While sitting in his car outside the gas station, Prescott is knocked out by Debs' chauffeur (Kelly Thordsen).

Prescott returns to the inn and chokes the bartender until he reveals Lila's last name, Kirby. He finds the Kirby home, where he meets Lila's mother (Claudia Bryar) and gets her to agree to go up to Lila's room to fetch her. While Prescott waits in the study, Debs enters – in a wheelchair. Debs tells her that Lila is dead – "She went off Lookout Point three years ago in her car..." – and shows him three-year-old newspaper clippings to prove it. This is Lila's second reappearance since her death; Debs has been trying to drive Prescott away for the sake of his sister Mrs. Kirby, Lila's mother, who has already been slightly unhinged by the tragedy. Prescott goes to the foot of Lookout Point and recognizes the three-year-old wrecked sports car he finds there.

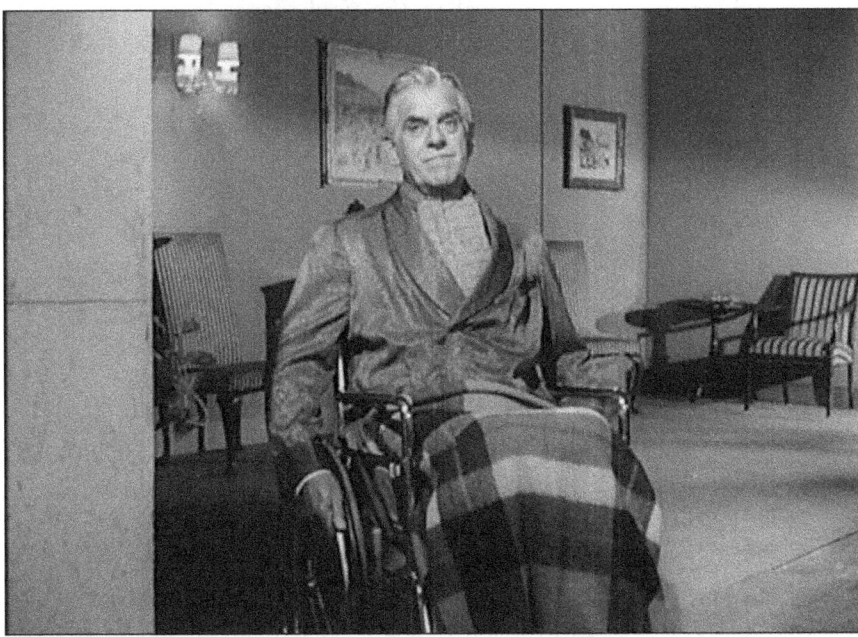

In Debs' (Karloff) first scene, he sits in the back of his big chauffeur-driven car and, per the script, speaks "in the quiet tones of one accustomed to command." It comes as a surprise when we see in the Kirby house scene that he's confined to a wheelchair.

A one-week break followed the back-to-back shooting of "Summer Heat" and "A Chapter of Genesis," and then the *Veil* went back to work with "Girl on the Road" and "The Doctor."

"Girl on the Road" steers *The Veil* into the "ghost story" genre. It was directed, and this time also written, by george waGGner and it's the best of his four *Veil*s — but it could have been better. Tod Andrews isn't the right age to be playing Galahad to Eve Brent – he looks about old enough to be her father – and there are a few unintentionally funny moments that disrupt the grim mood.

Throughout much of the second-act scene where Debs reveals that Lila is long dead, Karloff looks and talks into the camera, an unexpected touch.

"Girl on the Road" avoids a few of the potholes hit by the first two *Veil*s. The word count is down a bit, and characters get to see the light of day (i.e., parts of the episode were shot outdoors). Prescott is a good identification figure as he woos the girl, makes it his business to find out what's frightening her, and defies local "big cheese" Debs. He comes to one dead end after another but manages to learn a bit more in each encounter, which helps to hold audience interest. Until Debs reveals that Lila is long-dead, there isn't the faintest hint of the supernatural in anything that happens, but this total avoidance of spooky touches is the only reason Debs' climactic revelation that Lila is three years dead comes as a surprise. But the scene was carelessly written: Debs says that he was Lila's guardian after the death of her father and was at Lookout Point with her discussing some things she didn't want to hear when she "started to drive away." Drove off the cliff on purpose? Started to drive away and accidentally went off the cliff? Debs is in a wheelchair because of Lila's actions – was he in the car when it went off the cliff or did she run him over or … ? After Debs explains, you'll have more questions about that night than you did before he started talking.

"Girl on the Road" is just as good, or perhaps a bit *better* on a second viewing: There's no more mystery (natch), but the viewer will now know throughout that Prescott is canoodling with a ghost, which gives the whole thing an agreeably eerie quality. On a second viewing, however, you can't help but marvel at how unfazed the bartender (Jack Lomas) is, when a woman he knows is dead sits down at his bar; he casually serves her her drink and goes to the phone to give her uncle a heads-up. Well, maybe he gets a lot of ghosts in there. Again according to David Schecter, the creepy music we hear when Debs talks about Lila's death and her subsequent return "has got to be Jack Cookerly and his 'Magic Box,' a contraption that was made up of about seven different keyboards that had new electronics put inside them."

As the mysterious Debs, Karloff underplays very effectively as he attempts to dissuade Andrews from delving into past events. Claudia Bryar, briefly seen as the dead girl's dotty mom, played "Mother" in 1983's *Psycho II* and was killed by Anthony Perkins with a shovel in the final scene. Into their respective roles as sheriff and gas station attendant, Pitt Herbert and Rusty Lane inject a bit of personality.

Script-to-screen changes: My September 29, 1958, version of the script has a different Karloff opening:

> Shakespeare said it years ago … "There are more things in Heaven and Earth than are dreamt of in your philosophy…" These are the things of which this program is made, these things beyond that very thin veil which on occasion lifts, allowing us to see deeper into beauty and sadness, permitting us perhaps, a glimpse of eternity itself. However, I'm sure that Mr. John Prescott of Boston was not thinking of these things as he drove north from a Florida vacation. He and the night were young and the world was his for the asking.

In this script, the opening scenes with Prescott and Lila are set at night. Debs is *not* in a wheelchair, and he tells Prescott that today was Lila's third appearance since her death. In the episode, he says it was her second.

The *Veil* company didn't leave the Roach lot much but, as indicated above, for "Girl on the Road" they did, spending the first day (October 27) shooting the Prescott-Lila roadside scene and the Lookout Point scene. The production paperwork makes it appear that some of the other exteriors (outside the inn, outside the sheriff's office, outside the garage) were shot on the Roach lot. On the third day of production, the half-day, they shot the Kirby house scenes plus the finale with Prescott finding the smashed car at the base of the cliff. After lunch that day, the shooting of the next *Veil* episode, "The Doctor," began. Karloff didn't work on "Girl on the Road" on October 28 but he nevertheless put in a long day at Roach, shooting intros and closings for this episode, "Summer Heat," "Genesis" and "The Doctor." Series creator Frank P. Bibas directed this second unit.

In his end-of-episode comments, Karloff says of the events in "Girl on the Road," "In my pursuit of these strange and unusual happenings, I have come across several other such occurrences." You buy it when John Newland (*One Step Beyond*) says things like that, but Karloff? Naaah. But then again, is he even supposed to *be* Karloff in these scenes, or just a mysterious castle denizen and student of the supernatural? At no point in any episode does he introduce himself as Boris Karloff.

The Veil Episode 4: "The Doctor"

Production No. 9207, Shot on October 29, 30 and 31, 1958; Directed by george waGGner; Produced by Frank P. Bibas; Executive Producer: Hal Roach Jr.; Teleplay: David Evans; Production Supervisor: E.H. Goldstein; Photography: Howard Schwartz; Production Coordinator: William Sterling; Production Manager: D'Estell Iszard; Assistant Director: James W. Lane; Editor: Otho Lovering; Art Director: McClure Capps; Photographic Effects: Jack R. Glass; Set Decorator: Rudy Butler; Music: Leon Klatzkin; Sound: William Russell and Joel Moss; Casting: Ruth Burch; Costumer: John Zacha; Makeup: Sid Perell; Hair Stylist: Margit McEllroy; *The Veil* Created by Frank P. Bibas; **Uncredited:** Script Clerk: Verna Moran; Second Assistant Director: Miles Middough; Wardrobe Woman: Muriel Pool; Gaffer: Paul Grancell; Best Boy: Gordon Wells; First Grip: Larry Milton; Second Grips: Jerry Walton and Dean Rose; First Prop Man: Mitch Grimes; Second Prop Man: Ray Pedigo; Laborer: Bob Brian; Camera Operator: Cy Hofberg; First Assistant Cameraman: Ed Wade; Second Assistant Cameraman: Palmer Belmont; Sound Recorders: Tom Rennings and Hank Woehler; Boom Man: John McDonald; Cable Man: Malcolm Rennings; Grips: Leo Sperry and Dean Rose; Greensman: Hank Ford; Special Effects: Bob Overbeck; Stand-ins: Mildred Jean Olsen and Ralph Stein; Welfare Worker: Barbara Frank; Electrical

The "Doctor" script description of Karloff's character ("old and looks frail") makes this the only *Veil* script that doesn't flatter the septuagenarian actor. Usually Karloff's *Veil* characters are described in the scripts as being in their 40s or 50s, 60 tops.

Wind Machine: Hal Calwell; **Second Unit (Boris Karloff's Opening and Closing, shot on October 28, 1958):** Directed by Frank P. Bibas; Photography: Jack Glass; Assistant Director: William Forsyth; Makeup: Sid Perell; Gaffer: James Ferguson; Best Boy: A.H. McPhearson; First Grip: T. Joiner; Second Grip: Bill Forcade; First Prop Man: E. Trickle (Eddie Trickle?); Laborer: Bert Steinman; Camera Operator: Hugh Wade; First Assistant Cameraman: Al Colombo; Sound: Jack Goodrich; Sound Recordist: Ben Remington; Boom Man: Orrick Barrett; Cable Man: Earl

Winegarden; Special Effects: Bob Overbeck; Electricians: Bill Robinson and Jack Barbee; Stand-in: Ralph Stein

Cast: Boris Karloff (*Host/Dr. Carlo Marcabienti*), Tony Travis (*Dr. Angelo Marcabienti*), Argentina Brunetti (*Maria*), Elvira Curci (*Mother Bianchi*), Ernest Sarracino (*Father Bianchi*), Bruno Della Santina (*Guiseppe*), Domenick Delgarde (*Toni*), Inez Palange (*Grandmother*), Dominica Hauser (*Neighbor*), Laurie Perreau (*Francesca Bianchi*)

Synopsis: On a blowy night in (according to the script) 1927, Angelo Marcabienti (Tony Travis) returns after a long absence to his tiny Italian village. His elderly father Dr. Carlo Marcabienti (Karloff) has worn himself out caring for the child-like peasant locals, and now he anticipates that Angelo will take his place as the community's *doctore*. But Angelo's a rising surgeon with visions of "the big city" and up-to-date hospitals dancing in his head; he has no intention of burying himself in these backwoods.

While Carlo is out on a late-night call, Angelo receives word that a child is deathly ill. He rushes through the dark and still windy night to the cottage-home of Mother and Father Bianchi (Elvira Curci, Ernest Sarracino) – who instead of letting Angelo treat their little Francesca (Laurie Perreau), are upset that he, not his father, has arrived. The father refuses to allow Angelo to tend to Francesca, who is dying of diphtheria. There's a lot of arguing and hectic comings and goings, the night (and the episode) wear on, and then a stone-silent Carlo moseys in through the Bianchis' door, his mere presence calming the excited parents. Still mute, Carlo stands by and watches as Angelo performs a tracheotomy. Angelo and Carlo leave separately. When Angelo returns home, he learns that his father was there, asleep in a chair in his office, at the same time that his doppelganger had appeared in the peasant cottage.

"The Doctor" is one *Veil* episode that I think *could* conceivably be based on an actual preternatural occurrence. The reason I feel this story might be authentic is because it makes for such dull viewing that it's difficult to picture anyone making it up from scratch.

Maybe *Veil* host Karloff's backside was getting overheated by the flames of the castle fireplace; he parks himself in the nearby chair (rather than standing in front of the fire) to introduce "The Doctor," a ten-minute story they managed to squeeze into 30. In the play itself, Karloff sports glasses, curly white hair, a white mustache and a beard as Dr. Marcabienti. While the Italian accents of the supporting players are thick enough to cut with a pizza wheel, Karloff makes no attempt at an accent, merely adopting a halting delivery that gives the impression he's struggling with the language. Meanwhile, Tony Travis, who plays his son, speaks English perfectly. If Karloff is unimpressive in this episode (and yes he is), perhaps he was giving more attention to another current project, rehearsing for *Playhouse 90*'s live presentation of "Heart of Darkness," based on the novel by Joseph Conrad, Karloff's favorite writer. When it aired on CBS on November 6, "confused and confusing … one of *Playhouse 90*'s least auspicious productions" was *Variety*'s verdict.

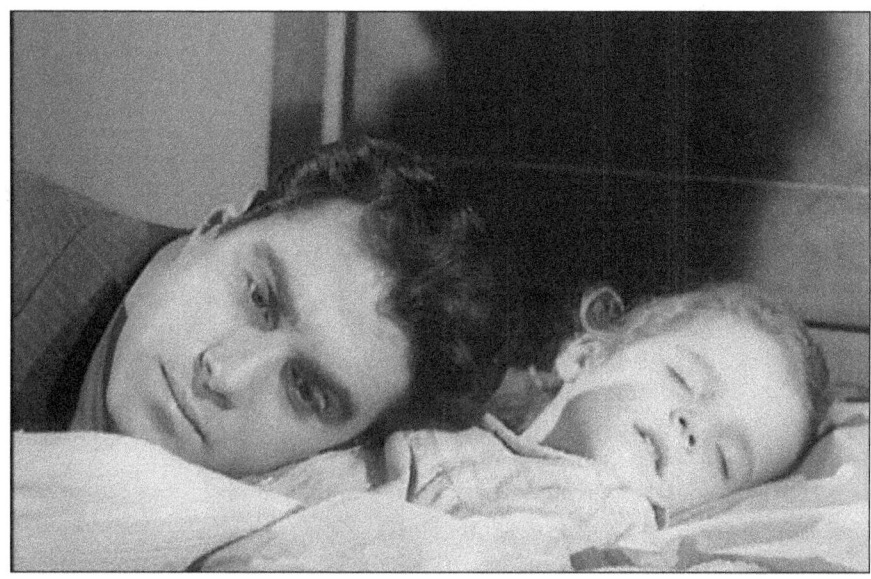
Angelo (Tony Travis) attends little Francesca (Laurie Perreau, younger sister of 1940s child actress Gigi Perreau).

"Doctor" co-star Travis was a singer and, in the late '50s and early '60s, a TV actor. In 1960, he starred as the young hoodlum turned TV singing star in writer-producer Paul Frees' *The Beatniks*. I would add that he was also a Pasadena Playhouse protégé and a veteran of 17 plays there, except that that factoid comes from a 1960 publicity item which adds that he was under contract at MGM (I doubt it), co-starred in the movie *The Outward Room* (there's no such movie) and that he went to Italy to film "The Doctor." When I called him in 2017 to ask about Karloff, he was very charming and sounded eager to please but told me that, while he knew who Boris Karloff *was*, he'd never worked with him. I nicely told him that yes he *had* and then, just for fun, as a "thank you" for talking to me, I offered to send him a DVD of "The Doctor." He sounded pleased as punch. But when I asked him for his address, he paused and then laughed and admitted that he couldn't remember that either. Yet another sad reminder that 2017 is awfully late to still try to be talking to the older Hollywood folks, even from the 1950s.

There's no feeling of buildup in "The Doctor," nor the slightest clue what the story could possibly be building up *to*. For nearly the entire running time, characters bicker and ignorant peasants insist that the aged, dog-tired Carlo be at their beck and call day and night, rain or shine and even in a tremendous windstorm (the Roach wind machine is set on HIGH throughout). The viewer feels frustration rather than suspense as the father of the sick girl rejects all offers of help from Angelo; only after the appearance of Carlo does he yield to sanity and let Angelo treat the child. If by some unthinkable circumstance you need to show a *Veil* episode to someone who doesn't like spooky stories, "The Doctor" would be the one because, minus the Karloff intro, there's not the most microscopic hint that it's a story of the paranormal until the last 20 seconds. (The just-finished "Girl on the Road" runs a close second: We don't learn that we're watching a story about a ghost until there's only a few minutes to go.) The idea of the image of a still-living man making a wordless materialization elsewhere in an hour of need was the punchline of *Telephone Time*'s "The Vestris," which had served as *The Veil*'s pilot.

Adding to the aggravation of "Doctor" viewers, Karloff mentions in his closing comments that Angelo eventually did come around to his father's way of thinking: "The glamour of big city medicine gradually lost its power and he stayed with his father to help what soon became ... *their* people." Since we have never seen the "good" side of these simpletons – and are given reason to wonder if they even *have* a good side – this seems like a waste of an ambitious, resourceful young doctor. The fact that the story takes place at night in a windstorm makes the region appear that much *more* hope-forsaken.

The draft of the script I own is dated September 25, 1958, the title on it is "The Medical Consultant" and it's every bit as painful reading as the episode is painful watching. It features one extra character, Rita, a local girl, "dark, pretty, about 21" – and sweet on Angelo. At least in this script, there's a silver lining (dark, pretty Rita) for Angelo to stay and babysit the backward, selfish peasants.

The Bianchis' kitchen looks like the same set seen as the Haney kitchen in "A Chapter of Genesis." Production on "The Doctor" ended with the filming of scenes in the Bianchi kitchen and bedroom on Friday, October 31. The date may have been Halloween but this dull, annoying story with 20 seconds of spooky punchline was all trick, no treat.

On November 13, Karloff shot intros and outros for more *Veil*s, again directed by Frank P. Bibas. The paperwork I could find doesn't specify which episodes, but the process of elimination makes me confident they were "Vision of Crime," "No Food on the Table" and *perhaps* "Jack the Ripper."

The Veil Episode 5: "Vision of Crime"

Production No. 9205, Shot on November 17, 18 and 19, 1958; Directed by Herbert L. Strock; Produced by Frank P. Bibas; Executive Producer: Hal Roach Jr.; Teleplay: Fred Schiller; Associate Producer: Sidney Morse; Production Supervisor: E.H. Goldstein; Photography: Howard Schwartz; Production Coordinator: William Sterling; Production Manager: D'Estell Iszard; Assistant Director: James W. Lane; Editor: Otho Lovering; Art Director: McClure Capps; Photographic Effects: Jack R. Glass; Set Decorator: Rudy Butler; Music: Leon Klatzkin; Sound: William Russell and Joel Moss; Casting: Ruth Burch; Costumer: John Zacha; Makeup: Sid Perell; Hair Stylist: Margit McEllroy; *The Veil* Created by Frank P. Bibas; **Uncredited:** Script Clerk: Verna Moran; Second Assistant Director: Miles Middough; Gaffer: Paul Grancell; Best Boy: Gordon Wells; First Grip: Larry Milton; Second Grip: Jerry Walton; First Prop Man: Mitch Grimes; Second Prop Man: Ray Pedigo; Laborer: Bob Brian; Camera Operator: Cy Hofberg; First Assistant Cameraman: Ed Wade; Second Assistant Cameraman: Palmer Belmont; Sound Recorders: Jim Masterson and Tom Rennings; Boom Man: John McDonald; Cable Man: William Delamare; Grip: Dean Rose; Special Effects: Bob Overbeck; Stand-ins: Mildred Jean Olsen and Ralph Stein

Cast: Boris Karloff (*Host/Sgt. Chester Willmore*), Robert Hardy (*George Bosworth*), Jennifer Raine (*Julie Westcott*), Patrick Macnee (*Constable Hawton*), Betty Fairfax (*Bertha Clink*), Terence DeMarney (*Albert Ketch*), Donald Lawton (*The Captain*), Kendrick Huxham (*The Scotsman*)[1]

Staring down into a water-filled wash basin, George (Robert Hardy) gets a "Vision of Crime" (the murder of his brother). Unfortunately for George, someone behind the Veil has photographed and directed the vision in such a way that he never sees the killer's face.

Synopsis: In an English village, under cover of darkness, a woman (Jennifer Raine) enters an apothecary shop as the owner Hart Bosworth is closing for the night. Producing a derringer, she fires two deadly shots. At that same moment, on a ship 150 miles out at sea, passenger George Bosworth (Robert Hardy) — Hart's brother — watches as images appear on the surface of the water in his wash basin: He sees the murder of Hart, but not the face of the killer.

Frantic with worry, he returns home and learns the awful truth from his fiancée Julie — whom we the audience recognize as the killer. George describes his vision, and Julie tries to convince him not to tell the police this unbelievable story. Undeterred, George goes to the apothecary shop, where Sgt. Willmore (Karloff) and Constable Hawton (Patrick Macnee) are searching for clues. By behaving strangely, George makes himself a suspect. That night, at the Blue Goose Inn, tipsy Mrs. Clink (Betty Fairfax) tells George that she saw Julie at the shop around the time of the murder. George, his suspicions running high, returns to Julie's and — hoping to force her hand — tells her he intends to sell the shop. Shocked, the avaricious Julie admits that she killed Hart so that she and George would inherit it. Stalking out on the girl, George heads off to notify the police.

"Vision of Crime" was predestined to fail before the ink was dry on the script. The episode might have worked better as a whodunit, but even with that story modification, the bland acting and economical staging would have been a lethal combination.

Director Herbert L. Strock saw his three *Veil* episodes ("Vision of Crime," "The Crystal Ball," "The Return of Mme. Vernoy") for the first time in October 1998 when I sent him copies of the Something Weird tapes. The veteran editor-director subsequently told me:

It was really a mind-boggling thing to see them completed, with the music and the effects in them, and to recall some of the things that happened. First off, I want to say that last Saturday [October 24], I was invited to Sierra Madre, where some people were holding a remembrance of the TV series *Highway Patrol*. They ran three episodes and invited the *Highway Patrol* "dignitaries": myself, actor Bill Boyett and the original technical adviser Frank Ryan, who put in 60 years of service with the Highway Patrol.

For decades, director Herbert L. Strock's résumé read like the history of television.

The reason I mention this is, they ran two of my shows. I sat there, and I said to Geri, my wife, "I don't remember *doing* these!" I didn't remember the actors, I didn't remember the stories, I didn't remember the shots — although some of them certainly had the "Strock imprint," they looked like things that I might have shot. But until my name came up as director on the screen, I was really unsure.

I mention this because the same thing holds true on *The Veil*. I looked at these three episodes, having remembered the shows completely differently than I saw them. I did notice that the movement of the people and the camera were things that I *might* have done, and I did pretty much recall "Vision of Crime," the one where Boris Karloff played the English bobby.

Strock had a long history on the Roach lot: It was on rented sets at Roach that he shot the pioneer TV series *The Cases of Eddie Drake* (1948) with Don Haggerty and Patricia Morison. "I was being observed by the old man [Hal Roach Sr.] *and* by Jr. *and* by other people who were around," Strock continues. "And I was the talk of the town, having made the first film made for television [*Eddie Drake*], having made the first sale of 13 episodes to CBS. I was the king of the hill: Anything that had to be known about television, everybody came to me." In the ensuing years, Roach got into TV production and hired Strock to direct. According to Strock, Roach Jr. "hired a lot of people that I didn't have much faith in; anybody who came along, that could do anything, he would hire. However, he was a very nice guy and I liked Jr. He was a *big* guy, about six-foot-three or -four, and weighed about 250 pounds. But affable, a charming guy. Not that knowledgeable, but willing to learn."

A period piece, "Vision of Crime" is a slow, indoorsy episode that shares the affliction of many *Veil* episodes: wall-to-wall talk. Karloff narration is heard over the shooting death of Hart and over the first shots of George aboard the ship. It is at this point that the dialogue floodgates open wide and stay open right to the end.

Contributing his full share of "chin music" is Karloff, seen here as Chester Willmore. an officious Cockney police sergeant. There's a bit of E.E. Clive's "Constable Jaffers" (from *The Invisible Man*, 1933) and "The Burgomaster" (*Bride of Frankenstein*, 1935) in Karloff's comical Sgt. Willmore, who blusters and states the obvious and takes offense whenever he's called by his first name instead of "sergeant." Playing a self-important, hard-to-take character with few funny lines, Karloff goes down fighting. Patrick Macnee, playing Karloff's much smarter assistant Constable Hawton, subtly registers exasperation at his superior's ineptitude, and gently tries to keep the older man on track. Without half-trying, Macnee gives a more winning performance than Karloff, and in much less screen time. It's fun to see future stars Macnee and, in "The Return of Mme. Vernoy," George Hamilton in *Veil* episodes, a nice relief from all the *Veil*s whose supporting casts are made up of the who's-who of "Who cares?"

Robert Hardy and Jennifer Raine fare no better than Karloff. Like Karloff, Hardy has the deck stacked against him contending with the bland role of the assistant chemist who wanders through the episode stammering out bits and pieces of the story of his bizarre "vision." British actor Hardy is now in his 90s and still going strong; modern audiences might know him best as the Minister of Magic in the Harry Potter movies.

The one good part in the episode, the grasping, murderous wife, is played ineptly by Raine, who makes faces, strikes poses and stares into space as she delivers some of her key lines. (In mid-episode, there's a four-minute scene recorded in a single shot, with Hardy and Raine moving back and forth across a room as they talk about the murder and Hardy's shipboard vision of it.) Raine was the great-great-granddaughter of Charles

Patrick Macnee and Karloff at the apothecary shop "scene of the crime." In 1958, Macnee, TV's future John Steed (*The Avengers*), resided at 770 Napoli Drive in Pacific Palisades and picked up $150 a day for his two-day "Vision of Crime" gig.

Dickens and the stepdaughter of actor Alan Napier. In Napier's posthumously published autobiography *Not Just Batman's Butler*, he wrote about her:

> Her career as an actress, which started with some promise, since she was pretty and talented, somehow failed to develop. Perhaps she wanted to be a success more than she wanted to act. … Perhaps her [real] father's dream of turning her into a child star gave Poppet [Raine's nickname] a secret feeling that she only had to wait for this to happen to her. However that may be, she seemed to be waiting for something wonderful to happen to her instead of going out into the mainstream of life to look for it.

In 1967 when Raine married for the third time, Napier didn't lose a (step)daughter, he gained a son … his own age. Husband #3 was actor Whit Bissell, just a few years Napier's junior. Back in the 1980s, in the days before the Internet and the IMDb, how was I to know that I was talking to Jennifer Raine every time I called the Bissell home to talk with Whit? Although decades younger than Bissell, Raine died first, in 1993.

The primary problem with "Vision of Crime" is the way the episode shows all its cards in the opening scene. Julie is seen entering the shop and killing the chemist, so the audience is way ahead of all the other characters for the balance of the episode. George tells one person after another the increasingly dull story of his vision while Sgt. Willmore and Hawley attempt to solve what is a mystery to them but not the viewer; they even interrogate an unsavory local (Terence DeMarney) spotted at the crime scene. The Karloff-DeMarney scene is pure padding, perhaps devised for the purpose of giving Boris a bit more screen time.

If we the audience had seen the murder the way George saw it in the wash basin, with the face of the killer hidden, the story would have taken on a whodunit flavor, and the revelation of Julie as the culprit might have come as a surprise. Instead, we wade through torrents of talk toward the only wrap-up this story could possibly have. Also: "Vision of Crime" re-gifts us with the paranormal element found in "Summer Heat." In "Summer Heat," Paige, looking out his window, got an advance peek at a murder that would happen in the future while in "Vision of Crime," George, looking in his wash basin, gets a "live" look at a murder taking place miles away. In both, the drama comes from the fact that Paige and George can't tell anyone about it without sounding crazy.

Annoyingly, the supernatural aspect of "Vision of Crime" doesn't advance the plot one bit. Having seen his brother's murder in the wash basin, George returns to England sooner than he would have; but once he does, everything happens the way it would have happened anyway. Mrs. Clink tells George something she neglected to tell the police, that Julie was at the shop minutes before the killing, and a now-suspicious George gets Julie to 'fess up. It woulda-coulda happened that way whether he'd had the vision or not.

Regarding Karloff, Strock told me:

> Here's a man [Karloff] many, many years advanced of myself—I was a kid – and he had to rely on me as the director. I would tell him where to move and how to do things, and he would do whatever I asked him to do as pleasantly as possible, coming up with suggestions (as any actor will do). It was a pleasure working with this man.
>
> Boris was the kind of man who would arrive on the set long before anyone else. I would give him a ten o'clock call and he would show up at eight

o'clock. Sometimes I would come on the set, figuring to be the first person there, and there was Boris and his wife Evelyn sitting there, she doing her knitting and him reading. I would say to him, "What are you *doing* here so early? I gave you a ten o'clock call." (He was no spring chicken at the time, and I didn't want him to be worn out.) But being the professional that he was, and having Evelyn at his side constantly, guiding him, and doing his own makeup, he wanted to be available if and when we ever needed him. That was greatly appreciated. I think, of all the actors I've worked with over the years (including some of the better-known actors), he was *the* most professional, the most willing. And a very capable actor. He could play from a bobby to a gentleman to … *any*thing! There was nothing this guy couldn't do, and I loved working with him. I enjoyed doing these [*Veil*] shows very much, although the budgets were *extremely* limited.

Terence DeMarney as the poacher suspected of murder. He was later seen in episodes of *Thriller* (remember the back-from-the-dead Uncle Julian in "Trio for Terror"?) and in Karloff's *Die, Monster, Die!* He died under the wheels of a London subway in 1971.

Fred Schiller must have scripted "Vision of Crime" before the castle setting for Karloff's intros had been decided upon, because he calls for Karloff to do his bit in a study. "In the back we perceive shelves lined with books. As we open the scene, BORIS KARLOFF is standing before a desk, perusing the pages of a book. As he turns another page he suddenly becomes aware of the watching viewers. Smiling gently, he sits down behind the desk, the book before him." At this point, Karloff greets us with a spiel that sounds like something that was written for the purpose of beginning *every Veil* episode:

Good evening… I've just been reading a fascinating story in this book of case histories.

(somberly)

What makes this story different is that it's reported to be true…

After a FADE OUT and COMMERCIALS, the script calls for Karloff to return with this intro, which is *not* the intro heard in the episode:

Very likely you will be as much amazed as I have been about some of the strange and mystifying things that are revealed in the story and for which there is no explanation… It all began in the year of 1880. Two brothers, George and Hart Bosworth, residing in the old market town of Trebodwine, England, had an extremely close relationship throughout their lives. As the owner of the town's apothecary shop they were highly regarded in their community… then one day, George, the younger of the two brothers, sailed on a packet-boat to Marseilles…

The version of the script in my possession isn't at all like the episode that was filmed. It starts on the boat with George (but not the viewer) seeing the vision of the murder in a mirror. He cries out, "Hart! What have they done to you!" and rushes to the bridge to talk to the captain. George tells the captain that in the mirror, he saw two sailors enter the shop and shoot his brother to death.

In this script, Sgt. Willmore is described as "a tall and serious looking man of about 55" and he's nothing like the dunderhead Karloff plays on screen. Hart's murder takes place in the morning, as he is opening the shop. As Sgt. Willmore and Hawley investigate, Agnes Roberts (not the clapper-tongued Mrs. Clink) says she was near the scene of the crime at the time, heard the shots, hurried to the shop and saw Michael Westcott, the brother of George Bosworth's fiancée

Julie, run out. That night, Willmore arrests Michael, who says he was just yards from the shop when he heard the shots, looked in, saw Hart's body and panicked. He also says that he went to the shop to try to borrow money from Hart, having already gotten George to make him some loans.

George returns and tells Julie – and then Sgt. Willmore – about his vision. Willmore is unimpressed. George now recalls that in his vision, he saw one of the sailors drop the gun into a dustbin; at the shop, he goes through back room dustbins until he finds it. Willmore and Hawley are summoned, and Hawley finds on the floor near the back door a button from a German sailor's uniform. Willmore, now a believer, says there are two German freighters in the harbor and encourages George to go to a local pub (sailors' favorite hangout) and watch for the sailors he saw in the vision. When the sailors enter the Green Lantern Tavern at closing time, Julie rushes off to alert Willmore as George crosses to the bar where the sailors are sitting. As the sailors rise to leave, they are met at the door by Willmore and Hawley. Willmore has brought along the derringer and button as evidence, and makes the pinch.

Needless to say, when a TV episode is supposedly based on an actual event, and you read a version of the script that's *this* different from the finished product, you start to wonder which script more accurately depicted the actual event. Then you wonder if either one accurately depicted the actual event. At this point, you would be forgiven for wondering if there ever *was* an actual event.

"Vision of Crime" began shooting on November 17, five days after the L.A. opening of King Karloff's *Frankenstein 1970* (on a double bill with *Queen of Outer Space*). It was the first of two *Veil*s shot the week of November 17-21 – the only *Veil*s shot that whole month. Karloff worked all day the first day and briefly on the morning of the second. The shipboard scenes were finished early in the afternoon of the 19th and there was a break for lunch … and then Karloff was back to commence work on the best *Veil* Karloff-wise, probably the best *Veil* period: "No Food on the Table."

The Veil Episode 6: "No Food on the Table"

Production No. 9209, Shot on November 19, 20 and 21, 1958; Produced and Directed by Frank P. Bibas; Executive Producer: Hal Roach Jr.; Teleplay: Jack Jacobs; Associate Producer: Sidney Morse; Production Supervisor: E.H. Goldstein; Photography: Howard Schwartz; Production Coordinator: William Sterling; Production Manager: D'Estell Iszard; Assistant Director: James W. Lane; Editor: Otho Lovering; Art Director: McClure Capps; Photographic Effects: Jack R. Glass; Set Decorator: Rudy Butler; Music: Leon Klatzkin; Sound: William Russell and Joel Moss; Casting: Ruth Burch; Costumer: John Zacha; Makeup: Sid Perell; Hair Stylist: Margit McEllroy; *The Veil* Created by Frank P. Bibas; **Uncredited**: Script Clerk: Verna Moran; Second Assistant Director: Miles Middough; Gaffer: Paul Grancell; Best Boy: Gordon Wells; First Grip: Larry Milton; Second Grip: Jerry Walton; First Prop Man: Mitch Grimes; Second Prop Man: Ray Pedigo; Laborer: Bob Brian; Camera Operator: Cy Hofberg; First Assistant Cameraman: Ed

Wade; Second Assistant Cameraman: Palmer Belmont; Sound Recorder: Jim Masterson; Boom Man: John McDonald; Cable Man: William Delamare; Grip: Dean Rose; Special Effects: Bob Overbeck; Stand-ins: Mildred Jean Olsen and Ralph Stein

Cast: Boris Karloff (*Host/Capt. John Elwood*), Kay Stewart (*Ruth Elwood*), Tudor Owen (*Capt. Barney*), Russ Bender (*Calvin Logan*), Eleanor Luckey (*Bessie*), **Uncredited:** Carl Sklover, Dean Carruthers

Synopsis: Capt. John Elwood (Karloff), master of a sailing ship, has a roving eye, a love of money — and little interest in his plain wife Ruth (Kay Stewart), whom he married for her father's dough. The mariner returns from a trip to Florida (during which his ship was infested with poisonous snakes) and, instead of going home, beelines to the Captain's Harbor Inn for drinks and dinner. Finding him there, the long-suffering Ruth loses her temper and pulls the tablecloth off a large club room table set for the elaborate dinner. The angry Elwood brings her home and the two argue. Ruth opens Elwood's trunk and is bitten by a poisonous snake that Elwood inadvertently sealed inside. She survives thanks to the quick action of Elwood, who realizes too late that he missed a perfect opportunity to allow her to die.

When Elwood later sets his cap for a wealthy widow, he invites Ruth to accompany him on a sea journey, and begins to poison her after they set sail. Ruth finally realizes what is happening, rising from her stateroom bed of pain to confront Elwood, and swearing as she dies that Elwood will be "repaid with evil." After Elwood returns from the sea, he visits the inn, where once again tablecloth and settings are torn from the club room table, this time by an unseen force, and in front of eyewitnesses. When a panicked Elwood starts putting fallen items back on the table, the whole table is tipped over by invisible hands. Onlookers realize it is the ghost of Ruth and instantly realize that Elwood snuffed out her life.

It's safe to assume that, as producer of *The Veil*, Frank P. Bibas had his choice of which stories he wished to direct. As his one and only directing job, he selected "No Food on the Table," shot on November 19 (half a day), 20 and 21, 1958. "No Food" could pass as a birthday present for Dear Boris (who turned 71 on the 23rd), providing him with the biggest and best part he had in the short-lived series. It's a *Veil* that's worth half an hour of any Karloff fan's time.

Boris receives top billing in all the *Veil* episodes, most times undeservedly, but here he fully rates the top spot. It's funny to think that, just a few weeks earlier, he was convincingly frail in "Girl on the Road" and "The Doctor" while here the actor is every bit as convincing

The "No Food on the Table" script describes Capt. Elwood (Karloff) as "about 45." Two days after the episode wrapped, the actor turned 71. This was one of just three *Veil* episodes ("The Doctor" and "Destination Nightmare" were the others) where Karloff worked all three days.

as the robust and roguish sea dog Capt. Elwood. He looks a bit like *Bedlam*'s Master Sims in his dark toup and sideburns, laughing and carousing with his pals at the Captain's Harbor Inn and then putting on his stony "Gloomy Gus" expression in scenes with his loyal and unloved wife (Kay Stewart). In the scene where he saves her from the snake poison, then realizes he should have let her die, the look in his eyes speaks volumes. It's at this point that Elwood goes from cad to full-fledged villain; he knows that his first mate (Russ Bender) is suspicious but Elwood nevertheless steers a steady course to murder, poisoning her on his next sea trip. "You've had enough poison to kill *two* people," he snaps after she's figured out his plan. "You might as well know it now: I've wanted you dead, and now you *will* be."

Karloff as Capt. Elwood and actor-screenwriter Russ Bender as his first mate Mr. Logan. In their first scene, Karloff flubs and calls *him* "Mr. Elwood."

Payback's a bitch for Elwood, who is exposed as a killer right in front of all his mateys, ostracized by the community and then (we learn via dialogue) is the one casualty when his next ship unaccountably breaks up and sinks in fair weather on a calm sea. Unmoved by news of his death, Capt. Barney (Tudor Owen) tells several men of the sea in the pub room of the Captain's Harbor Inn, "It's retribution. The Devil has claimed his own." At that very moment, as if on cue, waitress Bessie (Eleanor Luckey) emerges from the club room and happily chirps, "Gentlemen. The food is on the table!" – an ironically timed announcement. The room gets as quiet as if a needle had been lifted off a record and the men hold their poses like figures in a tableau. But then they all laugh, and they're still laughing as they head into the club room to put on the feedbag. (You *know* you've failed at the game of life when the reaction to news of your death is happy laughter!) One of the more pitiless figures in the deep roster of Karloffian depravity, Elwood has come to a fitting end.

Karloff looks right at home in the period setting, but Kay Stewart and Russ Bender seem a bit too twentieth century. Bender doesn't bother with the slight Irish accent the script writer wanted him to have.

Even though everything happens just the way you think it will, the story has the right amount of forward momentum, at least partly because of Boris' star presence. Howard Schwartz keeps his camera on the move to distract the audience from the length of the takes, and rocks it during shipboard scenes to create the proper seagoing mood. The low budget rears its ugly head when the story calls for an establishing shot of the Elwoods' home and instead we get a shot of a so-so painting of a house. Paintings stand in for exteriors in other *Veil*s, including "The Doctor" (the Bianchi cottage), "Vision of Crime" (the Blue Goose Inn) and "Truth in the Crystal Ball" (various abodes – including one with motionless ripples in a body of water out front).

In his introduction, Karloff claims that this story was developed from a report "contained in the files of the Gloucester Historical Society," which may or may not be true. Frank Bibas' daughter Barbara tends to think it might be. "My father had files of these stories [actual 'paranormal' occurrences] that he collected. I remember seeing it when I was younger, it was like a listing of short synopses of real-life supernatural cases. So the stories are based on fact – at least the ones in his files were." On the subject of *The Veil*'s star, she adds, "I don't think my father and Boris Karloff were *real* close, but he liked Karloff very much. He thought Karloff was a very likable man, a real professional and a good person. And he thought Karloff was just perfect for the [job of host] – Karloff did exactly what was expected of him."

The "No Food on the Table" script is included in this book, starting on page 101. There are a number of variations from the episode as filmed: Karloff narration throughout (probably not a good idea, with Karloff also starring as a different character), a Mrs. Elwood with more backbone, etc. Toward the end, as narrator Karloff talks about the gale that wrecked Capt. Elwood's next ship ("an old hulk, with a long record of bad luck"), the script calls for a stock shot of a schooner being tossed about in a storm.

On the episode's shooting schedule are several short scenes that were planned but not filmed or filmed but not used. After Ruth is snake-bit and faints to the floor, we were to have seen Elwood draw a knife and kneel, preparing to drain out the poison. The shipboard death of Ruth was to have been followed by a burial at sea, the paperwork calling for Elwood, Logan and four sailors as attendees plus the props "burial canvas w/weights, plank." And, at the end, we were to have had the satisfaction of seeing the evil Elwood hit the skids: a montage as he goes from one shipping office to another unsuccessfully trying to get work. Makeup- and wardrobe-wise, he was supposed to look all right at the first shipping office and "very seedy looking" at the second, and then "down & out" at the docks as the sequence ended.

Most of the second day of shooting, November 20, was devoted to the cabin and stateroom scenes of Elwood poisoning Ruth and her dying denunciation of him. If the mood on the set was serious during the shooting of these grimly dramatic scenes, it was surely dispelled in the mid-afternoon when *The Veil* went on hold for a half-hour so that a test could be shot for Roach's upcoming *The Dennis O'Keefe Show*!

Despite Karloff's rep as the screen's top terrornaut, "No Food on the Table" is the only *Veil* that finds him in a less-than-humanitarian mood. Even though the actor's darkest movie deeds were now on coast-to-coast late-night TV display (and getting big ratings) via his old movies in the *Shock!* package, casting directors were often giving him roles as kindlier characters, probably partly because of his age and perhaps also partly due to the fact that his off-screen "gentle as a kitten" persona was permeating all his interviews. The January 11, 1958, *TV Guide* article "Love That Monster" includes quotes from his friend of 19 years, actor Carl Esmond, who revealed that the garden in one of Karloff's past Hollywood homes was partly destroyed by marauding birds. The punchline to Esmond's story: "Do you know what Boris did in retaliation? He built half-a-dozen bird baths and bird houses."

Elwood (Karloff) puts the liquid- in liquidation, closing the chapter on his marriage to Ruth (Kay Stewart) with poison. This might be Karloff's best *Veil* performance.

Dave Kaufman's *Variety* column "On All Channels," November 25, 1958

[Boris] Karloff feels TV is a breeze, be it film or live, although he has a preference for the latter. "It's a hangover from my days in stock; and that helps me considerably. TV is not so tough compared to stock work. My new series, *The Veil*, calls for me to play a different part in each episode; that's what I did in stock." Actually, Karloff began toiling in stock in 1910 in Western Canada and the Northwest U.S. "I played all the tanks," he recalls. He came here in 1920, became a truck driver to keep eating, finally getting his break in 1931 with *Frankenstein*.

The vet describes *The Veil* as a series dealing with the supernatural, "more or less, and authenticated stories that couldn't happen but did."

Karloff observes: "TV to me is the most intimate form of communication there is. You should play a part for the small set, with an average audience of two people. To hell with the millions they tell you are looking; they're dying to tune you out and go to another channel at the slightest provocation. TV is over-producing for the small screen; I'm convinced of that. And if a show is cluttered up with too many characters, the show means nothing. Mickey Rooney's fine show, *Eddie*, had just the one actor. But you understood his problem, and the show wasn't divided up with six or eight other people, so that you get lost … I also don't know why they have all those long shots; they're lost on TV. There's a helluva lot of waste in TV. The temptation is to use a budget for a lot of speaking parts and sets. … The foundation of the whole operation is in the story; the man who puts words on paper is the most important man in the whole operation," he claims.

The Veil Episode 7: "The Return of Mme. Vernoy"

Twice The Veil nodded to the 1950s fad for reincarnation yarns, "The Return of Mme. Vernoy" and "Peggy?" (the two episodes were shot on the same sets). Here's Karloff in "Mme. Vernoy" as Goncourt; according to the script, he's 55 or 60, a professor of mathematics at the Sorbonne in Paris.

Production No. 9206, Shot on December 1, 2 and 3, 1958; Directed by Herbert L. Strock; Produced by Frank P. Bibas; Associate Producer: Sidney Morse; Executive Producer: Hal Roach Jr.; Teleplay: Stanley H. Silverman; Production Supervisor: E.H. Goldstein; Photography: Howard Schwartz; Production Coordinator: William Sterling; Production Manager: D'Estell Iszard; Assistant Director: James W. Lane; Editor: Otho Lovering; Art Director: McClure Capps; Photographic Effects: Jack R. Glass; Set Decorator: Rudy Butler; Music: Leon Klatzkin; Sound: William Russell and Joel Moss; Casting: Ruth Burch; Costumer: John Zacha; Makeup: Sid Perell; Hair Stylist: Margit McEllroy; *The Veil* Created by Frank P. Bibas; **Uncredited:** Script Clerk: Verna Moran; Second Assistant Director: Miles Middough; Wardrobe Woman: Hazel Allensworth; Gaffer: Paul Grancell; Best Boy: Gordon Wells; First Grip: Larry Milton; Second Grip: Jerry Walton; First Prop Man: Mitch Grimes; Second Prop Man: Ray Pedigo; Laborer: Bob Brian; Camera Operator: Cy Hofberg; First Assistant Cameraman: Ed Wade; Second Assistant Cameraman: Palmer Belmont; Sound Recorder: Jim Masterson; Boom Man: John McDonald; Cable Man: William Delamare; Grips: Dean Rose and Robert Higgins; Greensman: Hank Ford; Stand-ins: Mildred Jean Olsen and Ralph Stein

Cast: Boris Karloff (*Host/Prof. Charles Goncourt*), Lee Torrance (*Santha Naidu*), Jean Del Val (*Armand Vernoy*), Iphigenie Castiglioni (*Mme. Naidu*), George Hamilton (*Krishna Vernoy*), Julius Johnson (*Rama Mukerjee*)

Synopsis: The story is set in India during World War II (the script says 1943). Rama Mukerjee (Julius Johnson) is in love with Santha Naidu (Lee Torrance) and asks her mother Mme. Naidu (Iphigenie Castiglioni) for permission to marry Santha. But Mme. Naidu drops a bombshell: Santha was born with the memory of a previous incarnation; knows that she was married and had a son in that earlier life; and, just one day earlier, finally remembered the name of her husband. Mme. Naidu and Rama accompany Santha to the city of Muthra, where they call at the home of Armand Vernoy (Jean Del Val), who was married to the late Sita Vernoy (Santha in a past life). Santha's claim to be the reborn Sita stuns Armand, intrigues Armand's friend Prof. Goncourt (Karloff) and appalls Armand's son Krishna (George Hamilton), who is about Santha's age.

Armand has admitted to Prof. Goncourt that he has made some unwise investments and has been financially ruined, and therefore cannot send Krishna to New York's Columbia College as planned. When Santha hears this news, she reminds Armand that he gave his late wife a fortune in jewels. Armand says that the jewels have been missing for years, at which point Santha reveals where Sita kept them (inside a box hidden in the base of a pedestal). Armand finally accepts that Santha is his wife reborn.

The mysteries of the East are touched upon in this *Veil* episode which (as usual) host Karloff claims is "based on a true and authenticated incident."

Unlike "Girl on the Road," "No Food on the Table"

and "The Doctor," which save their supernatural elements for the end, "The Return of Mme. Vernoy" introduces the outré plot device (reincarnation) early on. Unfortunately, it works to this story's disadvantage: For 20 minutes, Santha tries to convince people that she is Mme. Vernoy reborn, and this is more than enough time for everything to succumb to silliness. Lee Torrance's performance doesn't help. In order to seem "spiritual" and wise beyond her years, she delivers many of her lines with a glance heavenward. But the young actress overdoes it, rolling her eyes so far up into her head that she looks like she's simply making faces. The far-out dialogue, Torrance's face-making and the sitcom-like situations (young Santha "mothers" young Krishna, who gets annoyed) are a fatal combination.

Torrance is a bust acting-wise, but Jean Del Val, playing the widower, does a good job of registering shock and dismay, as the situations dictate. In this episode, Karloff hosts, provides some narration (to help jump-start the complex story) and also plays the bearded and bespectacled Prof. Goncourt, the Vernoy family friend and advisor. In the wrap-up, host Karloff tells us that Armand Vernoy and Santha went their separate ways following the events depicted in this story; "Their decision to part, this time forever, undoubtedly avoided future unhappiness for all concerned." It also undoubtedly avoided unhappiness for censors who kept a weather eye on TV scripts, and would have taken a dim view of Santha shacking up with old cocker Armand for the final fadeout. The script describes Santha as 14 or 15, "a youthful, introspective Hindu 'Madonna.'" We also learn via the script that Armand is an archaeologist.

Also featured in the cast is George Hamilton, who in 1958 was at the beginning of his screen acting career. He worked two days on "Mme. Vernoy," pulling down $125 a day. In his 2008 autobiography *Don't Mind If I Do*, a *New York Times* bestseller, Hamilton wrote about the day when he used his last savings to buy his agent Buster Vogel a bottle of Jack Daniel's "to bribe him to get me something [some acting jobs]. He put the bottle in his desk drawer and promised me good news if I called him on Monday." The "good news" was a bit part on a *Rin Tin Tin* TV episode and "even more insignificant" acting chores on *The Donna Reed Show* and *Cimarron City*. Hamilton continued:

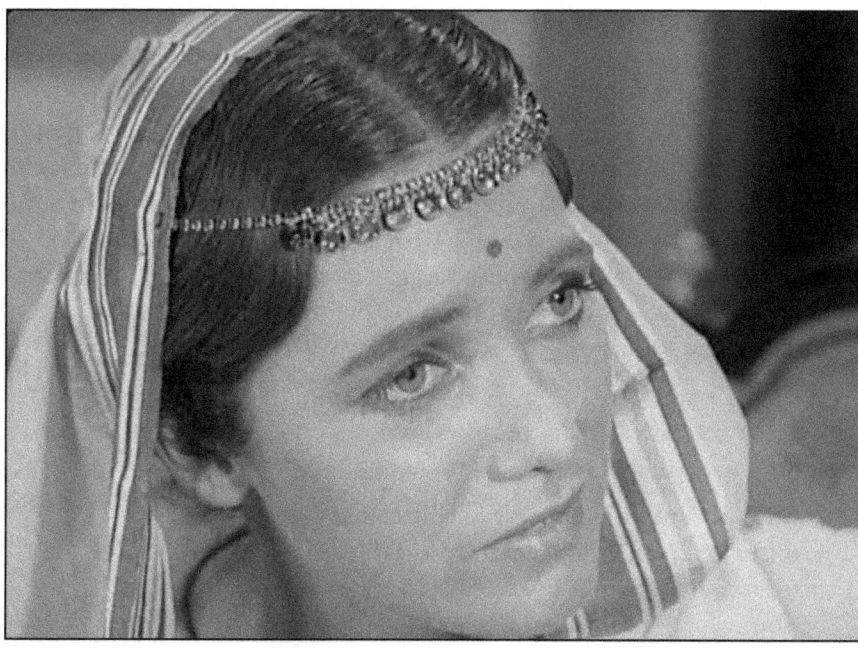
With a TV career of three 1958-59 episodes (one of them, her *Veil*, never broadcast), Lee Torrance went on to neverlasting show biz fame.

Many 1950s TV series happened to feature up-and-coming stars. *The Veil* provided early glimpses of Patrick Macnee, Denise Alexander and, in "The Return of Mme. Vernoy," George Hamilton (pictured here with Jean Del Val).

Best of a bad lot was a bit on *The Veil*, a *Twilight Zone*-ish anthology of horror shows hosted by Boris Karloff. Instead of playing cowboys, this time I played an Indian. Meeting Frankenstein was a thrill that mitigated the ignomiy of my situation. That was something to write home about. Boris himself honored me with a bit of useful advice: "Never let your jacket gap away from your neck. It's the sign of the bad politician and the bad actor."

"George Hamilton was a rising young thing, and he was not the easiest character to work with," director Herbert L. Strock told me. He continued,

> It was only out of his respect for Boris that I got George to do *anything*; George was rather difficult to move around, and would always want to be somewhere else. When Boris showed George that he [Boris] had faith in *me*, George then got faith in me. But up to that point, he wasn't the easiest guy to work with.
>
> Ruth Burch [who cast the *Veil* episodes] knew a lot of people. She got the best she could get for the price she could pay, and once in a while we'd come up with a decent actor.[2] It was a pleasure to have people like Pat Macnee and Leonard Penn and some of the others, and George Hamilton as well. I enjoyed doing *The Veil*, and I know that Roach was pleased with what I was doing. By planning very carefully and letting the assistant director Jimmy Lane know the order of shots I would shoot, I was able to start at eight o'clock, nine o'clock in the morning and get *through* by six o'clock. I never never went beyond six or seven o'clock at night, I never went into overtime and I always brought them in *under* budget. That was one of the things that Roach liked, because it was tough getting money. The studio was in dire trouble. Hal Roach was interested when we were shooting; he would come down on the set once in a while.

Another regular on the set, Strock recalls, was Karloff's wife Evelyn. "Mrs. Karloff was a charming elderly lady, and she did her knitting or read while he worked. She stayed there – came with him first thing in the morning and stayed with him. I *guess* she did the driving – I'm not sure. She saw to it he had his hot tea and that he had lunch, and she was actually very helpful in rehearsing lines with him, things like that. I *liked* her."

The "Mme. Vernoy" script, dated September 25, 1958, starts on page 142 of this book. (Apparently the original copy passed through the hands of the series' art director McClure Capps, whose name [Mac Capps] is handwritten on the cover.) Karloff may have received this script around the time that the article "Karloff, First 'Monster,' Says Current Horror Pix in Bad Taste" appeared on the bottom of page one of the November 21, 1958, *Variety*:

> Today's producers of so-called "horror" pix are violating all precepts of good taste and making "sensational pictures for the sake of being sensational," and it means "the people will start yawning at these efforts if they're not already," it was asserted yesterday by Boris Karloff, who appeared in one of the first of all "monster" or "shocker" pix as the Frankenstein monster in 1931. Karloff deplored the product being made today, saying, "They're beginning to do things in bad taste. They're rubbing your nose in it. An audience can only be interested if it's allowed to take part, but today they show people a bucket

Karloff wasn't averse to beefing about the low quality of some of his own movies, including 1958's *Frankenstein 1970* (with Jana Lund, pictured). He said in one interview that that movie convinced him that no one nowadays (the late '50s) could make a horror movie with taste: "[But] I guess they'll go on as long as people are stupid." (Photo courtesy John Antosiewicz)

of guts just to show a bucket of guts. The audience isn't permitted to use its imagination."

…Although he frowns on the type of pix now being made, Karloff emphasized: "I'm completely opposed to any kind of censorship – that's wrong. The public is the best censor. It boils down to good taste. When things are made in bad taste, the public will take care of it by not seeing such pictures.

"This is a great revival, but like in all things fashions will change, in this case because the revival is being abused. You can't eat beefsteak three times a day and enjoy it, and now there's a rash, a flood of such pictures," he commented.

At that point, November 1958, two of Karloff's newest features were *The Haunted Strangler* and *Frankenstein 1970*. In the former, he chokes and slashes a dance hall girl (Vera Day) to death with his scalpel, chokes and stabs his wife (Elizabeth Allan) to death with the scalpel, and he also drags a piece of broken glass across the face of an asylum guard. In *Frankenstein 1970*, playing a 20th-century Frankenstein descendant, he carries a human heart around his lab, massaging it in a close-up, and later totes a jar containing eyeballs. His other recent feature (not yet released as of 1958), *Corridors of Blood*, featured an on-screen knifing, a villain getting a face-full of acid in close-up, and more.

How funny … and hypocritical … to find Karloff looking down his nose at the makers of movies such as these, when *he* was one of the makers of movies such as these. In fact, since he "carries" these pictures, and they probably wouldn't have been made if he'd refused to do them, he was the *most* responsible. For most of his post-*Frankenstein* career, Karloff had to have been in high cotton, and the cotton had to be higher than ever in his twilight years; and yet he continued making increasingly horrific horror movies, some so gruesome they make *Haunted Strangler* and *Frankenstein 1970* look restrained.

Take their money and run – *and then complain and badmouth your producers* – Dear Boris.

The Veil Episode 8: "Truth in the Crystal Ball"

Novelist Vallier (Booth Colman), cast aside by a girlfriend who marries his wealthy publisher, realizes that "Girls Just Want to Have Funds" in "Truth in the Crystal Ball."

(The title on the script is "Truth in the Crystal Ball" but Roach production paperwork calls it "Truth in a Crystal Ball." All modern sources refer to the episode as "The Crystal Ball.") Production No. 9203, Shot on December 3, 4 and 5, 1958; Directed by Herbert L. Strock; Produced by Frank P. Bibas; Executive Producer: Hal Roach Jr.; Teleplay: Robert Joseph; Associate Producer: Sidney Morse; Production Supervisor: E.H. Goldstein; Photography: Howard Schwartz; Production Coordinator: William Sterling; Production Manager: D'Estell Iszard; Assistant Director: James W. Lane; Editor: Bruce Schoengarth; Art Director: McClure Capps; Photographic Effects: Jack R. Glass; Set Decorator: Rudy Butler; Music: Leon Klatzkin; Sound: William Russell and Joel Moss; Casting: Ruth Burch; Costumer: John Zacha; Makeup: Sid Perell; Hair Stylist: Margit McEllroy; *The Veil* Created by Frank P. Bibas; **Uncredited**: Script Clerk: Verna Moran;

Second Assistant Director: Miles Middough; Wardrobe Woman: Hazel Allensworth; Gaffer: Paul Grancell; Best Boy: Gordon Wells; First Grip: Larry Milton; Second Grip: Jerry Walton; First Prop Man: Mitch Grimes; Second Prop Man: Ray Pedigo; Laborer: Bob Brian; Camera Operator: Cy Hofberg; First Assistant Cameraman: Ed Wade; Second Assistant Cameraman: Palmer Belmont; Sound Recorder: Jim Masterson; Boom Man: John McDonald; Cable Man: William Delamare; Grips: Robert Higgins and Dean Rose; Greensman: Hank Ford; Special Effects: Bob Overbeck; Stand-ins: Mildred Jean Olsen and Ralph Stein

Cast: Boris Karloff (*Host/Andre Giraud*), Booth Colman (*Edmond Vallier*), Roxane Berard (*Marie*), Leonard Penn (*Charles Montcour*), Albert Carrier (*Philippe Jussard*), **Uncredited:** Mildred Jean Olsen (*Maid*)

Synopsis: Another *Veil* with a period setting (circa 1900, according to the script) and a foreign locale (France). Edmond Vallier (Booth Colman) is a writer of love stories whose real-life romance with Marie (Roxane Berard) has reached its unhappy final chapter: Behind his back, the pretty little sexpot has fanned a new flame, Vallier's wealthy publisher Charles Montcour (Leonard Penn), and now she's casting Vallier aside to marry Montcour. As a going-away present, Marie gives Vallier a crystal ball, "a symbol of the future to commemorate our past."

After Montcour and Marie marry, Montcour plans a business trip and asks Vallier to occasionally visit Marie while he is away. Vallier, combating writers' block, is too busy in the ensuing days to call on Marie – but he does keep tabs on her via the crystal ball, in which he is able to see images of Marie and her artist-lover (Albert Carrier) carrying on an affair at the artist's Paris apartment. Haggard and unshaven, Vallier becomes obsessed with the crystal; not even his roguish "ladies man" uncle Andre Giraud (Karloff) can coax him out of his morbid new mindset. Montcour, returning from his trip, visits Vallier, senses his agitation and badgers him to explain the situation. When Vallier says he sees Marie in the crystal, Montcour scoffs. To settle matters, Vallier and Montcour travel together to Paris, to the apartment house in Vallier's crystal ball visions – and they catch Marie and the artist together in the love nest. Vallier returns home and smashes the crystal ball.

Once again, Karloff's closing commentary is a John Newland-*One Step Beyond*-style spiel, meant to convince viewers that the events in "Truth in the Crystal Ball" were taken from a true and documented incident: "Based on Edmond Vallier's testimony of what he had seen in the crystal ball, Montcour was granted a divorce – the only time that evidence of this kind has ever been accepted in a court of law."

"Where these stories came from is beyond me," "Crystal Ball" director Herbert L. Strock told me. He continued,

> Bibas, being the producer, would hire the writers. [The stories] were *supposed* to be based in some way on *fact*. I honestly don't think they really *were*, but *maybe* they were, maybe some *iota* of the story [was true], and then the writers would embellish it into whatever they wanted to do. These writers – I don't recall ever having met with any of them, I don't *know* any of them, I never used any of them on anything else. They must have been friends of Bibas' or had worked for Roach – I don't know.

> The stories themselves were talky. What bothered me was that they never had any action, we were never allowed to go outside and shoot. Roach had a stock library

Right at the start of the "Crystal Ball" script, writer Robert Joseph lets us know what to think of Marie (Roxane Berard) as she gives Vallier the brush with the hard bristles: "This is basically a cruel dame, and she plays the rest of the scene casually and lightly, with no thought of his feelings."

and he would pull scenes. As you saw in ["The Return of Mme. Vernoy"], they'd get footage of an Indian railroad station and things like that, in order to get a little "expanse." I felt the stories were talky, and therefore I tried to *move* actors. I moved actors from two-shots into singles, and then back into two-shots and three-shots, in order to save the time of cutting them up into individual close-ups. To try to keep them *moving*. Which was a very difficult thing to do, with nothing but yak-yak going all the time.

"Truth in the Crystal Ball" is nothing but yak-yak, but at least it's halfway-interesting yak-yak, and the plot does keep a (tenuous) hold on the viewer's interest. The idea of mystically spying on one's own ex-lover appeals, naturally, to the voyeur in all of us; it goes without saying that Vallier, who keeps his nose to the crystal ball like it's been Krazy Glued there, is seeing them do more than play footsie. This is made a bit more obvious than one would expect in a 1958 TV episode: When we first see Marie in the artist's apartment, she's stepping out from behind a screen adjusting her clothes, creating the impression they've just had a nooner. In the episode, a nighttime scene of Marie and the artist making out is followed by a shot of Vallier watching them in the crystal; in the script but not the episode, this is followed by a morning-after shot of Vallier *still* keeping vigil on them: "It is entirely possible he hasn't moved from this spot all night." The episode also features the same sort of sticky situation found in "Vision of Crime": Through supernatural intervention, a man gets an eyeful of distant events, but can only talk about them at the risk of being considered insane. Eerie library music, some of it glommed from the spooky sand pit scenes of *Invaders from Mars* (1953), evokes memories of past goosebumps.

Except for the bogus French accents, the actors do a good job of putting forth the far-out story. Booth Colman might be a bit unglamorous to perfectly fit the role of a romance novelist-jilted lover, and yet he comes across well. In the scene in which Colman can't bring himself to tell Karloff about the crystal ball visions, Colman cries, wipes the tears, sniffles and finally sobs, "Uncle Andre, I fear I'm going *out of my miiind!*" This

Marie and Philippe (Albert Carrier and Roxane Berard) in the crystal ball (a matte shot), as seen by Vallier as he obsessively monitors the lovers' trysts.

emotional outburst is not found in the script (well, not in my draft of the script), so perhaps it was suggested by the actor. "Booth Colman was one of the better actors to appear on *The Veil*," Strock told me. "I think I found him at a little theater and brought him to [casting lady] Ruth Burch. I thought he was an excellent actor and I wanted to use him — and I used him in other things *after* that."

The real-life father of Sean Penn, Leonard Penn plays the part of the pompous publisher with the proper amount of bluster. Roxane Berard looks and acts just right as the little tease who gives Vallier the air to marry his publisher, and then instantly strays off the marital reservation. Mildred Jean Olsen, a *Veil* series stand-in right from Day One, has a silent bit as the Montcours' maid. Acting schools must teach students to wag their index fingers – a lot – when they play Frenchies, because the actors here do it — a lot.

The "letdown" performance is, again, Karloff, who had no business playing the girl-crazy Andre Giraud. Karloff actually *looks* funny in his fancy clothes and bowler, garish bow tie and monocle, and *sounds* funny speaking with zee Frrrench ac-*cent*. Uncle Andre calls himself "a seasoned campaigner in the game of love," but he comes across just like your everyday, garden variety, standard-issue dirty old man. "You have heard, no doubt, of my little black book," Giraud, smug and self-satisfied, tells Vallier. "Ho, ho, ho, ho, it is well-known in Paree. Perhaps as famous as the Arc de Triomphe

Karloff as Uncle Andre the Paris Boulevardier. The script describes this roué as 60 and likens him to Maurice Chevalier in *Gigi*. Uncle Andre appears to be an attempt at comic relief but viewers may be more embarrassed than amused. Pictured: Colman, Karloff.

and the Champs d'Elysees!" Women are all that Giraud ever seems to have on his mind, but you have to wonder how often this conceited old cocker would score if he started leaving his checkbook at home.

"Truth in the Crystal Ball" began production on the afternoon of December 3, 1958, after the morning was spent finishing "The Return of Mme. Vernoy." Karloff was on hand that first (half-)day. At 5:45 that evening, the company moved to Stage 6 to shoot Karloff's intros and outros for "Mme. Vernoy" and "Crystal Ball."

Booth Colman saw "Crystal Ball" for the first time when I sent him a VHS tape in 1998, and "it was the most extraordinary experience watching it!" exclaimed the veteran stage-film-TV actor. "The entire thing was long gone from my memory and I couldn't believe it was me up there. Vaguely I recalled sitting on the sofa with Boris Karloff saying lines, but that's all."

"Crystal Ball" was a reunion for Karloff and Colman, who first met when Karloff was a silent partner in Maurice Evans' Broadway presentation of *Hamlet* (1945-46) and Colman played the part of Guildenstern. "And Boris was courting one of the ladies in the company," Colman recalled.

> She wasn't an actress, she was an English lady who handled Evans' business and personal details. Boris and Evie were married when we were on our break-in tour. In our company, playing Osric, was Morton DaCosta, who later became a very important director — *Auntie Mame* [1958] and *The Music Man* [1962] were some of his film credits. I remember he sent Evie a telegram for the wedding: **DON'T LET HIM SCARE YOU OUT OF BED**. [*Laughs*] I saw the Karloffs for, oh, 20-odd years after that, whenever they came out here [to California]. We were very friendly.

One of the things Karloff mentioned to Colman about *The Veil*, years after the fact: that he was never paid! "I think Karloff told me that nine or ten were made, and then they ran out of money or something," Colman told me.

When I told Strock what Colman had said, he scoffed, "Karloff *did* get paid, that story is a lot of baloney. What Karloff probably *didn't* get was any money from the show — he may have had a participation. But the shows never *went* anywhere, they were never sold. In fact, until now [1998], I never saw them."

Scott Allen Nollen's 1999 book *Boris Karloff: A Gentleman's Life* addresses the money situation. According to this book, Karloff "entered into a contract with Hal Roach Studios to host and appear in 25 episodes of *The Veil*.... For each half-hour installment, he was to be paid $2000 plus an additional $1000 as an advance against syndicated reruns, for a total of $75,000." Nollen says that for the *Veils* Karloff did before Hal Roach Studios went belly-up, he netted $12,500, a "far cry" from the $75,000 he was promised he would earn. Apparently he felt he was entitled to the additional $62,500.

Karloff's opening speech in my copy of the script is all spook talk, and makes no reference to the story about to unfold:

> *The Veil* tells stories of strange and mysterious origin, and often of unexplained outcome ... Our stories are based on fact, as they were reported to authorities and officials by participants or eyewitnesses ... and, in some cases ... by the dead.
>
> We do not ask you to believe ... We ask only that you observe and that you listen, that you reflect, and only then make up your minds about the truth ... that truth which is beyond the veil of our own ignorance ...

"Crystal Ball" was the last *Veil* episode shot in 1958: With eight episodes now completed, the show went on hiatus, the shutdown timed to coincide with that of *The Gale Storm Show* so that the studio would not have to remain operative for only *The Veil*. On the bottom of December 5's Daily Work Sheet (a list of "Crystal Ball" crew members), M.S.M. – presumably second assistant director Miles S. Middough – wrote nice and big: **MERRY CHRISTMAS & HAPPY NEW YEAR!!**

For at least two *Veil* principals, this hiatus was short on Christmas cheer but long on drama – more drama, in fact, than could usually be found in the series! In mid-December, *Veil* creator-producer Frank Bibas exited his own show. *Variety* reported this on December 16, adding that he retained an interest in the property as its creator. On December 17, the paper revealed that Bibas left because of a "policy hassle." Given Hal Roach Studios' financial difficulties, perhaps the "hassle" was Bibas' expectation to get paid once in a while, and the studio's inability to do so … ? On page 3 of this book, his daughter Barbara writes about the effect this unexpected development (Frank's departure) had on the family.

Stressful as this must have been for Frank Bibas, he surely wouldn't have wanted to swap troubles with Boris Karloff: On December 18, in Haslemere, England, his brother Sir John Pratt's daughter Diana Bromley, 39, drugged and then murdered her sons Martin, 13, and Stephen, 10. She strangled one with a belt, drowned the other in a bathtub, and then hacked at both their throats after they were dead. Newspapers in England and the U.S., and probably other countries, plastered the **KARLOFF** name in their headlines: "2 Relatives of Karloff Knife Victims," "Police Arrest Karloff's Kin," "2 Sons of Boris Karloff's Niece Slain — Throats Cut," "Karloff Niece Held for Death of Two Sons," "Karloff Niece Insane Killer" and more. Karloff knew his niece; in fact, in 1940 when she was perhaps 21, she came to California and spent the summer with him, and might have visited the sets of some of his movies during those months (*Doomed to Die*, *The Ape*, *Before I Hang* and *You'll Find Out*).[3]

When *The Veil* went on hiatus, it was supposed to resume on January 5, 1959. But, perhaps as a result of the Pratt family tragedy, the next *Veil* didn't begin shooting until February 9. A number of newspaper articles about the crime and Diana's trial appear on pages 246 and 247.

Gale Storm flanked by *Veil* producer Frank P. Bibas and his wife Susan.

Boris Karloff Meets Gale Storm

Throughout 1958, Hal Roach Studios tried to create the impression (via the trade papers) that it was a beehive of TV production activity, with a long list of announced pilots and series. But all an industry insider had to do to learn the truth was to check out the trade papers' weekly production charts to see that in the fall of that year, all that was being made under the Roach banner was *The Veil* and *The Gale Storm Show*. The latter, also known as *Oh Susanna!*, starred Storm as kooky Susanna Pomeroy, social director of the luxury liner *Ocean Queen*. Karloff crossed over into the cast of a *Gale Storm* episode, "It's Murder, My Dear," which according to *Variety* was slated to begin shooting on December 8 (the Monday after "Truth in the Crystal Ball" finished).

In "It's Murder, My Dear" (aired on January 31, 1959), Susanna and her friend "Nugey" (ZaSu Pitts), operator of the ship's beauty salon, get passes to visit a movie studio. The first half of the Alex Gottlieb-scripted episode is horrendously un-funny as Susanna and "Nugey" conspire to break quarantine and get off the docked ship; when they do, they hurry to the Roach Studios, where the first celebrity they spot is ZaSu Pitts, wearing out-of-date clothes and driving an old-fashioned car. ("Nugey" says, "My mother used to take me to see her in silent pictures!") The girls now traipse over to Lake Laurel and Hardy, where they encounter Boris Karloff, standing at the water's edge reading a script. As charming and self-deprecating as everyone says he was in real life, Karloff talks about his new series *The Veil*, signs "Nugey"'s autograph book and asks them if they'll be visiting the *Veil* set.

> SUSANNA: Are you shooting something
> exciting today?
> KARLOFF: Oh, it might be, possibly. [What
> an optimist!]

Susanna and "Nugey" are on the *Veil* set watching Karloff in action when a man who is Karloff's spitting image appears on a catwalk and shoots at him with a rifle. (Only Susanna and "Nugey" see the sniper.) Karloff, his shoulder grazed by the bullet, is understandably perplexed: "Why would anybody want to shoot me? My old pictures weren't that bad. Or were they?" (Perhaps, Boris, it's some of your more recent pictures that are the problem!) As Karloff is taken to the studio hospital, Susanna tells the director (Frank Cady) that Karloff was shot by a man who looked just like him; the director laughs them off. "What a pair of characters," he marvels. "They'd be great in a television series ... " (*Another* optimist!)

At the studio hospital, Susanna, "Nugey," Karloff and a nurse are imprisoned by the Karloff double, a frustrated actor who can't get a break because he looks just like Karloff. The imposter now returns to the *Veil* set posing as Karloff and acts in a scene. Then, seeing that Karloff and the others have freed themselves and are watching from the sidelines, he calmly asks to be arrested. "He wasn't half-bad," Karloff says of his twin's *Veil* performance. He then adds a line that sounds like something he himself might have suggested: "The only difference is, I'm a bit hammier and a great deal *luckier*."

The first half of the episode (aboard the ship) is dreadful, but for Karloff fans the second half is highly entertaining — although I must admit that if the story's "TV star" had been anyone other than Karloff, I probably would have hated both halves equally. Karloff plays a very affable, approachable, chatty Karloff (precisely the Karloff we all would like to have met); in his other role as the lookalike who wants a chance to act before the cameras, he hams it up like he's back in a Canadian stock company, circa 1914. (The frustrated lookalike just can't catch a break: Karloff acted in untold hundreds of movies and TV shows, and this poor schnook picks for his first and only screen appearance an episode of the never-released *The Veil*!) Frank Cady, *Green Acres*'

"A Double-Dealing Boris Karloff" is the title of this *Gale Storm Show* still from CBS's Photo Division. The caption: "Boris Karloff dons the dual demeanors of a dastardly dispenser of death and a damaged duplicate of himself for his Saturday, Jan. 31 visit to *The Gale Storm Show* (CBS Television Network, 9:00-9:30 PM, EST). Karloff alternately charms and frightens Gale Storm and her zany sidekick ZaSu Pitts."

store owner Mr. Drucker, plays the *Veil* director, who is named William Seiter after the real-life director of this *Gale Storm* episode. Real-life director Seiter had a long history at the Roach lot: That's where he'd started his career, on camera, as one of the Keystone Cops.

It would have been cute to let the actual *Veil* crew play themselves, but they didn't. I supplied a tape of this episode to Herbert Strock, who told me that he didn't recognize a single one of the on-camera set workers, and said they were definitely a pack of extras.

The original plan, mentioned in *Variety* (November 14, 1958), was for "It's Murder, My Dear" to guest-star Karloff, Guy Madison and Dennis O'Keefe. The blurb said that an "extra large budget has been allotted by CBS-TV for filming by Hal Roach Productions of [this] special segment." Madison and O'Keefe would be involved, again according to *Variety*, because they (like Karloff) had their own Roach series. The Hal Roach Studios may have *wanted* to give Madison and O'Keefe their own series, but it doesn't look like this ever happened. Madison apparently came closer than O'Keefe: His proposed series *The Sword and the Arrow* was mentioned many times in the trades, and a pilot may have been shot. My guess is that by December 8 when "It's Murder, My Dear" was set to begin shooting, the possibility of Madison and O'Keefe series was looking bleak and so the plan to feature them in the *Gale Storm* episode was dropped.

Columnist Erskine Johnson called "It's Murder, My Dear" "a nice little plug for the new Karloff series" and, regarding the title, reported that Gottlieb told him, "I thought of a better title too late, 'Let Me Kill You, Sweetheart.'"

No Funds A-*Veil*-able?

If you worked at Hal Roach Studios in 1959 and read the papers, you knew that the Lot of Fun was in a Lot of Hot Water. The Wednesday, February 4, *Variety* story "Scranton Corp. in Payroll Crisis at Roach Studios" revealed:

> Bloom may be off the rose of the Scranton Corp.'s wide-ranging show biz plans. A temporary crisis last week at Hal Roach Studios, one of the Scranton subsids, was the tipoff, as the studio for some time was unsure whether it would be able to meet its payroll. As it turned out, the payroll was met, and will be met next week, but nobody could predict anything beyond that.
>
> Payment for production personnel was slated for last Thursday [January 29], and by that afternoon Roach execs were phoning the unions asking them for wage waivers, for permission to delay wage payments by one week. They told the unions that money had been held up in New York, due to a short-term financial squeeze that would shortly be overcome. Late that afternoon, word arrived from New York that money would be forthcoming, and Friday afternoon everyone was paid off.
>
> Whatever the nature of the squeeze on Scranton's resources ... fact remains there's grave speculation over the studio's future here....
>
> Meanwhile, studio is operating as usual. [*The Gale Storm Show*] is the only show currently shooting; *The Veil* has laid off for a couple of weeks....

The Veil Episode 9: "Destination Nightmare"

A vision of the long-dead Wally Huffner (Roy Engel) reflected in the cargo plane's windshield in "Destination Nightmare."

Production No. 9222, Shot on February 9, 10 and 11, 1959; Directed by Paul Landres; Produced by Ben Fox; Executive Producer: Hal Roach Jr.; Teleplay: Ellis Marcus; Associate Producer: Jerry D. Lewis; Production Supervisor: E.H. Goldstein; Photography: Howard Schwartz; Production Manager: D'Estell Iszard; Assistant Director: Richard Maybery; Editor: Danny B. Landres; Art Director: McClure Capps; Photographic Effects: Jack R. Glass; Set Decorator: Rudy Butler; Music: Leon Klatzkin; Sound: Jack Goodrich and Joel Moss; Casting: Ruth Burch; Costumer: John Zacha; Makeup: Sid Perell; Hair Stylist: Margit McEllroy; *The Veil* Created by Frank P. Bibas; **Uncredited**: Script Clerk: Verna Moran; Second Assistant Director: Ray Taylor; Gaffer: Paul Grancell; Best Boy: Gordon Wells; First Grip: Larry Milton; Second Grip:

Jerry Walton; First Prop Man: Mitch Grimes; Second Prop Man: Ray Pedigo; Laborer: Bob Brian; Camera Operator: Cy Hofberg; First Assistant Cameraman: Alfred Baalas; Second Assistant Cameraman: Palmer Belmont; Sound Recorder: Jim Masterson; Boom Man: John McDonald; Cable Man: William Delamare; Still Photographer: Stax Graves; **Second Unit (Boris Karloff's Opening and Closing, shot on March 3, 1959):** Directed by John Meredyth Lucas; Camera: Ed Fitzgerald; Sound Recordist: Charles Althouse; Assistant Director: Marty Moss; Second Assistant Director: George Walls; Stand-in: Fred Walton

Cast: Boris Karloff (*Host/Pete Wade Sr.*), Ron Hagerthy (*Pete Wade Jr.*), Myron Healey (*Bill Tighe*), Roy Engel (*Wally Huffner*)

After holding court on a castle set for the *Veils* shot in 1958, host Karloff found himself stuck on a small office set for the last two episodes.

Synopsis: Pete Wade (Karloff), head of a European air service, is double-tough on his son Pete Jr. (Ron Hagerthy) because it worries him that Jr. doesn't have a take-charge attitude and may never learn to be a proper flyer. While flying a run in a cargo plane, Jr. is at the controls and Bill Tighe (Myron Healey) is in the cargo compartment. Jr. is blinded by a small, bright beam of light and then sees a man's face (Roy Engel) reflected in the windshield. The man's hypnotic voice puts Pete into a trance: He changes the plane's heading to 135 and steers a course straight for a hillside. Bill struggles to take the controls away from Jr., and must kayo him to make him let go.

That night, at home, Mr. Wade has a nightmare and calls out the name Wally until Jr. wakes him. Wade tells Jr. that, during World War II, he piloted a B-17 bomber that was hit by the Germans over France; Wally was a war buddy who bailed out with a chute that didn't open while Wade rode the plane down safely. At his father's office, Jr. notices a framed nightclub photo of his father and Wally, and recognizes Wally as the face in the windshield. Later that night, at Jr.'s request, he and Bill go up again to recreate the earlier experience. Once more the face appears, and once again Jr. becomes entranced; there's another near-crash, this one averted when the control wheel moves back sharply *by itself*. Obeying the face's command "Bail out," Jr. parachutes from the plane. Coming to earth in a lonely valley, Jr. finds himself just steps from his father's wrecked bomber and begins to wonder about the truth of the war story he was told. A showdown between father and son brings to light the convoluted true story and the father's long battle with many self-doubts. This leads to a better understanding between them, Jr. astutely observing, "Dad…I think Wally may have helped us both."

For Boris Karloff fans, 1959 began with a January 6 column by Associated Press Motion Picture Writer James Bacon, indicating that Boris was celebrating 50 years as an actor that year. (Unmentioned by Bacon: It was also Karloff's 40th anniversary as a *movie* actor, Boris having made his bow in Douglas Fairbanks' *His Majesty, the American* in 1919.) In the interview, Karloff mentioned that he played his favorite film role in *The Doctor from Seven Dials* (aka *Corridors of Blood*), then recently completed. Bacon also slipped in a plug for *The Veil*, calling it "[Hal Roach Studios'] answer to the saturation of TV Westerns. …It's a chiller, but as Karloff says, 'in an intellectual way.'"

After a hiatus lasting more than two months, *The Veil* went back onto the Roach stages with a new head man: Replacing the series' creator and producer Frank Bibas in the top spot was Ben Fox, a veteran of the Roach Studios' TV series *Code 3*. His first episode "Destination Nightmare" began shooting on February 9.

Starting with this episode, *The Veil* got a slight overhaul: "Destination Nightmare" begins with a pre-credits scene, then features a new title sequence: The series title and **STARRING BORIS KARLOFF** are

Don't be so sure, Boris; "Destination Nightmare" is a flight of fancy that hits one air pocket after another. The story is highly confusing and full of little bloopers and unintentionally funny situations. It's also quite reminiscent of the "restless dead" plots of some past *Veil* episodes.

Pete Wade Sr., cranky head of the air service, lectures Jr. on the destructive effects of doubt upon the human mind; at the end, we learn that Sr. has been suffering from this "malady" since World War II. His very befuddling account of the doomed flight involves intelligence operatives, a secret identity, a false report to the O.S.S., Nazi Germany's Wehrmacht, a poison capsule, a plane that may or may not have crashed and parachutes which may or may not have opened. For utter confusion, this tops the clear-as-mud exposition at the end of "Girl on the Road." I still didn't understand it even after several viewings, so I won't attempt to recount it here. Suffice to say that Sr.'s longtime bouts with doubts, *and* Jr.'s issues, are cured – or at least out in the open – after dead flier Wally's reappearance prompts father and son to thrash things out.

Unintended humor sends the story into a tailspin. In the episode's second half, Jr. and Bill take the plane up in search of the weird sun-reflecting phenomenon – at night! ("I guess I'm wrong," Jr. mutters glumly. "It's not the same now." Well, *duhhh*!) Jr. sends Bill into the cargo compartment for coffee, then immediately changes course with a sharp turn that would have put

In the "Destination Nightmare" script (dated January 26, 1959), the family is named Rumson. What do you want to bet the name became Wade once the *Veil* folks made arrangements to shoot outside this existing business, which I believe was located at the Santa Monica Airport?

shown over what looks like a rumpled piece of satin. Following the titles, Karloff – now situated in an office or den with a bookcase, lamp and world map – talks about the story in progress. He has a new base of operations and new prop (a pipe and tobacco pouch), but the same crummy polka dot tie, which he even wears in the damn episode! "I *do* think you'd be interested in exploring with me that ... strange world that lies [*one eyebrow shoots up*] behind the Veil!"

Bill *and* the coffee up on the ceiling (but doesn't). To prevent Bill from interfering, Jr. locks him in the back and tells him to bail out, even though they're flying over countryside a hundred miles from nowhere, at an altitude of just a few hundred feet.

Hagerthy is too all-American to be playing the son of Karloff's European air magnate. When I contacted him, he had the usual nice things to tell me about Karloff: "He was just a *very* nice guy. A very gentle man, kind…gentlemanly." He continued,

You *know* a show is slipping when its title sequence, formerly superimposed over a large, fabulous castle set, is now seen over what looks like a satin sheet on an unmade bed. Or is this supposed to *be* the Veil?

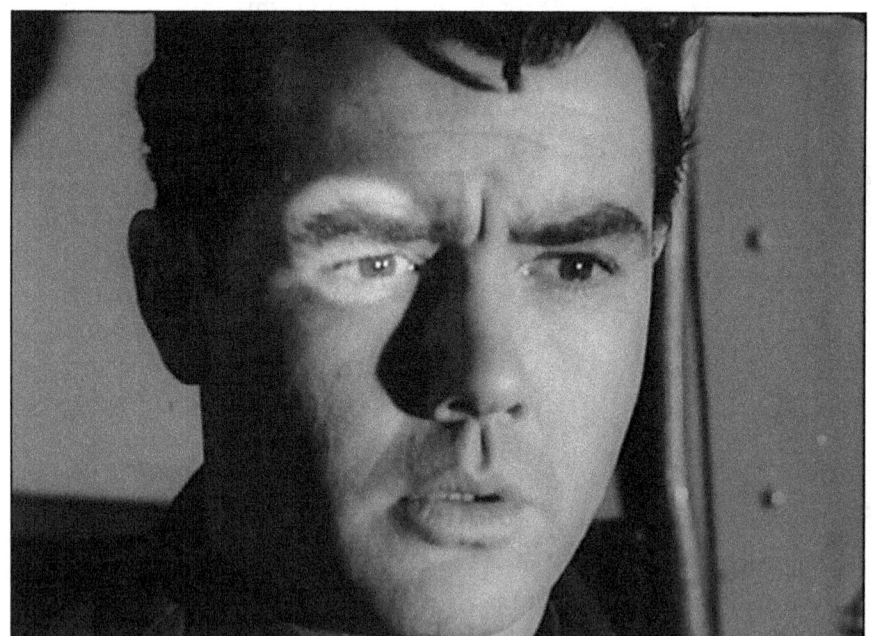

Decades before laser pointers were dangerously directed at pilots, Ron Hagerthy contends with light shining from behind the Veil.

One thing I remember about *The Veil* is one of those horribly embarrassing things. There was a scene where Boris is in bed and I'm standing beside the bed talking to him—he's supposed to be asleep, having nightmares. That scene was just a whole bunch of one-liners – there was no long, lengthy dialogue. It got to be fairly late in the evening, and I went blank – I could not remember more than one line at a time. I did my close-up for that scene just one line at a time, because that was all I could remember. When that happens to you – and it's happened to everybody – there's nothing you can do, you're just helpless. And what it does *technically* is put the editor into a position where he can only use the film a certain way, because he can't "stay" in one shot for more than one line! So you've kind of edited that scene for him [*laughs*] – oftentimes not in your own best interest! I've never forgotten that scene, which was one of the dark moments of my life.

Coincidentally, or maybe not, it was during the shooting of *The Veil* that Karloff talked to *Variety*'s Dave Kaufman and sounded uncharacteristically cross when he got onto the subject of actors who couldn't remember their lines. "I've worked on shows with actors who use cue cards, and it's just plain hell," he bellyached. "If you're playing a part, you ought to damn well know it. When these actors should be looking at the other persons in the scene, they're staring in the camera, reading their cards." Perhaps Karloff was just a little envious that he couldn't employ that trick himself: "I don't use cue cards or teleprompters," he said, adding with a twinkle and a more "Karloffian" attitude, "It wouldn't do me any good. If I took off my glasses, I couldn't see the cards." (Pull my *other* leg, Boris: You're obviously reading from cue cards or a teleprompter in your "Vestris" intro.)

The airport scenes, shot on the first day of production, are among the few exteriors in the whole *Veil* series, and one of the few times the company left the Roach lot. At least we didn't get a painting of an airport.

The script specifies that Jr. and Bill were bound for Italy on their Act One run, and that the mountains where Jr. nearly crashes are the Alps. In the episode, Bill

Drama between father and son (Karloff and Hagerthy). Of all the actors who could have been hired to play the lad who disappoints his dad by not wanting to be a pilot, the producers selected Hagerthy, co-star of the airplane adventure series *Sky King*!

gives Jr. a karate chop to make him release the controls, while in the script Bill "belts Jr. across the face twice, as hard as he can." Wally's face, reflected in the windshield, is described in the script as "strong, fascinating … its eyes deep and hypnotic," but later, when Jr. asks his dad to describe Wally, he calls him plain-looking.

Hagerthy apologized to me for not recalling very much about working on *The Veil*, "but, if you've looked at it, you can see that it's sort of forgettable [*laughs*]! It was just a very weak attempt at *Twilight Zone*." Episode director Paul Landres remembers less: At my request, he watched the episode and had zero memory of the entire experience!:

I didn't remember it, but I did [recognize] my technique of directing. So I went back into all my notes of everything that I've ever done, and sure as hell, there it was!

One of the reasons I didn't remember it was because it was one of the *few* shows that I did only one episode of. Everything else, I've done *multiple* episodes of — 99 percent of the time. I looked at it, and thought it was very amateurish. It was pretty much of a sit-down-and-talk show, and those are shows that I very, very greatly dislike.

Landres' brother Danny edited the episode (and also the last *Veil* episode, "Peggy?").

Of course, Paul Landres has to have *some* memory of working for several days with the great Boris Karloff … *doesn't* he? Landres: "No, strangely enough!"

The Veil Episode 10: "Peggy?"

(Modern sources refer to this episode as "Whatever Happened to Peggy.")
Production No. 9219, Shot on February 11, 12 and 13, 1959; Directed by John Meredyth Lucas; Produced by Ben Fox; Executive Producer: Hal Roach Jr.; Teleplay: John Bennett [Jack Bennett?]; Production Supervisor: E.H. Goldstein; Photography: Howard Schwartz; Assistant Director: Richard Maybery; Editor: Danny B. Landres; Sound: Jack Goodrich; Costumer: John Zacha; Makeup: Sid Perell; Hair Stylist: Margit McEllroy; *The Veil* Created by Frank P. Bibas; **Uncredited:** Script Clerk: Verna Moran; Second Assistant Director: Ray Taylor; Gaffer: Paul Grancell; Best Boy: Gordon Wells; First Grip: Larry Milton; Second Grip: Jerry Walton; First Prop Man: Mitch Grimes; Second Prop Man: Ray Pedigo; Laborer: Bob Brian; Camera Operator: Cy Hofberg; First Assistant Cameraman: Alfred Baalas; Second Assistant Cameraman: Palmer Belmont; Sound Recorder: Jim Masterson; Boom Man: John McDonald; Cable Man: William Delamare; **Second Unit (Boris Karloff's Opening and Closing, shot on March 3, 1959):** Directed by John Meredyth Lucas; Camera: Ed Fitzgerald; Sound Recordist: Charles Althouse; Assistant Director: Marty Moss; Second Assistant Director: George Walls; Stand-in: Fred Walton

Additional, unconfirmed credits: I've never seen a copy of "Peggy?" with complete end credits; since it was the last *Veil* shot prior to the abrupt closing of Hal Roach Studios, perhaps proper end credits were never created for it. Here are the names of people who received screen credit on the next-to-last episode "Destination Nightmare" so I assume they would have also received screen credit on "Peggy?": Associate Producer: Jerry D. Lewis; Production Manager: D'Estell Iszard; Art Director: McClure Capps; Photographic Effects: Jack R. Glass; Set Decorator: Rudy Butler; Music: Leon Klatzkin; Sound: Joel Moss; Casting: Ruth Burch

Cast: Boris Karloff (*Host/Ira Perry*), Denise Alexander (*Ruth Cooper*), Whit Bissell (*Dr. Madison*), Shirley Mitchell (*Mrs. Cooper*), Olive Blakeney (*Martha Perry*), Frances O'Farrell (*Nurse*)

Synopsis: Ellie Cooper, a middle-aged widow living in Chicago, wants her 15-year-old daughter Ruth to see Greenville, the town where Ellie grew up. They arrive in Greenville and stay in a hotel the first night – and Ruth wakes up not knowing that Ellie is her mother.

Dr. Madison examines Ruth, who has never been to Greenville but says she finds it familiar. Ruth reminds Dr. Madison of Peggy Perry, a teenager who died in a staircase fall in her home, ten years earlier. At the end of the examination, Ruth shocks Dr. Madison by calling him "Uncle Dar" — Peggy's nickname for him.

Dr. Madison and Ellie bring Ruth to the home of Peggy's parents Ira and Martha Perry. Peggy acts like she's been there before; she says to the limping Mrs. Perry, "Oh, your leg seems worse again"; she fixates on a framed photo of Peggy; she recognizes Peggy's porcelain statuette of a ballerina; and she greets the Perrys' dog Duffer by name. And the dog acts like he knows *her*. Ruth even calls Mrs. Perry "Mother." Dr. Madison thinks that it would be a good idea for Ruth to stay with the Perrys for a while.

Ruth continues to act like Peggy, even giving Mrs. Perry a list of friends (Peggy's friends) she wants to invite to her birthday party next Wednesday (Peggy's birthday). Of course, the long-dead Peggy's friends can't be invited (they're all grown women now) so the party guests are Dr. Madison and Ellie. Ellie struggles with her emotions as she sees that Ruth is now a happy part of the Perry family. When Ruth stands at the top of the staircase where Peggy took her fatal fall, Mrs. Perry freaks out, telling her not to come down, but Ruth starts anyway. With a shout, Mr. Perry rushes up the stairs and catches the stumbling girl. He takes her to her room, where an upset Ruth throws the ballerina statuette against a dressing table mirror, shattering both. It appears as though the breaking of the ballerina breaks Peggy's spell over Ruth: Herself again, she asks the Perrys, "Who are *you*? Where's my mother?" Mr. Perry says they're friends of her mother's, adding, "Now let's go home and give her a surprise."

It isn't every day that you get to hear Boris Karloff sing "Happy Birthday" but he does in this tale of a girl's possession by a spirit. The script describes his character as 57 years old and "distinguished, a big man with natural charm and strong, irregular features." According to the script, Mrs. Perry is 55 but actress Olive Blakeney was 65. Karloff and Blakeney give good performances but they're too old for their characters: It's confusing that Ruth has a still attractive mother but the parents of the not-all-that-much-older Peggy look like refugees from the geriatric unit. In fact, Blakeney died several months after "Peggy?" was shot. You might remember her from Paramount's "Henry Aldrich" movies of the 1940s, where she played Henry's (Jimmy Lydon) mother. (In 1952, she became Lydon's real-life mother-*in-law*.)

Host Karloff is apparently still locked out of his castle: Again (after "Destination Nightmare") he holds forth on a very ordinary office set. And again he has the pipe and tobacco pouch and he proceeds to fill the pipe while he speaks. This seems disrespectful to the viewer; his job is to talk to us for two minutes a week, why can't he give us his full attention? Is his life so crowded, his time so limited, that he has to multi-task (host a TV show and perform a chore at the same time)? Well, at least the chore is filling a pipe, rather than (say) picking dried mud out of the cleats in his cricket shoes or cleaning his ears.

According to the Internet Movie Database, "Peggy?" was written by Stanley H. Silverman, who also penned *The Veil*'s reincarnation story "The Return of Mme. Vernoy." But I've got the "Peggy?" script and *it* says "Teleplay by John Bennett." I don't know of any TV writer named John Bennett. A Silverman pseudonym? Possibly. "Peggy?" and Silverman's "Mme. Vernoy" *do* tell the same story: The spirit of a dead girl possesses a young girl who creates consternation by visiting the dead girl's family. But more likely the "Peggy" writer was *Jack* Bennett, a TV scribe busy in the '50s, with a list of credits that includes Roach's *Code 3* and *Telephone Time*.

At the end of the episode, Ruth throws the ballerina statuette and breaks the mirror. The viewer assumes she did it because she was upset; what else *is* there to assume? The script, however, called for something director John Meredyth Lucas didn't do, or perhaps couldn't figure out *how* to do:

With a sudden gesture, Ruth brings both hands toward her face, as if to weep in her hands. The Ballerina flies out of her hands, strikes the mirror of the dressing table, shattering both the figure and mirror. The force of the impact seems especially violent to have been exerted by Ruth's wracking sob, or the gesture of her hands. Perhaps the force *was* something else, something we don't understand.

Speaking of the script, the first two pages are set in a hotel room as Mrs. Cooper wakes Ruth, who asks her mother, "Who are you?" Presumably this would have been the pre-credits sequence. The Roach production paperwork for February 11 makes it look like the scene was shot, but it's in no version of "Peggy?" that I've ever seen.

On the script and production paperwork, the title is "Peggy?" but all modern sources call the episode "Whatever Happened to Peggy." I'd bet that the title "Whatever Happened to Peggy" was cooked up long after the fact, by God knows who, because it seems to be styled after movie titles like *What Ever Happened to Baby Jane?*, *What Ever Happened to Aunt Alice?* and *What's the Matter with Helen?*, movies that didn't exist in 1959. Also, the title "Whatever Happened to Peggy" isn't appropriate: There is no mystery about what happened to Peggy, she fell down some stairs and died.

Monster Kids can't fail to notice that Whit Bissell looks, acts and, in his doctor's office scene, dresses just as he did in his Herman Cohen Teenage Monster movies. Outside of Karloff, Bissell got the fattest paycheck of any actor to appear in a *Veil*. (If he *got* paid, that is!) There were $500 paydays for Harry Bartell ("Summer Heat"), Tod Andrews ("Girl on the Road"), Tony Travis ("The Doctor") and Ron Hagerthy ("Destination Nightmare"), but Bissell got $600. "Peggy?"'s Denise Alexander, then 19 but playing a 15-year-old, was also a member of the $500 club. Though still a teenager, she'd already been acting for years on TV, a movie (Don Siegel's *Crime in the Streets*, 1956) and, perhaps her best showcase, the stage (top roles in little theater productions of *The Children's Hour* and *The Diary of Anne Frank*). Long-running roles on the daytime dramas *Days of Our Lives*, *General Hospital* and *Another World* brought her lasting fame.

"Peggy?" is one of the better-made *Veil*s. The photography and music are a bit above the series norm, and there are a few inventive touches, like showing Ruth re-

If *The Veil* had made it to TV in 1959, there would have been comparisons with *One Step Beyond*. That series' "Guide Into the World of the Unknown" John Newland (pictured) may have been taking a shot at the competition when he told a TV columnist, "We're going to play the stories straight. We're not going to scare with the mood, trick lighting or spider webs. We're endeavoring to show reality. We will never use Boris Karloff."

flected in a broken mirror shard as she finally becomes herself again. But the tale is hard to follow, with too much backstory. In addition to being similar to "The Return of Mme. Vernoy," the two stories take place on the same house sets, including a large entrance hallway with checkerboard floor and wide, winding staircase.

Whatever actual events (or urban legend, or screenwriter's pipe dream) provided the basis for "Peggy?" was dramatized again in *One Step Beyond*'s "Who Are You?" The nearly identical episode's cast of characters included a 12-year-old (Reba Waters) who recovers from scarlet fever thinking she's a recently drowned girl; her parents (Phyllis Hill and Ross Elliott); and the bereaved parents (Philip Bourneuf and Anna Lee). The latter couple even has a dog that treats Waters as if she were the dead girl come back, and it all builds to the same happy ending as in "Peggy?" – in fact, an even happier ending. In his outro, host John Newland calls these cases of "purposeful possession" and adds, "Nobody could say that it won't happen tomorrow … to *you*."

It looks like the last time Karloff acted in a *Veil* was March 3, 1959, weeks after "Peggy?" wrapped, when "Peggy?" director John Meredyth Lucas shot the actor's openings and closings for "Destination Nightmare" and "Peggy?" The company toiled from 5:15 in the afternoon until 8:30 at night.

The Veil: "Bonus Episode": "Jack the Ripper"

Walter (Niall MacGinnis) and his wife (Dorothy Alison) read about the Ripper's newest atrocity – a murder matching Walter's dream.

Directed by David MacDonald; Screenplay: Michael Plant; Photography: Stephen Dade; Art Director: Denys Pavitt; Editor: Ann Chegwidder; Production Manager: Victor Peck; Casting Director: Robert Lennard; Music: Edwin Astley; Recording Supervisor: Harold King

Cast (in order of their appearance): Boris Karloff (*Host*), Niall MacGinnis (*Walter*), Dorothy Alison (*Judith*), Robert Brown (*Constable*), Mai Bacon (*Fat Woman*), Clifford Evans (*Inspector*), Robert Brooks-Turner (*Warden*), Nora Swinburne (*Myra Willowden*), Charles Carson (*Dr. Hatherley*)

Note: This quote-unquote "*Veil* episode" must have originally been a segment of some English TV series, perhaps one with the same basic premise (eerie tales with some foundation in fact). It was made at Associated British Studios, Elstree, England, acquired by Roach no later than January 1959 and transformed into a *Veil* via the addition of a *Veil* opening and closing plus footage with host Karloff.

Synopsis: In 1888 London, Walter (Niall MacGinnis), a professional clairvoyant, dreams that he is a witness to the murders of Jack the Ripper. He explains this to the police, but only succeeds in making himself the prime suspect. A Ripper murder takes place just as Walter had already described it and *while* he is in jail, prompting a befuddled police inspector (Clifford Evans) to ask for Walter's professional help.

Psychic vibes lead Walter and the police to the home of Willowden, a surgeon who, they learn, has just passed away (the casket is in the library). A distraught Mrs. Willowden (Nora Swinburne) breaks down and admits that she, too, suspects that her husband may have been the Ripper. In a lengthy, effective close-up, she describes how he recently stuck a hatpin through the paw of the family dog, and derived pleasure out of dipping bats in paraffin, setting them afire and then letting them fly around the room(!). Walter opens the casket and finds books instead of a body, forcing the wife and her doctor (Charles Carson) to admit that the husband has actually been committed to an asylum for life; the false announcement of his death, and the phony funeral, will enable them to avoid scandal. "Inspector," the wife murmurs, "is it a terrible thing to hope there will be *more* murders in Whitechapel?"

The creepy and highly entertaining "Jack the Ripper" features several cast members familiar to fans of horror and fantasy films (Niall MacGinnis, Clifford Evans and also Robert Brown, "M" in the James Bond movies of the 1980s). The "dream sequences" in which Walter sees the Ripper in action are effective. The only downside to the episode *Veil*-wise is that it's yet *another* variation on "Summer Heat," a beaten-to-death favorite of the series' writers.

Karloff provides the intro and closing comments, as usual, and also turns up in mid-episode to talk about the real-life Whitechapel murders — which took place when he was not yet one year old, about two miles from the London district where the infant Boris was living. Due to his tender age, most Ripperologists have eliminated Karloff as a suspect.

The Hal Roach Studios' Tra-Veils

The Roach Studios' 1959 plan for *The Veil*, according to a January 20 memo by production supervisor E.H. Goldstein, was to do two episodes a week, skip a week and then do two more, continuing that production schedule until a total of 39 was reached around the end of August or the early part of September. "There are so many things that can happen between the 10th picture and the 39th that anything I would say [about the completion date of the 39th episode] would merely be a wild guess," Goldstein wrote.

"So many things that can happen," indeed.

"Then there were the *bats* … !": The best bit of acting in this well-acted story was Mrs. Willowden's (Nora Swinburne) harrowing account of her husband's descent into madness, emotionally told in an uninterrupted 90 second-plus take.

HAL ROACH STUDIO CLOSES DOWN was the top story in the April 3, 1959, *Variety*. According to the paper's account of the studio's April 2 closing, the Scranton Corp.'s board of directors had decided to ask a federal court to appoint a receiver or trustee over the company; and as a result, as Roach Studios' story editor Martin Varno told me, "an army of U.S. marshals came through the front gate." Telephone service was cut off because, according to *Variety*, the lot had not paid its phone bill: "With the studio's own lines dead, personnel scrambled for public phones and made use of the tenants' private lines on the lot."

Varno, 21 at the time, recalled that the marshals announced, "This lot is now closed, it belongs to the United States government." He went on:

> Roach Jr. screwed the studio into the ground. He didn't know anything about the business. The old man [Hal Roach Sr.] was *so* frail by that time. We saw him every once in a while because the house where he and Mrs. Roach lived was on the back lot. The kid, hell, he didn't know anything about making pictures. Hal Roach Sr. had put everything into the hands of his son, Hal Roach Jr. – who was an imbecile [*laughs*]. A big imbecile who knew how to play football. He *looked* like a linebacker, he was huge. Every once in a while you'd see him with some people, probably people who had money, or represented people who had money, and Jr. was trying to sell them on the idea of coming in and saving the studio's ass. But he didn't know what the hell he was talking about. He was interested in only three things in the world: football, p***y and food. Not necessarily in that order! Whatever happened to come first, he was interested! He knew *nothing* about running a studio. Papa knew that … but Papa was too old to take it back.

Beginning on page 189 of this book is Varno's essay "The Monster Was Very, Very Good to Me," about working at Hal Roach Studios at the time when *The Veil* was being made.

How much of a "fine mess" (thank you, Oliver Hardy) was the financial pyramid that came tumbling down and caused the studio to close? I've found contemporary news stories that contain admissions by their writers that the Roach set-up was so complicated that it was beyond their comprehension, perhaps beyond *any*one's comprehension. But reliable ol' Herbert L. Strock dumbed it down and put it in a nutshell for me so that even I could understand it: "Hal Roach Jr. got in trouble – the studio owed money, they got tied up with the Mafia and were sold, and all the pictures [TV episodes] went down the drain."

> Boris Karloff put in several weeks on a projected TV series that may never see the light. Ten half-hour dramatic films under the general title of *The Veil*, an extra-sensory perception series, were completed at the Hal Roach Studio in Hollywood.

But then all work was stopped at the studio because of its involvement in the Guterma financial investigation. [Alexander L. Guterma was chairman of the Roach Studios' board of directors.] – May 1959 United Press news item

Karloff apparently never got his dough. The actor was down to the last few months of his life in July 1968 when it was reported that the reorganized Hal Roach Studios Inc., based in New York and again headed by Hal Roach Sr., was objecting to some $4,000,000 in claims, among them Karloff's for $62,500. In the meantime, it appeared that the Roach firm would be settling many of the other claims against it on a basis of less than two cents on the dollar. And payments would not be in cash, but in preferred stock of the Roach firm instead. Poor Boris! However: Keep in mind that most of the money Karloff felt he was owed was for *Veil* episodes that he never did (they were never made).

How steamed was Karloff? Probably plenty steamed. Could the *Veil* debacle have prompted this announcement, published in *The Stage* just 21 days after Uncle Sam lowered the boom on Roach?:

KARLOFF MAKES LAST TV APPEARANCE

Boris Karloff announced in New York that the present filmed TV drama he is making will be his last. He said he is going to retire from show business and live in England.

A 1960s Monster World without Karloff ... would it have been better or worse? Would his Lifetime Record have been helped or hurt by a 1959 bow-out? True, his fans would have been done out of *Thriller*, *Black Sabbath*, *Targets*, the Grinch ... but on the plus side, there would not have been the ordeal of *The Terror*, *The Ghost in the Invisible Bikini*, *Route 66*, *Shindig*, "Mother Muffin," *The Venetian Affair*, *The Crimson Cult*, *Cauldron of Blood* and of course his four Mexican movies, which were more like a swan dive than a swan song. We'd also have been spared seeing life's candle burning lower for Dear Boris, the sad spectacle of Karloff acting out of a wheelchair, and showing less spark in each passing project (see the *Name of the Game* photo on the page opposite.) Greg Mank wrote in his 2009 book *Bela Lugosi and Boris Karloff*, "[For Karloff] to carry on with boots and greasepaint was one thing, but in *these* films?" [the Mexi-movies]. Then, writing generally about the Karloff of the late '60s: "[I]f Lugosi had been a drug addict, it now appeared Karloff had become an acting addict. The inspiration of a man who wanted to work to the very last was, while often heroic, dangerously approaching pathos."

Perhaps while Karloff did his Oliver Hardy-like slow burn over the *Veil* screw job, he just needed to remember the old truism that, no matter how bad off you are, someone else is doin' worse:

> Hal Roach Jr., son of the famed producer of early-day film comedies, says his assets total $39,633 and his debts $1,050,802. In other words, he's bankrupt.
>
> Roach, 43, filed a bankruptcy petition in federal court Thursday. He described himself as an unemployed motion picture producer and said he made $2500 last year and $500 this year. – the Associated Press story "Yes Indeed, This Guy Is Bankrupt," March 30, 1962

In December 1962, high bidder Ponty-Fenmore Realty Fund acquired the Hal Roach Studios for $1,326,000 in an auction held in California under the jurisdiction of the U.S. District Court in Scranton, Pennsylvania. The new owners renamed it Landmark Studios and announced that as soon as they took over, they would begin a modernization program costing between $400,000 and $600,000. After this costly facelift was performed, a full-page *Variety* ad (April 9, 1963) featured an aerial photograph of the lot and a cartoon LANDMARK STUDIOS flag, and boasted:

> Complete facilities of the 14½ acre former Hal Roach Studios have been refurbished for immediate occupancy and full-scale production. Featuring 57 buildings including seven massive sound stages, LANDMARK offers the latest in modern equipment and resources: 65 Executive Offices >> 3 Projection Theatres >> 35 Film Editing rooms >> 20 Film Vaults >> Finest Camera and Optical departments >> Fully equipped Sound, Electrical and Property departments >> Extensive backlot and outdoor sets >> Abundant covered scene dock storage >> Parking for more than 350 cars.

Exactly six weeks later, most everyone who read that ad or saw the pricey improvements was probably appalled by *Variety*'s top story: **HAL ROACH LOT TO BE RAZED**. Fenmore and Ponty had had no luck making satisfactory lease arrangements with prospective tenants and reluctantly decided to make the land available for commercial use.

A month before the studio was demolished, Roach

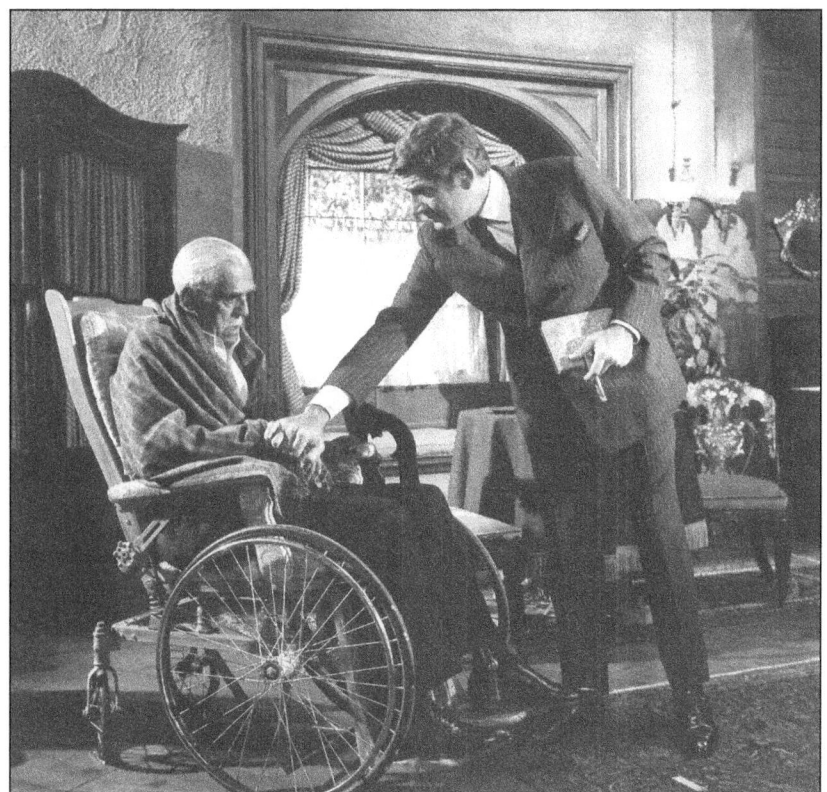

Dear Boris stayed active right to the end of his life: According to his own count in an October 1968 interview, "five films, guest appearances on two American television series and several British TV commercials — all done within these last 12 months." For the studio that made him a star, Universal, he played his final role in a 1968 *Name of the Game* episode, "The White Birch," with Gene Barry. (Photo courtesy John Antosiewicz)

Sr. made a film in which he acted as guide, showing viewers around the doomed movie plant. In July 1963 came the announcement that the lot's half-century collection of production paraphernalia and props would be auctioned off starting on August 1. The first day's sale was attended by several thousand people who bought around 1000 items, from Moviolas to cameras, booms, theater seats and special effects equipment. On *Variety*'s list of the "more bizarre artifacts" on the auction block: 20 tomahawks, a wide selection of bearskins, a six-foot pencil, a ten-foot beer bottle and 10,000 stills, mostly of "Our Gang"-sters and Cesar Romero. According to the auctioneer, "Everything will be sold; if we get no bids, then we give it away."

Less than a decade after bulldozers leveled the Laugh Factory, the man responsible for its downfall died at St. John's Hospital in Santa Monica. Hal Roach Jr. complained of feeling unwell on Monday, March 27, 1973, entered the hospital, and died of pneumonia early on the morning of the 29th. He was 53. His obituaries called him a TV pioneer and reminded readers that he was one of the founders of the Academy of Television Arts and Sciences as well as its second president.

Veil creator Frank Bibas continued to work in the industry; he was an Academy Award winner for his 1962 documentary *Project Hope*, a short subject about the hospital ship commissioned by the Kennedy administration to sail to third-world countries needing medical assistance. (The maiden voyage was to Indonesia, where the documentary was filmed.) After receiving his Oscar, Bibas went into business on his own, working out of New York producing industrial and training films for various companies. In the late 1980s, Barbara Bibas was living in Spain, where her father would occasionally visit. "I was getting involved with some of the TV stations there that needed programming," said Barbara, "so we thought, 'Wouldn't it be fun to take *The Veil* and dub these things, and see if we can revitalize them?' Well, unfortunately it didn't work out because the Ministry of Culture had sent a mandate: no more American films. They were inundated with them, and they wanted to promote more Spanish-made films. We went to three stations, and they all said the same thing." Frank Bibas died on October 16, 1997.

The Veil At Last Comes to TV!

The Veil never ran on television per se; the episodes were not seen in their original form prior to the 1998 release of the Something Weird tapes. But TV viewers were exposed to all 11 episodes (11 counting "Jack the Ripper") via three compilation movies that debuted in the late 1970s.

Imagine Monster Kids' excitement when *TV Guide*s from coast to coast included in their listings Boris Karloff movies that seemed to have sprung from nowhere: *The Veil, Jack the Ripper* and *Destination Nightmare*. The excitement level dropped a bit when showtime finally arrived and it became obvious they were not movies but TV episodes spliced end to end. Probably *none* of us knew what TV company's mysterious, long-sealed film vault had been plundered for these haunting half-hours, but that was okay; what we thought was a finite number of Karloff genre credits had unexpectedly been boosted by three. The feature-length *The Veil* consisted of the four episodes "The Crystal Ball," "The Doctor," "Summer Heat" and "Vision of Crime." Herbert L. Strock got the directing credit even though he only helmed two of the four; the names of cast members Booth Colman ("Truth in the Crystal Ball") and Argentina Brunetti ("The Doctor") were misspelled in the opening credits. The decision to put "Summer Heat" and "Vision of Crime" in the same compilation — one after the other, in fact — was a bad one, since they're basically the same story.

The compilation *Jack the Ripper* was made up of "Summer Heat" (again), "A Chapter of Genesis," "No Food on the Table" and "Jack the Ripper." David MacDonald, who directed the English-made "Jack the Ripper" and never worked on the *Veil* series — probably never even *heard* of it—received sole directing credit. The compilation *Destination Nightmare* gave the director credit to Paul Landres (his name misspelled Landers on-screen) and featured Landres' "Destination Nightmare" plus "The Return of Mme. Vernoy," "Girl on the Road" and "Peggy?"

These features were assembled without the sanction — or even the knowledge — of series creator Frank Bibas. Barbara Bibas recalled, "One night my father got up around three or four in the morning, because he couldn't sleep, and he flicked on the TV — and there it was [*laughs*]! *His* show, re-edited into one of those 'movies'! He was quite surprised!"

In addition to being aired as "movies," *Veil* episodes also showed up on public domain cable stations under the heading of "Chiller Theatre." Some or perhaps all of the episodes were retitled: "Girl on the Road" became "Lookout Point," "The Doctor" was called "The Medieval Healer" (huh??), "Peggy?" was rechristened "Invisible Ghost," "Destination Nightmare" was renamed "Heading 135," "Summer Heat" became "Grip of the Sun" and "The Return of Mme. Vernoy" was redubbed "Girl from Delhi."

For more information on the *Veil* "movies," we sought a consultation with the "Scripts from the Crypt" series' doctor in attendance, Robert J. Kiss, who now presents his findings:

The *Veil* Compilation Movies
By Dr. Robert J. Kiss

In email correspondence published in the 23rd issue of the British magazine *Headpress* (April 2002), Roger Watkins – director of the notorious *The Last House on Dead End Street* (1977) – claimed to have edited the feature-length compilation versions of *Veil* episodes during the summer of 1978 at the New York City facilities of EUE/Screen Gems, located at 222 East 44th Street. Watkins remarked that the hazily recalled paying gig "wasn't really an editing job at all, just a bit of tightening up and stringing together three [sic] episodes at a time." Either Watkins was wrong about the date, or else he may have been responsible only for the editing of *Destination Nightmare* and *Jack the Ripper*, since the feature-length *The Veil* had received a one-off screening on WQAD-TV (Moline, Illinois) on the night of March 5, 1977.

All three feature versions were first made available through John Ettlinger's Medallion TV Enterprises in the fall of 1978, with sales to several independent stations bringing them to the small screen (with no fanfare whatsoever) in early 1979. On the West Coast, San Francisco-based KBHK debuted the feature-length *The Veil* at 9 p.m. on January 26, 1979; one can only wonder how many tuned in, since this meant that it went head to head against the saturation-promoted first episode of *The Dukes of Hazzard* on CBS! The station subsequently debuted *Destination Nightmare* on February 9, but never screened *Jack the Ripper*, which would remain unseen on the West Coast until Sacramento-based KXTV aired it as a midnight movie on July 9.

On the East Coast, WOR-TV presented the three movies as the "1 p.m. Creature Feature" on three consecutive Saturdays: *Jack the Ripper* on March 10, *The Veil* on March 17, and *Destination Nightmare* on March 24. The following month, WOR became a nationwide superstation, meaning that its subsequent broadcast of the three features as midnight movies during Halloween Week 1979 constituted the first time that they could potentially be seen by cable and satellite viewers from coast to coast. Between then and New Year's Day 1986, WOR repeated each feature roughly a dozen times, primarily in post-11:30 p.m. "Fright Night" slots. A limited number of small independent broadcasters also continued to give the movies occasional play throughout this period until as late as 1987, with local Santa Fe, New Mexico, station KNMZ-TV once offering viewers the unique opportunity to watch all three features in the space of 26 hours during the weekend of December 28-29, 1985 – with Michael Findlay's yeti-with-a-zipper-fest *Shriek of the Mutilated* (1974) thrown in as an additional festive treat between *Destination Nightmare* and *Jack the Ripper*!

Between February and December 1990, *The Veil* and *Jack the Ripper* showed up anew in the programming of TNT.

Something Weird's Mike Vraney on Resurrecting *The Veil*

1998 interview by Tom Weaver

Mike Vraney: *The Veil* was one element of *thousands* of film elements I got my hands on all at one time. One day several years ago, I got off an airplane in Newark, New Jersey, and [exploitation movie producer] Dave Friedman was waiting for me there. The first thing he said to me was, "Mike, how would you like a print of *Mr. Peters' Pets*" [a rare nudist movie]—and half a dozen other titles, for video release. I went, "Okay, what's going on?" "Well," Dave said, "there's this black gentleman from Alabama in the city, he's the custodian of this building where Movielab used to be. The basement is just full of negatives and whatnot, all abandoned in the mid-1980s by a guy named Saul Jeffee" [the founder and longtime chairman and president of Movielab]. This black man was the custodian of the building, and Dave called him up and arranged for me to go there. If I'd give the guy $200 a negative, I could take whatever I wanted.

I went there with the sole purpose of getting four or five of Dave Friedman's "lost films." I walked into this basement, and it's bigger than a football field. The dust was two inches high, water had been leaking in certain areas—and there was film from floor to the ceiling, all racked. Amazing! And I'm so overwhelmed—I'm like the kid who buys one film at a time, and here's more than you could ever imagine. I went in there looking for four or five films, and I walked away with ten. And it was so easy, because I'd turn to my left and go, "Oh my God! *Naked Venus*!" Then I'd turn to my right: "Oh my God! *Horrors of Spider Island*!" I rustled up ten negatives and got 'em out.

I go home, and I'm tossin' and turnin', thinking, "There was the opportunity of a *lifetime*" – I didn't have a clue what else was in there, because I had no time even to look. About a week later, I called the custodian: "Listen, if I just show up there, and you give me three or four days, and I give you $5000 … will you let me walk with whatever I want?" He aid, "Yeah! Damn right!" So I call [producer-director] Frank Henenlotter and one of the guys he works with, Peter Clark, because I realized I would need help—not just physically, but help from someone with film knowledge, someone who could look at cans and know alternate titles and know what all this stuff *was*. So I brought Frank and Peter down there, and for two days we were like kids in a candy store. Frank's yelling out, "Mike! Do you want *Monster at Camp Sunshine*?" and I go "What the hell's that?" He goes, "How should I know? You want it though, right?" At that time, I took possession of about 120 features, a couple hundred shorts and trailers and some odds and ends. Not *The Veil* yet.

After I got this material shipped – like 15,000 pounds – it still bugged me about this huge collection. So a mutual friend of Dave Friedman and mine – let's call him Mr. X – he got hold of me and said, "What do you think is the value of that basement?" I said, "I didn't have enough time to even scratch the surface." Mr. X said, "Worse than *that*, Mike – there's two rooms that were locked off. You didn't even get into 'em." Oh, God! Next thing that happens is, Mr. X turns around and buys the whole basement! He puts it into storage in Jersey, with some idea that companies around the world – Paramount, 20th Century-Fox and all – will want to buy their own negatives. The guy didn't quite realize that what was there was made by little independent companies, foreign films – all stuff that fell through the cracks. Four or five years go by, Mr. X calls me again and we start having meetings about me taking possession of this stuff. We work out a deal and he sends the first batch, blindly. I took possession of this Movielab collection over a period of time, about a year and a half. It was only last February [1998] that the last semi showed up. It was 14 40-foot semis of material. (Out of that, there's still 80 skids that I have not even opened yet.) I'm going through it, and on (like) skid number eight I hit these *Veil*s. What I'd found were 35mm fine grain prints from England – fine grains that they struck negatives from, and *then* assembled [the *Veil* compilation movies]. I found the components that were used to make the movies, but they were unedited, clean as a whistle.

That's the story of the *Veil*s. They were sitting undisturbed all those years.

"Veil" Scripts

On the following pages, you'll find the *Veil* scripts "A Chapter of Genesis" (episode 2, written by Sidney Morse), "No Food on the Table" (episode 6, written by Jack Jacobs) and "The Return of Mme. Vernoy" (episode 7, written by Stanley H. Silverman).

PROD. NO. 9210

"A CHAPTER OF GENESIS"

Teleplay by

SID MORSE

T H E   V E I L

Created by

FRANK P. BIBAS

HAL ROACH STUDIOS

PRODUCER: FRANK P. BIBAS

"THE VEIL"

"A CHAPTER OF GENESIS"

by

Sidney Morse

CAST

JOHN HANEY, SR..........60-70. Hard-working farmer.

EMMA HANEY..............Several years younger. Sweet, gentle, passive.

JOHN HANEY, JR..........About 30, but looks 45. Has always worked on the farm.

JAMES HANEY.............About 27. Sharp, cocky, arrogant. A 1920's sharpie. Hasn't done a lick of work in ten years.

JONAS ATTERBURY.........About 60. Lawyer and friend of the family.

JUDGE DAVIS.............About 55. A strict jurist.

BLUE....................About 35. Young lawyer. A little too smart.

BAILIFF (no lines)

SETS

INTERIOR:

BEDROOM
KITCHEN
COURTROOM
ATTIC

FADE IN:

1   KARLOFF LIBRARY SCENE

              (DIALOGUE TO COME LATER)

                                                    FADE OUT.

    FADE IN:

2   KARLOFF INTRODUCTION

                                                    FADE OUT.

FADE IN:

3   EXT. OLD FARMHOUSE - NIGHT - ESTABLISHING SHOT (STOCK)

It is raining extremely hard, and we see and HEAR thunder and lightning.

                                        DISSOLVE THRU TO:

4   INT. BEDROOM - NIGHT - CLOSE SHOT - MRS. HANEY

sitting quietly in a rocking chair, rocking slowly. The chair SQUEAKS slightly as she rocks. She is looking intently o.s.

5   ANOTHER ANGLE

to include the bed, on which, eyes closed, lies JOHN T. HANEY. As she watches, he mumbles something unintelligible. She comes to bed and leans over, trying to catch it. He mumbles again, but she cannot hear. He lapses into silence. Suddenly she HEARS, o.s., the sound of somebody banging heavily on the outer door. As she reacts:

6   INT. KITCHEN - NIGHT - FULL SHOT

to show JOHN HANEY, JR. at the sink, where he has been washing up. He is reaching for a towel, head turned toward the door. Towel in hand, he starts for the door, when the BANGING sounds again.

                    JOHN
          All right! I'm coming!

7   ANOTHER ANGLE

to include the doorway, as John opens the door. Standing in the downpour is JAMES HANEY, a suitcase by his side. Throughout, it is obvious there's no love lost between them. At the sight of the figure, John reacts.

                    JAMES
          Well? You gonna keep me out
          here all night?

                    JOHN
                (recovering)
          Jamie...! Come in!

As James enters, shaking the water off:

8   ANOTHER ANGLE

to include Mrs. Haney as she enters the kitchen.

      MRS. HANEY
  Jamie.....!

      JAMES
  Hi, Mom.....

She rushes to him and embraces him.

      MRS. HANEY
  Oh, Jamie....

      JAMES
    (uncomfortable)
  You're gonna get all wet, ma...
    (disengages himself,
     starts removing coat,
     looking around,
     slightly mocking)
  You've changed, Johnny. Still
  not having any fun, are you?

      JOHN
  Running a farm by yourself
  doesn't leave much time for fun.

      MRS. HANEY
  John's been working awfully
  hard, Jamie.

      JAMES
  He would.
    (to John)
  Old, dependable Johnny.

Mrs. Haney misses the needle.

      MRS. HANEY
  Let me fix you something to eat.

      JAMES
  No thanks, Ma. I ate before I
  came.

      MRS. HANEY
  Some coffee then. And a piece
  of pie.

      JAMES
    (beat, he'll get her
     off his back)
  All right, ma. Just a small
  piece.

As John and James sit at the table and Mrs. Haney starts for the stove, we:

4.

9   INT. BEDROOM - NIGHT - MED. SHOT - JOHN HANEY SR.

eyes still closed. From below, we HEAR the murmer of voices, although we cannot hear what is being said. As we watch, Haney's eyes open, although they are still unfocussed.

>   HANEY
>   (murmers)
>   Jamie...? Jamie...?

With tremendous difficulty, he throws aside the covers, and manages to get to his feet. He staggers, then one step at a time starts for the closet door.

10   INT. KITCHEN - NIGHT

where Mrs. Haney is serving pie to the two men.

>   MRS. HANEY
>   I knew you'd get here in time,
>   Jamie. Pa's been asking for
>   you.
>
>   JAMES
>   (twisted smile)
>   He has, huh? Probably wants
>   to whale the tar outta me.
>
>   MRS. HANEY
>   Oh, Jamie!
>
>   JAMIE
>   All right, ma.
>   (beat)
>   Guess I might as well see him.
>
>   JOHN
>   (trifle sarcastic)
>   Yeah. Might as well. No sense
>   making the trip for nothing, is
>   there?

James starts to answer, but before he can, he is interrupted by a THUD overhead. They all react, then the two men shove back their chairs and dash out of the room, followed by Mrs. Haney.

11   INT. BEDROOM - NIGHT - FULL SHOT

to show Haney, Sr. crumpled on the floor near the closet door, now open, overcoats, etc., inside. Door to room bursts open and John and James stop. Mrs. Haney is behind them.

(CONTINUED)

11   CONTINUED:

                    JOHN
               Pa....!

He and James kneel beside the body.

                    JOHN
                 (continuing)
               He's all right.
                 (rising)
               Take his feet, Jamie...we'll
               get him back to bed.

They get Haney Sr. back into bed and re-cover him. Mrs.
Haney bustles about, tucking him in, as the boys watch.
Then James steps to the bed and looks down.

                    JAMES
               Pa.....
                 (beat)
               Pa, it's me. Jamie.
                 (beat)
               Pa....?

Slowly, the eyes of the man on the bed open. They are
unfocussed. He is obviously still in a coma, but James'
voice may have gotten through to him. When he speaks, it
is in a hoarse whisper, forcing the words out. He is unintelligible to Mrs. Haney and John.

                    MR. HANEY
               Will........

James leans over close to him, trying to hear.

12   CLOSE SHOT - JAMES, MR. HANEY

                    JAMES
               What'd you say, pa?

                    MR. HANEY
                 (still forcing)
               Jamie.... the .... will .....

James reacts, sliding his eyes sideways, to see if the
others heard.

                    JAMES
               I can't hear you, pa.

                    MR. HANEY
               ...the...will.......Ja---mie...
               the...will......

The effort is too much for him, and his eyes close as he
lapses back into a deeper coma. James straightens.

13   ANOTHER ANGLE - ALL

                    JOHN
          Did he make sense?

                    JAMES
          No. Just mumbling.

                    JOHN
          He's been like that for two days.

                    MRS. HANEY
          He knew you, Jamie! I know he
          did!

                    JAMES
               (throws look at
                John)
          Sure. Sure he did, ma.
               (beat)
          Let's go downstairs.

John looks undecided.

                    MRS. HANEY
          Go ahead, Johnny. I'll be down
          in a minute.

As the two men exit, Mrs. Haney starts back to the bed.

14   INT. KITCHEN - NIGHT

     as John and James enter, heading for the chairs and
     sitting.

                    JAMES
          How'd it happen?

                    JOHN
          His horse stumbled and fell on
          him.

                    JAMES
          Old as he is, you think he'd
          have more sense.

                    JOHN
          Where've you been all this time,
          Jamie?

                    JAMES
          All over. New York, Chicago,
          San Francisco........I've kept
          moving.

                              (CONTINUED)

14 CONTINUED:

>   JOHN
> For ten years?

>   JAMES
> Well... you know me, Johnny.

15 ANOTHER ANGLE

to include Mrs. Haney entering.

>   JOHN
> I'm a little surprised you came
> back.

>   MRS. HANEY
> Johnny!

>   JAMES
>   (touch of defiance)
> Why shouldn't I?
>   (as John stares)
> Oh, I get it. You're still
> sore 'cause I took off and
> you had to stay here and work.
>   (beat)
> Well, you could've gotten out,
> too!

>   JOHN
> And who'da run the farm?! Or
> did you forget that Pa was too
> old even then?!

>   JAMES
> All right! All right! So hate
> me! But don't forget...I was only
> seventeen years old! How much was
> I supposed to know?!

>   JOHN
> You knew enough to steal every
> cent Pa had in the house.

>   MRS. HANEY
> Stop it! Stop it right now!

>   JAMES
> No! Let him get it off his chest!
>   (to John)
> So that's it, huh? That's what's
> gripin' you all these years!
>   (beat)
> Well, lemme tell you! I didn't
> steal anything! That money
> <u>belonged</u> to me!

(CONTINUED)

15   CONTINUED:

> JOHN
> It did, huh? Just how do you figure that?
>
> JAMES
> You know how I figure it! Ever since I was ten years old Pa had me doing the work of a hired hand! Only I never got the money a hand would get! Just my food and your hand-me-down clothes! He owed me that money!
>
> JOHN
> And how about me, Jamie?! What was I doing all those years you were working your poor little fingers to the bone?! I was having a picnic, huh?!!
>
> JAMES
> That's your problem, Johnny boy! If you'd had any gumption you'd o' beaten me to the cash box!

As they stare at each other, hating one another:

> MRS. HANEY
> Enough! I won't have any more of this in my house! You ought to be ashamed! Both of you! Your father's dying right over your heads and you sit here fighting like animals!
>   (as they subside)
> Jamie, I'm going to fix your old room. When you're finished you march yourself upstairs and go to bed! And you, Johnny! Not another word! Remember...you're brothers!
>   (as she marches out)
> The very idea!

The two men wait in silence until she exits, then:

> JOHN
> Tell me the truth, Jamie...just for once. Why did you come back?

James takes a long beat, then his mouth thins.

(CONTINUED)

15   CONTINUED - (2):

                    JAMES
                (sneering)
            You never were very bright, were
            you, Johnny?
                (beat)
            All right, I'll tell you.
                (beat)
            Your telegram got me at the
            right time. I'm broke. And
            I figured in ten years the old
            man had enough time to build up
            another pile.

                    JOHN
                (long beat, as
                 he stares)
            You make me sick, Jamie.

                    JAMES
                (grins tauntingly)
            Then you should be sitting where
            I am. Look at you, Johnny boy...
            you're only three years older than
            I am, but anybody'd take you for
            my father.
                (beat)
            You _should_ be sick!

      John takes a long beat, then rises slowly.

                    JOHN
            You outsmarted yourself this time,
            Jamie. You made the trip for
            nothing.
                (beat)
            If pa dies, you won't get a dime.

      He turns and exits, as James watches.

16   CLOSER SHOT - JAMES

      as he sits watching after John. Then slowly, a smug
      smile crosses his face, as we:

                                        SLOW DISSOLVE TO:

17   INSERT SHOT - AN OUTER DOOR - DAY

      with a funeral wreath hung on it.

18   INT. KITCHEN - DAY - FULL SHOT

showing that it is empty. As we watch, the door opens and Mrs. Haney, followed by John and James, enters. They are followed by JONAS ATTERBURY, an attorney. The Haneys are in mourning, and have evidently come from a funeral. For a moment, they all stand around uncomfortably, then:

>   MRS. HANEY
>   (sighs)
>   I'll fix something to eat.
>
>   ATTERBURY
>   Nothing for me, thanks, Emma.
>   I just wanted to offer my
>   condolences.
>
>   MRS. HANEY
>   Just some coffee, then, Jonas.

Atterbury is about to refuse, but John catches his eye and nods slightly as though to say "Let her keep busy".

>   ATTERBURY
>   Coffee'll be fine, Emma.

Mrs. Haney removes her hat and veil and begins to fuss at the stove as the three men sit.

>   ATTERBURY
>   (continuing)
>   I'm afraid there'll be some
>   delay in probating the estate
>   what with your father not leaving
>   a will. I tried to get him...
>
>   JOHN
>   He _did_ leave a will.

There is a sharp reaction on the part of James and Mrs. Haney, but John and Atterbury don't notice.

>   ATTERBURY
>   (beat)
>   I don't understand. I was his
>   attorney and _I_ didn't draw it.
>   (beat)
>   Oh... he drew it himself.
>
>   JOHN
>   Yes, sir.

(CONTINUED)

18 CONTINUED:

>   ATTERBURY
>   (shakes his head,
>   wryly)
>   Your father was a strange man.
>   He didn't trust banks, he
>   didn't trust bookkeepers...and
>   now I find he evidently didn't
>   trust his lawyer.
>
>   JOHN
>   I don't think that was it, Mr.
>   Atterbury. He...he said he
>   wanted it kept a secret.
>
>   ATTERBURY
>   Mmm-hmm. May I see it?
>   (dry)
>   Or is it still a secret?
>
>   JOHN
>   No, sir.

John reaches into an inside pocket and withdraws the will.
Atterbury reads through it quickly.

>   ATTERBURY
>   (looks up)
>   Looks legal enough. He leaves
>   everything to you, Johnny...
>   (reads from will)
>   "...knowing that as head of the
>   family, you will take care of
>   your mother and young brother".
>
>   MRS. HANEY
>   (from stove)
>   Oh, I'm so glad, Johnny!...
>
>   JAMES
>   Wait a minute....
>
>   MRS. HANEY
>   (continues right on)
>   I guess there's no need now to
>   bother about mine.

All three men react, looking at her.

>   ATTERBURY
>   You've got one, too?

Mrs. Haney is puzzled at the fact that there should be any
reaction.

                                                    (CONTINUED)

18 CONTINUED - (2):

                    MRS. HANEY
            Why, yes...

                    ATTERBURY
            May I see it, Emma?

                    MRS. HANEY
            I don't see any need to fuss
            with it, Jonas. Johnny'll take
            care of everything.

                    JOHN
            Let him see it, Ma. It all
            should've been left to you in
            the first place.

                    MRS. HANEY
            I can't see what difference....
                (beat)
            Well, all right.....

It's completely unimportant to her, but if it will put a
stop to this fussing, she'll comply. She exits the room.
The men sit waiting, looking at each other.

                    ATTERBURY
            Your father and I were friends
            for years, but sometimes I
            wonder.....

He shakes his head. The two boys don't say anything, but
we can sense their agreement. Mrs. Haney returns with the
will. She hands it to Atterbury with an air of washing
her hands of the whole thing.

                    MRS. HANEY
            There!

She returns to her chores at the stove, as Atterbury reads
the will, the two boys watching intently.

                    ATTERBURY
                (sighs)
            Well...in _this_ one, he left
            everything to _you_, Emma. The
            boys aren't even mentioned.
                (beat)
            I wonder how many more he.....

Atterbury stops abruptly. Then, as if they all had the
idea at the same time, they all turn to look at James.
There is no expression on his face.

                              (CONTINUED)

18   CONTINUED - (3):

                    ATTERBURY
                (continuing,
                 quietly)
          You, too, Jamie?

James nods, reaches into his pocket and brings out a folded will which he hands to Atterbury. Atterbury reads to himself for a moment, in the watchful silence. Then;

                    ATTERBURY
                (continuing,
                 wearily)
          "To my youngest son, James, I
          leave all my worldly possessions,
          and trust that he will provide for
          his mother as long as she lives.
          It is my hope that he will also do
          what is fair for my oldest son,
          his brother John, Jr."

Atterbury stops. John looks at James, then back to Atterbury.

                    JOHN
          They can't *all* be legal!

                    ATTERBURY
          No.
                (lines up the wills)
          Your mother's is dated July
          18th, 1890.....

                    MRS. HANEY
                (smiling softly)
          The day after we were married.
          We'd just come here to live.....

She stops, looking up guiltily, as though apologizing for interrupting. They all look at her tenderly for a moment, then:

                    ATTERBURY
          Yours is dated January 12th, 1911.
                (beat)
          Yours takes precedence over your
          mother's.
                (beat)
          Jamie's is dated February 14th...
          1917.
                (beat, as it sinks in)
          Jamie's is the one that will
          stand up.

                                        (CONTINUED)

18   CONTINUED - (4):

There is a long silence, then John turns slowly to look at James. James tries to keep his face expressionless, but the hint of a smile plays at the corners of his mouth. John turns to look at Atterbury.

>   ATTERBURY
>   (continuing)
>   I can't imagine what he was
>   thinking of. Three wills...!
>
>   MRS. HANEY
>   (defending him)
>   John knew what he was doing!
>
>   JOHN
>   (almost disgust)
>   I know what he was thinking.....
>   (beat)
>   You knew his temper, Mr. Atterbury.
>   I'd like to bet about the time
>   he made my will, he and ma had
>   an argument.
>
>   MRS. HANEY
>   (surprised remembrance)
>   Why, that's right! I can't
>   remember why, but John said.....
>   (stops abruptly)
>   But I thought he was only joshing
>   me.....
>
>   JOHN
>   (short, bitter laugh)
>   And about the time Jamie's was
>   made out, Pa and me had a real
>   knock-down-and-drag-out over my
>   wanting to enlist. He said I'd
>   be sorry if I went. Well.....
>
>   MRS. HANEY
>   (stoutly)
>   Anyhow, I'd glad he remembered
>   Jamie.
>
>   JAMES
>   Thanks, ma.
>   (to all)
>   Look...why all the sour faces.
>   Ma's got nothing to worry about.
>   And you know I'll take care of
>   you, Johnny boy.....

                                              (CONTINUED)

18   CONTINUED - (5):

> JOHN
> (quietly, but there's
> a needle in it)
> Uh-huh. I'm sure you will.

> JAMES
> Mr. Atterbury, how long will it
> take to clear up all the legal
> stuff?

> JOHN
> What's your hurry, Jamie?

> JAMES
> Well, I'd like to put the farm
> on the market as soon as I can.

There is a shocked reaction from the other three.

> MRS. HANEY
> Jamie! You're not going to sell
> the farm! It's our home!

> JAMES
> Aw, now ma...you know I'm not
> cut out to be a farmer. Besides,
> we ought to get a good price for
> it right about now.

> MRS. HANEY
> (helplessly)
> But Jamie.....

She looks at John, who is staring at James.

> JOHN
> (quiet)
> Where'll Ma go, Jamie?

> JAMES
> Don't you worry about that.....
> I'll take care of her.

> JOHN
> (demanding)
> Where, Jamie?

> JAMES
> (he's ad-libbing)
> Well.....
> (to Mrs. Haney)
> You've always wanted to visit
> AuntMartha in Kansas! Now's
> your chance!

(CONTINUED)

18   CONTINUED - (6):

                    MRS. HANEY
          But Jamie...I only wanted to
          visit. It's....I can't imagine
          living any place but here, Jamie.

                    JAMES
          Now, ma...you know this place is
          too big for you! You gotta work
          too hard!

                    JOHN
               (deadly quiet)
          When she gets back from her
          visit,.....what then, Jamie?

                    JAMES
               (selling eagerly)
          Well...she deserves a rest...
          you know...at her age she oughta
          take it easy......so.....
               (now it's getting
                tougher)
          I thought...maybe we'd get her a
          room at Mrs. Chalmers'.....

                    MRS. HANEY
          That's an old folks' home!!

                    JAMES
          But it'd be good for you, ma!
          You...you wouldn't have to work
          any more, and...and there'd be
          people your own age to talk to...
               (to John)
          You know what I mean, Johnny!

                    JOHN
          Sure...I know what you mean...
               (beat, then builds)
          To get her off your hands you'd
          like her to sit on a porch for
          the rest of her life and rot!!

James takes a shocked beat, then flares up.

                    JAMES
          Now wait a minute! All of
          you!
               (self pity)
          That's what I get for trying
          to be a good guy!
               (MORE)

                                        (CONTINUED)

18   CONTINUED - (7)

                    JAMES (cont'd)
                (beat)
            This is my farm! Pa left it
            to me and I'll do what I like
            with it!
                (beat)
            If ma don't do what I want...
            okay! You take care of her!

With one bounce, John comes out of his chair, knocking it over backwards. He starts for James.

                    JOHN
            You dirty, little.....!!

Atterbury grabs John, halting him momentarily and hanging on. James jumps up and moves back in fear. Mrs. Haney comes running to hang on to John.

                    MRS. HANEY
            Johnny!!!!

                    JAMES
                (in fright)
            You touch me, Johnny, and
            you won't get a cent!

                    MRS. HANEY
            Johnny, stop it! Listen to me!
            Jamie's right!
                (John stops in surprise)
            I...I have been working too hard...
            I am tired.....
                (she's forcing this,
                 and trying to avoid
                 tears)
            You know I want to see Martha again...
            and...and when I get back...I..I'd
            like to live at Mrs. Chalmers'!
                (almost impossible
                 to control the tears)
            I...it's...I think it'd be...
            very nice!

They are all motionless. John is too deeply touched to struggle any further. Gently, he touches Mrs. Haney's cheek.

                    JOHN
                (gently)
            All right, ma. I'll be good.

                                        (CONTINUED)

18   CONTINUED - (8):

They release their holds on him. He turns to Mr. Atterbury.

                    JOHN
              (continuing,
               quietly)
          Mr. Atterbury, how do we go
          about breaking that will?

                    MRS. HANEY
          No, Johnny! Your father.....!

                    JOHN
              (interrupting)
          My father did enough, Ma. I'll
          handle this.

                    JAMES
              (defiant, but scared)
          You better not try, Johnny!

                    ATTERBURY
              (thoughtfully)
          I don't think you can, Johnny.
          Your father was of sound mind
          when he wrote the will. You
          don't have any grounds.

                    JOHN
          How about the part about taking
          care of ma? You call throwing
          her into a home taking care of her?
          You know pa didn't mean that!

As Atterbury thinks, they watch him intently. James goes unnoticed.

                    JAMES
          Don't you worry about ma! I'll
          take care of her! You just mind
          your own business!

                    ATTERBURY
          Nooooo...I'm sure that wasn't
          your father's intent....
              (beat)
          but I don't think that makes
          much difference.....
              (beat)
          I'll be honest with you, Johnny...
          I don't think you can win.

                                        (CONTINUED)

18   CONTINUED - (9):

                  JAMES
              (furious)
All right! You heard him! Now
I'll tell you something! Get
outta my house!

                MRS. HANEY
Jamie! He's your brother!

                  JAMES
Then why don't he leave me alone?!
He's been beatin' on me since I
got here! You heard him!
              (beat)
I want him outta here! It's my
house!

Mrs. Haney turns to John. She wants peace at any price.

                MRS. HANEY
              (pleading)
He's upset, Johnny...
              (beat)
Maybe for just a little while.....
till he cools off.....

                  JOHN
              (beat, then to
               Atterbury)
All I want is a chance! For
ma. As far as I'm concerned, I
don't want a dime of the money.
              (beat)
Will you take the case, Mr.
Atterbury?

Atterbury takes a long beat as he looks toward Mrs. Haney,
then at James, then back to John.

                ATTERBURY
              (nods)
I'll take it, Johnny.

                  JOHN
All right, Jamie...I'll get
out of your house ... for now.
              (beat)
Have your fun while you can.

As they all watch, he leaves, and we:

                                  FADE OUT.

<u>MIDDLE COMMERCIAL</u>

ACT TWO

FADE IN:

19 INT. COURTROOM - DAY

Presiding is JUDGE DAVIS. The courtroom is empty of jury and spectators. The only people present being Mrs. Haney, and Atterbury at one table. At the other, James and his lawyer, MR. BLUE. A BAILIFF is present. John is on the witness stand.

          BLUE
Objection! He's leading the witness!

          JUDGE
Sustained. Mr. Atterbury, please re-phrase your question.

          ATTERBURY
     (nods, turns to John)
Yes, sir. John...what is your own, _personal_ interest in attempting to void your father's will?

          JOHN
I have none.

          ATTERBURY
In other words, if the court should declare this will invalid... you would make no attempt to claim any part of your father's estate?

          JOHN
No, sir...I wouldn't.

          ATTERBURY
Will you tell us then why this case has been brought to trial at all?

          JOHN
I want to make sure my mother gets what's coming to her!

Atterbury returns the will to the judge and comes back to John.

          (CONTINUED)

19   CONTINUED:

                    ATTERBURY
                 (continuing)
            The wording seems to be specific
            enough. James is to provide
            for your mother. Do you have any
            reason to doubt that he will?

                    JOHN
                 (grim)
            I sure do!

                    ATTERBURY
            Will you tell the court why you
            doubt it?

                    JOHN
            'Cause I know Jamie. I know how
            he thinks! He's a liar and a
            thief!!

                    BLUE
                 (jumping up)
            Objection!!!

                    JUDGE
            Sustained!
                 (severely)
            Mr. Haney, I must warn you this
            court will not tolerate name
            calling! Another outburst like
            that and I'll cite you for contempt!

                    JOHN
                 (subdued)
            I'm sorry, your honor.

                    ATTERBURY
            John...you know of the three
            different wills. Would you say
            this was the act of a...stable
            man?

There is an instant reaction from Blue and Mrs. Haney. They
speak together:

                    BLUE
            Objection!!!

                    MRS. HANEY
            No!!!

The judge bangs his gavel.

                                        (CONTINUED)

19   CONTINUED - (2):

                    JUDGE
          Order!
               (much more gently
               to Mrs. Haney)
          Mrs. Haney, I know this is
          very difficult for you, but
          you must control yourself.

                    MRS. HANEY
          But he's trying to say John was
          crazy! That's not true! I don't
          care about the money or the farm!
          John was a good man!

                    JUDGE
          I can understand your feelings
          about your husband, but if there's
          anything you have to say, you'll
          be given a chance to say it.
               (beat)
          Now please...no more outbursts.

He looks at her for a moment longer to be sure she's
going to be quiet, then turns to Blue.

                    JUDGE
          Your objection is sustained,
          Counselor.
               (to Atterbury)
          Mr. Atterbury, you know better than
          that.

                    ATTERBURY
          I apologize to the court. I had
          no intention of intimating that
          the deceased was not of sound
          mind, but that he _was_ of a rather...
          mercurial disposition. Yet, despite
          that, his relationships with his
          wife were of the best.
               (quietly)
          No further questions.

                    JUDGE
          Mr. Blue?

                    BLUE
          No questions.

                    JUDGE
               (takes out pocket watch)
          It is now nearly noon. This court
          will adjourn until two-thirty o'clock.

He bangs his gavel and stands. As the rest rise, we:

                                        DISSOLVE TO:

23.

20   INT. KITCHEN - DAY

        showing Mrs. Haney and James at the table. Food is in
        front of them. Mrs. Haney is just pushing hers around,
        no appetite. James is gobbling up the last of it from
        his plate. Now he shoves back his chair and gets up.

                        JAMES
                I gotta run, ma. I got a
                date with a customer for the
                farm.

                        MRS. HANEY
                    (trying once more)
                Jamie...do you have to.....?

                        JAMES
                    (snaps)
                Yes! I have to! Don't _you_
                start on me, ma! I've had enough
                from Johnny!
                    (he starts for door)
                I'll pick you up in time for
                court.

        He exits, as Mrs. Haney sits hopelessly. In a moment,
        there is a KNOCK on the door. She gets up to open it,
        reacting as she sees it is John.

                        MRS. HANEY
                Johnny! You shouldn't be here!
                If Jamie sees you.....!

                        JOHN
                It's all right, ma. I waited
                for him to leave. I won't be
                long. Just wanted to get some
                of my things.

                        MRS. HANEY
                    (uncertainly)
                Well...please hurry, Johnny.
                I don't want any more trouble.

        John nods and starts out of the room as she watches him
        worriedly.

21   INT. BEDROOM - DAY

        SHOOTING TOWARD THE DOOR. From in BACK OF CAMERA, we HEAR
        the SQUEAK of the rocking chair. Now we HEAR John's
        footsteps nearing the door. They stop. Then the door
        opens and John stands in the doorway, a puzzled look on
        his face. Obviously he has heard the squeak and wondered
        who was causing it. He reacts in shocked amazement as
        the SQUEAK STOPS.

24.

22 POV SHOT

to show John Haney Sr. seated in the chair.

23 ANOTHER ANGLE - BOTH

      JOHN, JR.
 Pa!!!

When John, Sr., speaks, he has to force the words, as though it is terribly difficult to speak.

      JOHN SR.
 John--ny......over..coat......

      JOHN JR.
 What? What'd you say, Pa?

      JOHN SR.
 Over..coat...Johnny......my.....
 overcoat......

      JOHN JR.
 What about it? What about
 your overcoat, pa?

      JOHN SR.
 My......over..coat......

      MRS. HANEY'S VOICE
   (calling)
 Johnny......?

24 CLOSE SHOT - JOHN JR.

as he turns his head toward the door. Then he turns back, and reacts.

25 POV SHOT - THE ROCKING CHAIR

which is now empty, but still rocking gently, as though somebody just got out of it.

26 FULL SHOT

as John looks frantically in all directions.

          (CONTINUED)

25.

26　CONTINUED:

      MRS. HANEY'S VOICE
     (closer, outside
      the door)
  Johnny.....?
     (the door opens)
  Who are you talking to?

      JOHN
     (still in some shock)
  Uh....nobody, ma......

      MRS. HANEY
  I thought I heard voices.
     (beat)
  Are you all right, Johnny?
  What are you doing in here?

      JOHN
  Nothing... I was just.....
     (stops, beat)
  Ma...what'd you do with Pa's
  things? You know, his suits...
  overcoat...?

      MRS. HANEY
     (slight surprise
      at change)
  I packed them away. They're in
  the attic, I think. Why?

      JOHN
  Well...I thought I might take
  some of it. Nobody else can use
  them. The stuff'd be too small
  for Jamie.....

      MRS. HANEY
  I'm sure he wouldn't mind...but,
  Johnny...do it some other time.
  Jamie'll be back soon.....

      JOHN
  I'll only be a minute, ma.....

Before she can object, he leaves the room. Wearily, Mrs. Haney exits, heading for downstairs.

27　INT. ATTIC - DAY - FULL SHOT

It is completely dark, except for what little light fights its way in through a tiny window at the end. Now more light streams in as the trap door is lifted, and John pokes his head in. He climbs in, carrying a lighted lantern and looks around.

26.

28   POV SHOT

　　　as CAMERA PANS THE ATTIC, showing it is jammed with boxes, cartons, trunks. CAMERA STOPS at a big steamer trunk, which is in the foreground.

29   ANOTHER ANGLE

　　　to include John, as he spots the trunk and opens it to find it jammed with a man's clothes. He begins to pull them out, dropping each piece in a pile as it turns out to be something other than an overcoat.

30   INT. KITCHEN

　　　where Mrs. Haney paces nervously. She glances overhead at the ceiling, wondering what's keeping John so long. Now she walks to the window and looks out. She reacts.

31   INT. ATTIC - CLOSE

　　　the pile of clothes, now grown very large.

32   ANOTHER ANGLE

　　　to include John as he stares into the trunk.

33   POV SHOT

　　　of a folded overcoat in the trunk.

34   ANOTHER ANGLE

　　　as John reaches in slowly and pulls it out. He's almost afraid to search it. Then he looks in all the pockets, until he reaches into the inside breast pocket. He freezes, then slowly pulls out a sheet of paper. Unfolding it, he holds it close to the lantern.

35   INT. KITCHEN

　　　where Mrs. Haney has her hat and coat on, almost jittering in her nervousness. The door opens and James enters.

　　　　　　　　　　　　JAMES
　　　　　　　Hey...you're ready. That's
　　　　　　　good, ma.

　　　　　　　　　　　　　　　　　　　　(CONTINUED)

35   CONTINUED:

> MRS. HANEY
> (nervously)
> Yes. Let's hurry, Jamie...we don't want to be late.

> JAMES
> We're not in <u>that</u> much of a rush.

> MRS. HANEY
> Please, Jamie...I want to be on time.

James glances at her curiously, wondering at her nervousness. Then he shrugs.

> JAMES
> Okay...

As they turn to go, there is a sudden CLATTER of footsteps rushing down the stairs, and o.s.

> JOHN'S VOICE
> (excited)
> Ma! Ma!

James swings around, his face growing ugly. He looks at his mother, who grabs his arm.

> MRS. HANEY
> Jamie...he only came to get his things!

John rushes into the kitchen, stopping abruptly. He has the overcoat over his arm and the paper in his hand. There is a moment of silence, then:

> JAMES
> You got what you came for? Now beat it!

> JOHN
> (grim)
> I got more than I came for.
> (indicates paper)
> I found this in Pa's coat.

James comes to him slowly.

> JAMES
> What is it?

He reaches for the paper, and John lets him have it. James looks at it.

36   INSERT SHOT - THE PAPER

which reads: "Genesis: 27".

37   ANOTHER ANGLE - ALL

as James looks up.

> JAMES
> Genesis 27. What's it mean?

> JOHN
> That's what I'm going to find out!
> (turns, looking around)
> Where's the Bible?

He spots it on a shelf and starts for it. James grabs his arm.

> JAMES
> Everything in this house is mine!
> Keep your hands off!

John tries to shake him off, but James clings. Mrs. Haney is yelling.

> MRS. HANEY
> John!!! Jamie!!! Stop it!!!!

> JAMES
> I'm warning you!!

John swings a right that knocks James on his fanny. As he goes down, John heads for the Bible. James bounces up immediately and rushes for the shotgun that hangs on the wall. As John gets the Bible, James swings the gun toward him.

> MRS. HANEY
> (screaming)
> Jamie!!! No!!!

She rushes to James, grabbing the muzzle and trying to get it away. James has to struggle with her.

> JAMES
> I warned him...!!!

As this goes on, John is frantically shaking the Bible, but nothing falls out. A puzzled expression comes over his face, as he stops shaking it, and just stares at it. James sees it, and stops struggling with Mrs. Haney. A smug smile crosses his face.

(CONTINUED)

37   CONTINUED:

>   JAMES
>   (continuing,
>   mocking)
>   What's the matter, Johnny?
>   Nothing in it? What'd you expect
>   to find...a new will?

John is turning the pages slowly. Mrs. Haney makes sure James is not going to shoot, then walks to John, who is staring down at an open page. She takes the book from him and reads:

>   MRS. HANEY
>   "See, the smell of my son is
>   as the smell of a field which
>   the Lord hath blessed....."

As she looks from one to the other:

>   JAMES
>   There _is_ no other will! And
>   I'll tell you something else!
>   The next time I find you here,
>   even ma ain't gonna stop me from
>   putting a load of buckshot in you!
>   (beat)
>   Now get outta my house and stay
>   out!!

Still puzzled, but not frightened, John slowly walks toward the door. James reaches out and takes the Bible from Mrs. Haney.

>   JAMES
>   (continuing,
>   mocking)
>   Johnny boy.....

As John stops and turns, James throws the Bible to him.

>   JAMES
>   (continuing)
>   You might as well take this with
>   you.
>   (beat)
>   It's _all_ you're gonna get.

On the reaction, we:

DISSOLVE TO:

30.

38 INT. COURTROOM - DAY - CLOSE SHOT - THE BIBLE

lying on a table. Over this:

                BLUE'S VOICE
        Mr. Haney, much has been made
        of the fact.....

CAMERA PULLS BACK to show that James is on the stand, Blue alongside. Atterbury, Mrs. Haney and John are at their table; the Bible is in front of John, who is staring fixedly at it.

                BLUE
           (continuing)
        ...that you wish to sell your farm
        and place your mother in what has
        been called "an old folks' home".
        Will you tell the court exactly
        what it is you had in mind.

Over the above, John idly opens the Bible to the frontispiece. He stares down at it for a moment.

39 CLOSE SHOT - JOHN

staring down. Then a frown crosses his face as he thinks of something. An idea hits him. Over this:

                JAMES' VOICE
        Yes sir. Your honor, my mother's
        worked hard all her life. As long
        as I can remember, she's been
        cooking, sewing, washing. There've
        even been times when she's helped
        in the fields when we were short-
        handed.

40 POV SHOT

of frontispiece, on which is written in an old-fashioned hand: "To my son John on his tenth birthday. Isaac Haney". Over this, James' voice continues. He is being honest, open, boyish and a complete phoney.

                JAMES VOICE
           (continuing)
        Up until now I've never been
        able to do anything about it. But
        now I can, and I want to!

31.

41 MED. SHOT - JOHN, MRS. HANEY

as John leans toward her. James continues in the b.g.

                    JAMES VOICE
              (continuing, under
              following dialogue)
They call Mrs. Chalmers' place an old folks' home -- That's not true! Mrs. Chalmers takes in boarders! She's got enough help so her guests don't have to do a lick of work if they don't want to! And that's what I want for ma! For her never to work again!

Following dialogue over the above:

                    JOHN
Ma... this is Pa's bible!

                    MRS. HANEY
Of course.

                    JOHN
Didn't we used to have another one?

                    MRS. HANEY
Yes. Your grandfather's.

                    JOHN
              (getting excited)
Where is it, ma?

                    MRS. HANEY
              (puzzled)
I don't know, Johnny. In the attic, I expect.....
              (gets an idea)
Oh, Johnny! You're not going to make any more trouble!

                    JOHN
No...don't worry, ma.

As he leans back thoughtfully, we:

42 FULL SHOT - ALL

Over following, John leans over to whisper to Atterbury, who reacts, then shakes his head violently. John whispers again, urgently. Atterbury's reaction is as violently negative.

                    (CONTINUED)

42   CONTINUED:

>BLUE
>Your honor, isn't it obvious that Mr. Haney is not the cruel, hard-hearted son the plaintiff is trying to make him out to be? On the contrary...here is a devoted son who loves his mother, and whose only wish is to make the rest of her days happy ones!

>JUDGE
>Mr. Blue, are you making your summation or do you intend to question your witness any further?

>BLUE
>No further questions.

>JUDGE
>Mr. Atterbury?

>ATTERBURY
>(rising)
>Your honor, in view of the lateness of the hour, may I be permitted to start my cross examination tomorrow morning?

>JUDGE
>(looks at his watch)
>Very well. We will adjourn until ten o'clock tomorrow morning, at which time you may cross examine. Following that I will hear closing arguments.
>(BANGS gavel)
>Court's adjourned.....

As all rise:

43   MED. SHOT - ATTERBURY, JOHN

As Atterbury turns to him.

>ATTERBURY
>Have you gone completely out of your mind?!

He is interrupted by:

>JAMES' VOICE
>Ready, ma?

33.

44   ANOTHER ANGLE

to include James and Mrs. Haney. As James throws John a contemptuous glance, Mrs. Haney looks at John pleadingly as though asking him not to cause any trouble. Then she walks off with James. As they go:

45   CLOSE SHOT - ATTERBURY, JOHN

> ATTERBURY
> Johnny...if he catches you in that house he has every right to shoot you!

> JOHN
> (stubborn)
> I don't care! Pa wasn't the kind to play practical jokes! And I saw him as plain as I see you!

> ATTERBURY
> I'm too old to start believing in ghosts. And so are you. I will not break into that house with you, and I forbid you to do it!

As they stare at each other, we:

> SLOW DISSOLVE TO:

46   INT. ATTIC - NIGHT - FULL SHOT

to show it is pitch dark. Now a sliver of light appears as the trap door is lifted, and John and Atterbury climb in, both carrying lighted lanterns. Atterbury surveys the crowded room and shakes his head resignedly.

> ATTERBURY
> I must be getting senile, Johnny, to let you talk me into this.
> (beat)
> Well...let's get started...and please! Don't make any more noise than you have to!

> SLOW DISSOLVE TO:

47   INT. ATTIC - DAY

Through the little window, we can see that it is dawn. The attic is a mess. All boxes, cartons, trunks, etc., have been emptied and examined. John stands deep in one corner

(CONTINUED)

47   CONTINUED:

by an old roll-top desk on which papers have been scattered. The top drawer on one side is open, blocking his exit.

> ATTERBURY
> (completely beat)
> It's no use, Johnny. There's nothing here. We'd better get out before they wake up.

John nods bitterly. In frustration, he shoves the drawer back in order to get out, starting out as he does so. The drawer closes only about two-thirds of the way, blocking him. He stops and stares down at it.

> ATTERBURY
> (continuing,
> worried)
> Johnny...it's light out! We've got to go!

> JOHN
> In a minute.....

He pulls the drawer completely out, and sticks his arm in as far as it will go. He freezes, then slowly pulls out a Bible. He stands, holding it in his hands.

> JOHN
> (continuing,
> strained)
> Mr. Atterbury.....

48   CLOSE SHOT - THE BIBLE

as John lets it fall open. At the spot where it does so, there is a folded sheet of paper.

49   ANOTHER ANGLE - BOTH MEN

staring down at the paper. Slowly, Atterbury removes the paper and holds it to the light where he can read it. John watches, his heart in his mouth. Finally Atterbury shows grim satisfaction on his face.

(CONTINUED)

49   CONTINUED:

                    ATTERBURY
               (reading slowly)
          I, John Haney, hereby bequeath and
          provide that.....
               (beat)

Atterbury looks up at John.

                    ATTERBURY
               (continuing)
          The old man made it right after
          all. This will clearly supercedes
          all the others --

                                        FADE OUT.

                    FINAL COMMERCIAL

FADE IN:

50 KARLOFF

> KARLOFF
> Jonas Atterbury knew his law. The will found in Chapter 27 of Henesis was the legal one. And, as it turned out, much more equitable than the one being contested.
> (beat)
> John Haney, Sr. never appeared again. But to this day, no one has ever been able to explain his instructions to his son, and his disappearance.
> (beat)
> Was the veil lifted long enough to give John Haney Jr. a glimpse of what lies beyond...before it dropped again?
> (beat)
> We may never know. But we do know that this is the only record in modern times in which a ghostly appearance has been directly responsible for a court ruling.
> (beat)
> Be with us again when we bring you another true and documented chapter of "THE VEIL".

FADE OUT.

THE END

PROD. NO. 9209

"NO FOOD ON THE TABLE"

Teleplay by

JACK JACOBS

T H E V E I L

Created by

FRANK P. BIBAS

HAL ROACH STUDIOS

PRODUCER: FRANK P. BIBAS

1.

"NO FOOD ON THE TABLE"

FADE IN:

1   KARLOFF (DIALOGUE TO COME LATER)

                                          FADE OUT.

(FIRST COMMERCIAL)

FADE IN:

2   BACK TO SCENE - SHOT - KARLOFF

                    KARLOFF
There's an old saying..."Every man should marry. Happily if possible -- but if unhappily, let him not despair. He can always become a philosopher, and that is good for any man." Captain John Elwood of Gloucester, Massachusetts made a very big mistake. He got tired of being a philosopher.

As CAMERA MOVES CLOSER to bottle:

                                DISSOLVE THROUGH TO:

3   OCEAN GOING SAILING VESSEL AT DOCK - DAY - (STOCK SHOT)

                  KARLOFF'S VOICE
The time was 1855. The good Captain Elwood had just returned to Gloucester from a voyage to Florida.

                                DISSOLVE THROUGH TO:

4   INT. CAPTAIN'S STATEROOM - DAY - MED. SHOT - ELWOOD

CAPTAIN JOHN ELWOOD is about 45, a husky, good-looking man with smiling eyes and a cheery disposition. At least at the moment he has. He is putting clothing into his sea chest that lies open on his bed.

                  KARLOFF'S VOICE
                    (continuing)
The trip had been an exciting one and the Captain had a fine story to tell his friends at the Mariner's Club.

                                   (CONTINUED)

4   CONTINUED:

The chest is almost full. Elwood looks around for something, sees it in the cabin through the door and goes out of the stateroom.

5   INT. CABIN - DAY - MED. SHOT - ELWOOD

begins to HUM a sea chanty as he picks up a few pieces of clothing in the cabin. He opens the drawers of a bureau looking for forgotten items. Behind him we see into the stateroom and slithering down onto the chest is a snake! Elwood is about to go back to the stateroom when a KNOCK is HEARD.

                ELWOOD
   Come in.

6   MED. SHOT - SNAKE

SHOOTING through stateroom door, we see the snake coil on the clothing, then disappear to the bottom of the chest under the clothing.

7   REVERSE SHOT

Coming into the cabin and closing the door is FIRST MATE CALVIN LOGAN, a medium-sized, strong-looking man about 40. He carries a black log-book. Logan has an Irish accent. It should be slight, not heavy.

                LOGAN
   Here's the log-book, Captain.
   Everything's in order, sir.

                ELWOOD
    (taking the book)
   Thank you, Mr. Logan.

                LOGAN
   The crew's anxious to leave,
   sir. Most of their wives are
   waitin' for 'em on the wharf.

                ELWOOD
    (nodding)
   Aye, and the way they're be-
   havin' you'd think we were months
   overdue instead of two weeks.

                LOGAN
   They've likely heard of our
   trouble, sir. Happy to see
   us alive.

                (CONTINUED)

7   CONTINUED:

                    ELWOOD
              Nonsense. They'll grab their
              men by the ears and march 'em
              to the paymaster before kissin'
              'em.

                    LOGAN
                  (slight smile)
              Aye, sir, some. There's all
              kinds among 'em.

                    ELWOOD
                  (sudden terrible
                   thought)
              Is Mrs. Elwood out there?

                    LOGAN
                  (quickly)
              Oh, no, sir. The Captain's
              wife is too well bred to show
              her emotions in public.

                    ELWOOD
                  (relieved)
              Indeed.
                  (gestures for
                   Logan to follow
                   him)
              I want you to do something
              for me, Mr. Logan.

       Elwood walks to the stateroom followed by Logan.

8   INT. STATEROOM - DAY - ANGLE ON CHEST

       As Elwood comes into shot, tosses the few other clothes into
       the chest and closes it. Logan enters shot.

                    ELWOOD
              I have to go to the ship's
              company to make my report.
              See that my gear's taken
              directly to my home.

                    LOGAN
              I'll do it myself, sir.

       Logan goes to pick up the chest.

                    ELWOOD
              That's kind of you. Tell Mrs.
              Elwood I'm fine and that I'll
              be with her presently.

                                                  (CONTINUED)

4.

8   CONTINUED:

>   LOGAN
>   Aye, aye, sir.

As Logan walks out, we HOLD CLOSE on chest being carried.

                                              DISSOLVE TO:

9   INT. KITCHEN - ELWOOD HOME - DAY - MED. SHOT

The part of the kitchen we see contains a circular dining table and several chairs. Coming into the room from the adjoining living room is RUTH ELWOOD, a slender, almost frail woman about 35. She has the air of a fallen aristocrat. Following her with the chest is Logan.

>   RUTH
>   Put it anywhere here, Mr.
>   Logan. I do appreciate your
>   coming. I was so worried,
>   what with the hurricane, and
>   reports of the plague.
>
>   LOGAN
>   (putting down
>   chest)
>   It wasn't the plague, Ma'am.
>   Just a lot of poisonous snakes
>   that came aboard while we were
>   in Florida.
>
>   RUTH
>   Oh! There was talk that some
>   of the men died.
>
>   LOGAN
>   Aye. Two seamen. Three others
>   were bitten but we saved 'em.
>
>   RUTH
>   It must have been a terrible
>   experience.
>
>   LOGAN
>   We were findin' the snakes all
>   over the ship for two or three
>   days after leavin' the wharf.

Logan moves toward doorway.

>   RUTH
>   Did the Captain say how long
>   he'd be?

                                              (CONTINUED)

9   CONTINUED:

                    LOGAN
                (in doorway)
            No ma'am.

                    RUTH
            I'd best be getting his dinner.
            Thank you kindly, Mr. Logan.

                    LOGAN
            You're welcome, Ma'am.

    He salutes and exits. She watches him go, then looks at the
    chest. She goes to the chest, bends down and begins to open
    it, stops as she gets an idea which brings a slight smile to
    face, then goes quickly to where a shawl hangs over an chair.
    She throws it over her shoulders and starts for the living
    room.

                                            DISSOLVE TO:

10 INSERT - SIGN

    Reading: "GLOUCESTER INN"

                                        DISSOLVE THROUGH TO:

11 INT. DINING ROOM - INN - DAY - MED. SHOT

    In f.g. is a rectangular table about five feet by two which
    is set sumptuously. On it can be seen a ham, a roast fowl,
    piles of bisquits, etc. MR. RICHARDSON, a white-haired,
    beefy man is busy arranging dishes. In b.g. through the open
    door of the adjoining room we see Captain Elwood, the center
    of a group of some 10 or 12 middle-aged fellow CAPTAINS.
    As we hear Elwood's booming voice, CAMERA MOVES past food
    on table toward the door.

                    ELWOOD
            And there they came, slitherin'
            up the lines and gangplank
            like so many fiends a'hell.

    JESSE, a serving boy, walks toward CAMERA, carrying empty
    ale mugs on a tray.

                    ELWOOD
                (continuing)
            "There's hundreds of 'em,"
            somebody cries. "Don't let
            'em aboard till they pays their
            passage!" I says!

                                            (CONTINUED)

6.

11   CONTINUED:

There is a general convivial laughter as Jesse comes out of the room and closes the door behind them. On the door is a sign reading: "MARINER'S CLUB -- NO WOMEN ALLOWED" The sign is loosely nailed at the top.

12   REVERSE SHOT

Coming into the room a bit timidly is Ruth. She enters from a dim hallway. Jesse disappears into the kitchen with his tray. Richardson looks up and sees Ruth.

          RICHARDSON
    'Afternoon, Mrs. Elwood.

          RUTH
    Hello, Mr. Richardson, I'd
    like a bottle of that Spanish
    wine the Captain favors. He'll
    enjoy it with his dinner.

          RICHARDSON
    Be supper more'n likely, ma'am.
    Club's havin' dinner in his
    honor.

Ruth frowns as the club room door opens and a 2ND SERVING BOY comes out with a tray full of mugs. He leaves the door open. Ruth looks into the room as she HEARS Elwood's voice.

          ELWOOD'S VOICE
    Would'a been nobody hurt at
    all...

13   POV SHOT

Elwood drinking and surrounded by the others as before.

          ELWOOD
         (continuing)
    ...except some of the fools
    tried stompin' the snakes with
    their feet and got bit for their
    pains.

The smile on his face fades as he looks toward CAMERA and sees Ruth.

14   ANGLE ON RUTH

She stares at him, rigid and shocked. Richardson moves o.s.

15 BACK TO SCENE

Elwood comes away from the men who are now staring out toward Ruth. Elwood reaches the door, closes it and proceeds to Ruth.

16 ANOTHER ANGLE

Elwood has a frozen smile on his face.

> RUTH
> (trying to be calm)
> Hello, John.

> ELWOOD
> (close to her)
> So! Now it's come to you spyin' on me, is it?

> RUTH
> (hurt)
> Spying? I thought you were at...

> ELWOOD
> (commandingly)
> Go home! I'll be there presently!

CAMERA PANS UP as he turns on his heel and goes back to the door, opens it, then with a forced smile, goes inside and closes the door. The sign "Mariner's Club, No Women Allowed", flaps against the door.

17 ANGLE ON RUTH

As she grimly purses her lips and turns to go. Richardson enters with the bottle.

> RICHARDSON
> Here we are, Mrs. Elwood.

> RUTH
> (curtly)
> I won't be needing it now, thank you!

She walks o.s. leaving Richardson staring perplexed, holding the bottle of wine.

DISSOLVE TO:

8.

18   INT. KITCHEN - ELWOOD HOME - DAY - MED. CLOSE SHOT - CHEST

It remains on the floor in the same position as before. CAMERA PULLS BACK revealing Ruth sitting at the table, alone, the remains of her dinner on a plate before her, a cup of tea in her hands. She reacts as she HEARS the SOUND of a door open and close o.s. She looks toward the living room.

19   INT. LIVING ROOM - DAY - MED. SHOT - ELWOOD

enters and starts toward the kitchen. The room is furnished sparely and in the period, no frills.

20   INT. KITCHEN - DAY - MED. SHOT

Ruth sits sipping her tea. She turns her back on the doorway as Elwood appears. He looks at her, then goes to the table and stands there awkwardly beside her.

      ELWOOD
     (brusquely
      apologetic)
  I'm sorry for what I said to
  ya, Ruth. Mr. Richardson
  told me you came for a bottle
  of wine.

      RUTH
     (bitterly)
  For your dinner. I had the
  foolish notion that on your
  first day back, you'd prefer
  eating at home.

      ELWOOD
     (lamely)
  I didn't want to stay... It
  was in my honor, I couldn't
  leave.

      RUTH
  And what of me? After fearing
  you dead these past weeks, you
  hadn't the good grace to even
  see me before joining the company of your drunken friends!

21   ANOTHER ANGLE

Elwood sits in a chair next to her as she begins to sob softly into her napkin.

      (CONTINUED)

21   CONTINUED:

                    ELWOOD
        It was only a matter of a
        few hours...

                    RUTH
        How dare you humiliate me like
        that! Ever since our ship sank
        two years ago, you've treated
        me like a servant!

                    ELWOOD
               (he's heard this
               before)
        I've done no such thing...

                    RUTH
               (unheeding; crying
               with mixed bitter-
               ness and anger)
        Sometimes I think you only
        married me for the money to
        buy the ship. And when it
        was gone, you had no further
        use for me!

Elwood rises, a resigned, philosophic expression on his face.

                    ELWOOD
               (not harshly)
        Ruth, I'm sorry. Sorry for
        your complaints and your tears.
        But I do my best, and that's
        all I can.

Ruth looks up at him. She has him where she wants him now.

                    RUTH
        Is it your best to practically
        live in a saloon when you're
        ashore? Have _I_ no right to
        your company and affection?

                    ELWOOD
               (a little sorry
               for her)
        Well...I was plannin' to take
        ya to Boston for a week's holi-
        day.

                    RUTH
               (wide-eyed)
        Boston? Do you mean it, John?

                                 (CONTINUED)

10.

21   CONTINUED - (2):

                    ELWOOD
          If you'll see to my clothes and
          ready yourself, we'll leave in
          the mornin'.

He turns and walks toward the living room.

                    RUTH
              (rising, slight
               smile)
          Yes, John.

She goes to the chest.

22   INT. LIVING ROOM - DAY - MED. SHOT

Elwood comes in, takes off his jacket and goes to clothes tree to hang it. Behind him we can see Ruth opening the chest and taking clothing out of it.

23   CLOSER ANGLE - RUTH

As she blithely begins sorting the articles of clothing out on the floor. MUSIC underscores the movement toward danger.

24   ANGLE ON ELWOOD

Keeping Ruth in b.g. He picks up a pipe from a sideboard, when there is a sudden SHRILL SCREAM from Ruth.

                    RUTH
              (hysterically)
          John! John!

25   INT. KITCHEN - ANGLE ON RUTH

Almost mesmerized with fear, staring into the chest. Elwood comes in and she throws her hands to her face, crying with fright. He takes her in his arms.

                    RUTH
              (continuing)
          LOOK!!!

Elwood looks down at the chest.

26   INSERT

Dead snake lying on bottom of the chest, uncoiled.

11.

27 BACK TO SCENE

                    ELWOOD
               (kicks the chest)
          Dead. There, there, nothing
          to fear now. Why, if it were
          alive it might have killed
          you, my dear...

     He looks with narrowed eyes at the chest, and his expression
     tells us that he's now thinking. This might not have been
     such a tragedy, as we:

                                             DISSOLVE TO:

28   INT. LIVING ROOM - ELWOOD HOME - DAY - MED. SHOT (SILENT)

     Ruth sits smiling opposite Elwood, talking a blue streak,
     rolling yarn into a ball. Elwood holds the hank of yarn
     on his hands for her, his pipe in his mouth, an open news-
     paper on the table beside him which he glances at while
     suffering the tortures of the damned.

                    KARLOFF'S VOICE
          For a week after their return
          from Boston, Captain Elwood
          acted the proper husband. At
          least, he stayed home a reason-
          able number of hours.

                                             WIPE TO:

29   INT. LIVING ROOM - ELWOOD HOME - DAY - MED. SHOT - RUTH
     (SILENT)

     Winding yarn into a ball. Her hank of yarn is now stretched
     between the arms of a small chair. She is alone in the room.

                    KARLOFF'S VOICE
               (continuing)
          But in the weeks that followed,
          he resumed his old habits...

30   INT. MARINER'S CLUBROOM - DAY - FULL SHOT (SILENT)

     Elwood and a group of his cronies drinking and talking,
     some playing chess or darts in b.g.

                    KARLOFF'S VOICE
               (continuing)
          And always at the same cost.

                                             WIPE TO:

31   INT. LIVING ROOM - NIGHT - MED. CLOSE SHOT - RUTH

                    RUTH
               (angrily)
          But you said two hours, John!
          You were there five!

CAMERA PULLS BACK to reveal Elwood hanging his pea-jacket on the clothes tree near the front door.

                    ELWOOD
          I might'a been gone five, woman,
          but I was at the ship's company
          half the time.

                    RUTH
               (taken aback)
          Another voyage?

                    ELWOOD
               (nodding)
          We leave for Jamaica in two
          weeks.

He walks over to his tobacco can and takes a pipe from his pocket. She follows him a few steps. He seems pleased at announcing the news.

                    RUTH
          John...take me with you. You
          promised if you ever had another
          trip to the Indies...

                    ELWOOD
               (frowning)
          I did?

                    RUTH
          Last year. Don't you remember?

                    ELWOOD
          I don't know. I'll have to
          talk with the owners.

                    RUTH
          I can look after you. We can
          be together, John...

As she smiles hopefully, he hides his dissatisfaction and we:

                                        DISSOLVE TO:

32   INT. KITCHEN - NIGHT - MED. SHOT - RUTH

Setting the table. Elwood is seen in b.g. coming from the living room, putting on his jacket. Ruth turns and sees him, frowns at him.

                    RUTH
          Are you going somewhere, John?

                    ELWOOD
          I thought I told you. Captain
          Farnsley's sailin' tomorrow.
          We're havin' supper in his
          honor.

                    RUTH
          You didn't tell me!

                    ELWOOD
          I'm sorry. Don't wait up,
          I'll be late.

He turns to go and walks away. She runs to the doorway.

                    RUTH
          John!

33   INT. LIVING ROOM --NIGHT - MED. SHOT

Elwood stops and looks back at her. She comes to him.

                    RUTH
          When will you see the owners
          about taking me to Jamaica?

                    ELWOOD
          Oh, I'd forgotten...

                    RUTH
          There's only three days left.

                    ELWOOD
          It might be too late to ask
          now, my dear. Perhaps the
          next trip.

                    RUTH
             (flaring)
          You never intended to ask them!
          You never intended to take me.

                    ELWOOD
             (irritatedly)
          Oh, come now, woman. Can't
          a man have a little peace!

                                        (CONTINUED)

14.

33 CONTINUED:

He glares and goes to the door, opens it and is gone. Ruth looks at the plate she holds in her hand and with a cry of pure anger, throws it violently to the floor.

DISSOLVE TO:

34 INT. DINING ROOM - INN - NIGHT - MED. SHOT

The table is set with food. Mr. Richardson rearranging some of the delectables as Jesse enters with a large pot of coffee and puts it on the table.

> RICHARDSON
> I told ya to wash your face
> and hands, yer dirty lumpkin!
>
> JESSE
> (backing away)
> Yissir.

A shadowy figure is seen in b.g. near hall entrance. Jesse exits via the door leading to the kitchen, CAMERA MOVES past partition into Mariner's Clubroom, where the usual checker playing, dart throwing, drinking and talking is being indulged in by the members. In a corner we see Elwood and an older Captain. CAPTAIN BARNEY, sitting across a checker board, drinking from large ale pots.

35 TWO SHOT - ELWOOD AND BARNEY

> BARNEY
> (shaking head
> sadly)
> If only I was ten years younger...
> I'd be a wooin' and courtin' Eliza-
> beth Smith is the mornin'.
>
> ELWOOD
> Ruth and me was talkin' to the
> widow just a week ago...
>
> BARNEY
> (confidentially)
> She got the letter from London
> only yesterday!
>
> ELWOOD
> And you say her Uncle left her
> twenty thousand pounds?

(CONTINUED)

15.

35   CONTINUED:

                    BARNEY
               (nodding)
          Aye. It'll be a lucky man
          that gets her.

                    ELWOOD
               (nodding)
          He could buy most any ship in
          the harbor with that much money.
          Why don't ya give her a go,
          Barney?

                    BARNEY
          I would if I looked like you
          and had your manner, John.
               (shaking head sadly)
          The widda Smith can afford to
          be particular now...and she
          will be.

36   INT. DINING ROOM - NIGHT - MED. SHOT

       The dim figure in f.g. watching Richardson, who now leaves
       the table and goes to the clubroom. As Richardson opens the
       door and enters the room, the figure steps out of darkness.
       We cannot see who it is, but the person wears men's clothes,
       much too large, and a cap partially covers the face. The
       'man' hurries to the food laden table.

37   INT. CLUBROOM - NIGHT - MED. SHOT

       Richardson comes a few steps into the room.

                    RICHARDSON
          Gentlemen...the food is on the
          table.

       As the club members rise, still keeping up a stream of
       conversation, there suddenly comes a loud and SHATTERING
       CRASH from the dining room. Richardson whirls and runs
       to the door like a madman.

38   INT. DINING ROOM - NIGHT - WIDE ANGLE SHOT

       As Richardson runs into the room we can see the 'man' run
       out to the hall. The floor is littered with food and broken
       dishes, the table tipped over on its side. Richardson gives
       a horrified look at the food, then sees the disappearing
       figure.

                                                  (CONTINUED)

16.

38 CONTINUED:

                    RICHARDSON
          Stop! Stop!

He runs after the fleeing 'man'. Behind him, coming into the
room are the club members, who look with dismay at the mess
on the floor. Jesse runs in from the kitchen and stares
incredulously. There are scattered ad libs from the men.
"Someone turned over the table", "Who'd want to do a thing
like that?", "Couldn't have been..."

                    ELWOOD
          I didn't feel the place list
          to starboard!

The voices are interrupted by Richardson's voice o.s.

                    RICHARDSON
          Come here! Come in here, you
          devil!

They look up as Richardson pulls a very unwilling figure by
the scruff of the neck, into the lighted room. The men
stare with curiosity and surprise.

39 ANGLE ON RICHARDSON AND 'MAN'

Richardson grabs the cap off the head of the 'man and Ruth
is revealed! She cowers, frightened and ashamed.

40 TWO SHOT - ELWOOD AND BARNEY

Elwood reacts with a shocked expression. Barney looks at
him pityingly. CAMERA PULLS BACK as Elwood moves to Ruth,
who has been released.

                    RICHARDSON
          Mrs. Elwood...I must have made
          a mistake...

Elwood reaches her and stares at her hard.

                    ELWOOD
              (slowly)
          Did you do this, my dear?

Ruth can't face him, clasps her hands before her humbly.

                    RUTH
              (nodding)
          I'm sorry. I'm sorry!

                                              (CONTINUED)

40 CONTINUED:

She's ready to cry, like a child afraid of being spanked. Elwood doesn't seem angry, rather sympathetic. He turns and looks at the food on the floor, then at the men staring at him, waiting to see what will happen.

>   ELWOOD
>   (a deep sigh)
>   You'll charge the cost of the
>   spoilage to me, Mr. Richardson.
>
>   RICHARDSON
>   Yes, Captain.

41 ANOTHER ANGLE

>   ELWOOD
>   (to the men)
>   Gentlemen, my wife isn't to be
>   blamed. Hell hath no fury like
>   a woman scorned...You see, I
>   promised to take her on my next
>   voyage, and then...broke that
>   promise. I make it again in
>   front of all of you.
>   (he smiles for-
>   givingly to Ruth)
>   She will go on my next voyage.

The men begin to smile and look at one another knowingly. Elwood puts his arm around Ruth's waist.

>   ELWOOD
>   (continuing)
>   Come, my dear. Let us say no
>   more of the matter.
>   (to the others)
>   You will pardon us, gentlemen.

The men watch as Elwood escorts Ruth out of the room. They keep a discreet silence for a moment until Elwood and Ruth are well into the hall out of sight. CAMERA PANS the food on the floor.

42 GROUP SHOT

The men looking down at it. Jesse prominent in shot.

>   BARNEY
>   I do declare...What's gettin'
>   into women nowadays?

43   INT. HALLWAY - NIGHT - MED. CLOSE SHOT - ELWOOD

his arm around Ruth.

                    RICHARDSON'S VOICE (o.s.)
               Seems to me the Captain's only
               the First Mate in his own
               house.

as Elwood reacts to hearing this.

                              DISSOLVE TO:

44   INT. LIVING ROOM - ELWOOD HOME - NIGHT - MED. SHOT

The room is lit dimly by an oil lamp. We HEAR the door open and shut o.s., and in a moment, Ruth enters with Elwood. She moves in ahead of him, still frightened, unsure that John might just be waiting to get her alone before showing his wrath. He looks at her unemotionally.

                    ELWOOD
               We're leaving in three days,
               Ruth. You'd do well to spend
               most of your time getting ready.

Ruth now begins to cry in a whimpering way.

                    RUTH
               It was a terrible thing I did,
               John. Please forgive me.

                    ELWOOD
               I've been amiss, woman. I
               meant what I said at the Inn.
               Now go change those clothes,
               I'll put on the tea.

Ruth nods and starts for the hall. She stops near him and looks at him forlornly.

                    RUTH
               I couldn't help myself, John.
               I just couldn't help myself.

She turns and hurries out to the hall. Elwood watches her go, then lights another oil lamp on a table nearby and starts into the kitchen.

45   INT. KITCHEN - NIGHT - MED. SHOT

Elwood enters with the lamp, goes to a side door and opens it.

46 ANOTHER ANGLE

SHOOTING into a fairly well-stocked pantry. Elwood goes inside, looks up to the top shelf and reaches for something. He takes down a jar, blows the dust off and holds it close to the light.

47 CLOSE SHOT - JAR

On it is a label reading: POISON -- FOR RATS AND VERMIN.

48 BACK TO SCENE

Elwood looks out toward the kitchen, then pockets the jar and starts to back out of the pantry as we:

FADE OUT.

END OF ACT ONE

20.

ACT TWO

FADE IN:

49 STOCK SHOT - SAILING VESSEL RUNNING WITH WIND - DAY

> KARLOFF'S VOICE
> Captain John Elwood, accompanied by his wife, shipped out for the West Indies in the summer of 1855. A week after leaving Gloucester, Mrs. Elwood became ill.

DISSOLVE THRU TO:

50 INT. CAPTAIN'S STATEROOM - DAY - MED. CLOSE SHOT - RUTH

CAMERA PULLS BACK to reveal Ruth lying on a bed, fully clothed. She looks wan and tired and her breath is a little labored. From o.s. she hears Elwood's booming voice approaching.

> ELWOOD'S VOICE (o.s.)
> And have the carpenter repair the after deck stairway before somebody breaks his bloomin' neck!

> LOGAN'S VOICE (o.s.)
> Aye, aye, sir.

Ruth hurriedly sits up, pinches her cheeks, runs her hands over her hair which hangs to her shoulders and looks a little unkempt. She rises, forces a smile and goes to the cabin.

51 INT. CABIN - DAY - MED. SHOT

as the door opens and Elwood enters carrying a china teapot. He looks toward Ruth.

> ELWOOD
> How are you feeling, my dear?

> RUTH
> (trying very hard)
> Much better, John, much better.

(CONTINUED)

21.

51   CONTINUED:

She joins him at the small dining table. Elwood puts the
teapot down and gets a cup from a cabinet as he talks.

                    ELWOOD
          The cook's made more of his
          special tea. Sit down. Another
          calm day like this and you'll
          be completely well.

She sits as he pours the tea. She looks at him with wan
affection.

                    RUTH
          I didn't mean to be a burden
          to you, John...you've been so
          good to me.

                    ELWOOD
          Having you is a comfort, Ruth.
          I should have brought you along
          more often. Nothing lonelier
          than a Captain's life.

                    RUTH
          I should like to come with you
          as often as you'll let me.

                    ELWOOD
          So you shall. Drink up, my
          dear.

Ruth nods and sips her tea. Elwood begins to light his pipe.

                    RUTH
          I dozed off for a while...and
          had the strangest dream.

                    ELWOOD
          A good one, I hope.

                    RUTH
          Yes. I dreamt we were back on
          our ship...on the trip we made
          to Charleston...and instead of
          cotton, the holds were filled
          with money.

                    ELWOOD
               (slight smile)
          I could hardly improve on that
          myself.

                                        (CONTINUED)

22.

51   CONTINUED - (2):

                    RUTH
          We were so happy in the days
          we had money, John. I've been
          thinking about them more and
          more since we left home.

52   ANOTHER ANGLE - FEATURING RUTH

She smiles fondly.

                    RUTH
                 (continuing)
          You were a most handsome man,
          John.

                    ELWOOD
          Have five years destroyed me?

                    RUTH
          You've changed so little. It's
          I who feel the bitterness of
          age. And I know why, now.
                 (a beat)
          Serenity has never been in my
          character. My father used to
          say I had a bit of the devil
          in me.

                    ELWOOD
                 (jocularly)
          All of us do to some extent.

                    RUTH
          I proved my failing when I
          turned over the table at the
          Inn. I'm going to be different,
          John. You'll see...I won't
          complain, and I won't cry...
          and you may go to the Mariner's
          Club as often as you like...
                 (sudden thought)
          <u>If</u> you take me on your voyages
          as you said.

                    ELWOOD
          I accept the bargain, my dear.

She smiles, a far away look in her eyes as she drinks her
tea.

53   MED. CLOSE SHOT - ELWOOD

His eyes narrowing as he watches her. Now he looks alert. CAMERA PULLS BACK as he leans over and pours Ruth more tea. Ruth's eyes are closed and her head drops slightly.

> RUTH
> Some day you'll have your own ship again. I'll see to it.

> ELWOOD
> With the money from your dreams?

> RUTH
> (opening eyes)
> No. From my Uncle Calvin in Philadelphia.

Elwood frowns with puzzlement as he recognizes Ruth's lightheadedness.

> RUTH
> (continuing)
> Lizzie Smith's Uncle in London died and left her 20,000 pounds!

> ELWOOD
> But he was childless. Your Uncle has four sons.

> RUTH
> (back to reality, unhappily)
> Oh! Yes, I forgot. Maybe they'll die.
> (righteously)
> My father left Uncle Calvin a great deal. Therefore Uncle Calvin owes _me_ his inheritance. It'll be yours, John. Yours!

She suddenly whimpers with pain and holds her abdomen. Unable to continue the deceit of her feeling well, she begins to breathe fast and shallow. Elwood rises and goes to her.

> ELWOOD
> You're ill, my dear. Come let me put you to bed.

He helps her up and walks with her to the stateroom.

54 TRAVELING SHOT

As they go.

>   RUTH
>   (crying)
>   I didn't want to get sick.
>   I'm such a burden to you...
>   I should have stayed home...
>   I should have stayed home...

The final line takes them into the stateroom. CAMERA remains SHOOTING through doorway, as Ruth sits on bed.

>   RUTH
>   (continuing)
>   Forgive me, John. Forgive me
>   for doing this to you...
>
>   ELWOOD
>   You'll be fine in a few days.

He helps her onto the bed. We HEAR a knock o.s.

>   ELWOOD
>   (continuing)
>   Try to sleep, my dear.

Elwood comes out of the stateroom, closing the door behind him. He goes to the middle of the cabin.

>   ELWOOD
>   (continuing)
>   Who is it?
>
>   LOGAN'S VOICE
>   Logan, Captain.
>
>   ELWOOD
>   Just a minute.

Elwood quickly picks up the teapot, whirls its contents around as he walks to a porthole, takes the top off the pot and throws the contents out of the porthole. He quickly puts the pot on a shelf and moves away from it.

>   ELWOOD
>   (continuing)
>   Come in, Mr. Logan.

55 ANOTHER ANGLE

The door opens and Logan enters.

(CONTINUED)

25.

55   CONTINUED:

                    LOGAN
          You asked me to see you after
          my watch, Captain.

                    ELWOOD
          Oh, yes, Come in...

Logan comes further into the room as Elwood looks worriedly toward the stateroom.

                    ELWOOD
                    (continuing)
          Frankly, Mr. Logan, I'm worried
          over Mrs. Elwood's illness.
                    (growing chummy)
          You'll be gettin' your Captain's
          license after this voyage, won't
          ya?

                    LOGAN
          I hope so, sir.

                    ELWOOD
          I've seen ya reading up on
          doctorin'. You always had a
          good hand with the sick...I
          was thinkin' that maybe two
          heads are better'n one...

                    LOGAN
          Yes, sir.

                    ELWOOD
          I wonder if you'd mind havin'
          a look at Mrs. Elwood?

                    LOGAN
          I'd be glad to do anything for
          the Missus, sir. If I can.

                    ELWOOD
          Good. Come along.

Logan follows Elwood to the stateroom door. As they enter the stateroom:

                                        WIPE TO:

56   INT. CABIN - DAY - ANOTHER ANGLE

The tea pot in f.g. SHOOTING toward the stateroom door. Logan comes out followed by Elwood, who closes the door and they walk toward the table. Logan has a puzzled frown on his face.

                                        (CONTINUED)

56   CONTINUED:

                    ELWOOD
          I thought at first it was
          cholera...

                    LOGAN
                (shaking head)
          No, sir. I've seen nothin'
          like it. Not in a man.

                    ELWOOD
          Neither have I.

                    LOGAN
          She needs a doctor familiar
          with women's complaints, sir.

                    ELWOOD
                (nodding)
          If she's not better in a few
          days, we'll make a course for
          St. Augustine.

                    LOGAN
          Aye, sir.

Logan goes to the door, as he opens it, Elwood speaks.

                    ELWOOD
          Uh, be sure you put your diag-
          nosis in the ship's log, Mr.
          Logan.

                    LOGAN
          I will, Captain. I do hope
          she's better soon.

Logan closes the door behind him. Elwood smiles slightly, looks toward the stateroom door, then hurries to the cabinet and pulls out a small medicine chest.

57   ANOTHER ANGLE

Elwood lifts the chest to the top of the cabinet, opens it, and takes out the jar we had seen at end of act one. The label is gone and there is less than half the contents remaining.

                                        DISSOLVE TO:

58   SAILING VESSEL UNDER FULL SAIL - DAY - (STOCK SHOT)

                                        DISSOLVE THROUGH TO:

59 INT. CABIN - DAY - CLOSE SHOT - JAR

It is empty, being held by Elwood whom we see looking at it as CAMERA PULLS BACK. He has a quizzical expression on his face, looks at the stateroom door and goes to the porthole. He looks at the jar again, then throws it out. He turns and goes slowly to the stateroom, opens the door and enters.

60 INT. STATEROOM - DAY - MED. SHOT - RUTH

She lies in bed, covered, wearing a nightdress. Her eyes flicker open as Elwood enters and looks down at her.

>   RUTH
>   (labored)
>   How close are we to St.
>   Augustine?
>
>   ELWOOD
>   We ran into a storm during the
>   night. Took us a day off course.
>
>   RUTH
>   A storm? I didn't feel it.
>
>   ELWOOD
>   You were unconscious, I think.
>
>   RUTH
>   We must get there soon, John,
>   or I shall die, I know I shall...
>
>   ELWOOD
>   (fixes cover)
>   I doubt it. The devil in you
>   won't let you.

He means it but she smiles wanly at this 'joke', holds his hand in hers.

>   RUTH
>   John...I've never appreciated
>   you. I never have. If only
>   I'd allowed you to make me
>   laugh. The way you do your
>   friends at the Club.
>
>   ELWOOD
>   (harshly)
>   You laugh, my dear? Can a man
>   go against his nature.
>   (MORE)

(CONTINUED)

60   CONTINUED:

>   ELWOOD (CONT'D)
>   After we married, you fretted
>   at every dollar I spent. When
>   we bought the ship, you worried
>   constantly about losing it. And
>   when we lost it, you couldn't
>   accept the will of God!
>
>   RUTH
>   (distraught)
>   Don't say those things to me
>   now. Please, John!

He looks at her bitterly, then walks out, closing the door, on her faint cries of "John...John..."

61   INT. CABIN - DAY - MED. SHOT

As John comes away from the stateroom there is a KNOCK on the cabin door.

>   LOGAN'S VOICE
>   Captain Elwood!

Elwood goes to the door, opens it to reveal Logan. He is obviously perplexed.

>   LOGAN
>   Sir, we're passin' the longi-
>   tude. If we don't turn for
>   St. Augustine...
>
>   ELWOOD
>   (loudly, angrily)
>   I know our longitude, Mr. Logan.
>   My order stands! We remain on
>   course for Jamaica!

62   ANOTHER ANGLE

The stateroom door opens a crack in the b.g.

>   LOGAN
>   But I looked at Mrs. Elwood,
>   yesterday, sir. She won't
>   last that long!
>
>   ELWOOD
>   (firmly)
>   She and this ship are my respon-
>   sibilities, Mr. Logan! She'll
>   be alive when we reach Jamaica,
>   I warrant it!

(CONTINUED)

29.

62 CONTINUED:

                         LOGAN
               As you say, sir...

     The door is closed before Logan finishes the line. The
     stateroom door opens further and Ruth stands in the opening.
     Elwood whirls and sees her.

                         RUTH
               Liar! Liar!
                    (stumbles a few
                     steps holding
                     onto the door-
                     frame)
               You want me dead. You want me
               dead!

     Elwood walks toward her, a look of grim hatred on his face.

                         ELWOOD
               Get back in there!

     She backs up as he moves to her.

63   INT. STATEROOM - DAY - MED. SHOT

     Ruth backs against the bed.

                         RUTH
                    (her SCREAM is
                     hardly more than
                     a whisper)
               Mr. Logan! Mr. Logan!

     She lies on the bed on her back and covers herself, fear-
     stricken and hysterical, her breath now coming more shallow
     and difficult. Elwood comes in and looms over her.

64   MED. CLOSE SHOT - ELWOOD - RUTH'S POV

     His face is distorted with hate.

                         ELWOOD
               You've had enough poison to
               kill two. Know it now, woman
               that I wanted you dead, and
               I'm about to finish ya!

65   TWO SHOT - RUTH AND ELWOOD

                         RUTH
                    (with difficulty)
               You're an evil man, John Elwood...
               And you'll be repaid by evil!

                                                  (CONTINUED)

65 CONTINUED:

Her eyes burn up at him, then she turns her head on the pillow and goes limp...Elwood grabs a woman's hand mirror from a nearby bureau and holds it to Ruth's face. Satisfied she is not breathing, he straightens and sighs with satisfaction at this happy conclusion. Suddenly remembers himself and runs off toward the cabin, shouting.

>   ELWOOD
>   Mr. Logan! Mr. Logan!

CAMERA FOLLOWS him as he runs to the door of the cabin and we:

DISSOLVE TO:

(NOTE) Is it possible to find stock shot of sea burial on sailing ship?)

66 SAILING VESSEL RIDING IN FULL WIND - DAY - STOCK SHOT

Going opposite direction from previous shots.

>   KARLOFF'S VOICE
>   Mrs. John Elwood was buried
>   at sea. The Captain performed
>   the rites. Three months later,
>   at an inquest held in Gloucester,
>   her death was attributed to brain-
>   fever.

DISSOLVE TO:

67 INT. LIVING ROOM - ELWOOD HOME - DAY - MED. SHOT - ELWOOD

He sits in his favorite chair smoking his pipe. CAMERA PULLS BACK to reveal Captain Barney and a plump, sad-faced woman sitting nearby. The woman rises and Elwood escorts her to the door during the narration.

>   KARLOFF'S VOICE
>   As becomes any respectable, grief
>   stricken man, the Captain remained
>   in mourning for a month. Among
>   those who visited to pay their
>   respects was the Widow Smith.

>   ELWOOD
>   (at the door)
>   It was nice of you to come,
>   Elizabeth. And thank you for
>   the cake. Good day.

(CONTINUED)

67 CONTINUED:

He bows, closes the door and walks back into the room.

                    BARNEY
How many times that make she's been, John?

                    ELWOOD
I don't know. Three or four.

                    BARNEY
I think she's got her eye on ya, man.

                    ELWOOD
              (protesting)
Barney, it'll be some time before I...

                    BARNEY
I give ya a year. Nobody expects ya to wait longer.
              (rising)
John, it's time ya got outa the house now.

                    ELWOOD
You think so?

                    BARNEY
We're having supper tonight in honor of a new member. Your old first mate, Logan. You've got to come John, he'll expect ya to.

                    ELWOOD
I don't know...

68 ANOTHER ANGLE

                    BARNEY
I'm givin' you orders! Now stop actin' like a lost dog.

                    ELWOOD
              (nodding)
All right, Barney. If you think I've done my duty.

                    BARNEY
You have. And more!

As Barney smiles sympathetically and touches Elwood consolingly on the shoulder:

                            DISSOLVE TO:

69 INT. DINING ROOM AT INN - NIGHT - MED. SHOT

Jesse, and Mr. Richardson are busy at the table. It is full of food. The 2nd Serving Boy comes out of the Mariner's Club room carrying a tray of empty mugs. The buzz of men's voices is HEARD when the door opens. CAMERA MOVES PAST partition into the Mariner's Clubroom.

70 INT. CLUBROOM - NIGHT - PANNING SHOT

The usual smoke-hanging atmosphere exits. CAMERA FINDS several members playing chess and kibitzing. Elwood is the center of three of his friends. Finally, across the small room we find Logan shaking hands with an older member, two others standing by, wishing him good luck. These men soon drift away from Logan, who looks toward Elwood.

71 ANGLE ON ELWOOD AND FRIENDS

He holds a pot of ale in his hand, ad libs an 'excuse me' to the men around him and walks to Logan.

72 ANGLE ON LOGAN

As he watches Elwood approach. He is not overly cordial and does not smile.

          ELWOOD
        (offering hand)
    Captain Logan. Welcome to the
    Club, sir.

Logan hesitates a moment, then takes the hand for a brief shake.

          LOGAN
    Thank you, Captain.

          ELWOOD
    I haven't seen you since the
    inquest. Did I thank you for
    not bringing up the subject of
    our disagreement?

          LOGAN
    Makes no difference now,
    Captain.

(CONTINUED)

72   CONTINUED:

                ELWOOD
It does to me. I want your friendship, man. You know perfectly well, no matter when we changed course my wife could have never reached St. Augustine alive.

                LOGAN
I didn't know it then.

                ELWOOD
But I did...I suspected it. You were trying so hard to help her...I didn't want to upset you...
              (a beat)
For a while, you acted as though I wanted her dead, Mr. Logan.

                LOGAN
I beg your pardon for that, sir. I'm sure you didn't.

                ELWOOD
Thank you.

The door behind them opens and Richardson enters.

73   ANOTHER ANGLE

                RICHARDSON
Gentlemen...Gentlemen...

Someone raps on a table and the noise subsides.

                RICHARDSON
              (continuing)
The food is on the table, gentlemen.

As the men begin to rise and drift toward the door, the SOUND of a shattering crash and thump comes from the dining room. Richardson whirls and runs back through the door.

74   INT. DINING ROOM - NIGHT - MED. SHOT

The table lies on its side as before, the food and broken dishes on the floor. Richardson enters shot looking horrified at the mess, the club members entering behind him.

                        (CONTINUED)

74   CONTINUED:

CAMERA PULLS BACK to reveal Jesse, his hands on his face, petrified, standing only a few steps behind the fallen table. Richardson goes to him and hits him hard across the ear.

                    RICHARDSON
Clumsy Ox!

                    JESSE
               (high pitched,
               hysteric)
I didn't do it, sir! I didn't! I _didn't_!

                    RICHARDSON
You're the only one in the room!

                    JESSE
I didn't touch it, sir. I swear, I didn't touch it!
               (almost a scream,
               pointing)
Look! It's exactly the same as when Mrs. Elwood tipped it! 'Twas her ghost, sir! 'Twas her ghost that did it, sir!

                    RICHARDSON
               (hitting Jesse
               again)
Stop that nonsense!

75   ANGLE ON THE CLUB MEMBERS

Elwood and Logan are prominent in shot as Richardson moves to them.

                    RICHARDSON
               (to Elwood)
A thousand pardons, Captain.
               (to all)
Give me ten minutes, Gentlemen. In the meantime, the drinks are on the house.

Elwood can see the gaze of Logan and the others on him as he turns and goes back to the clubroom. The others follow.

                  JESSE'S VOICE (o.s.)
               (a whining lament)
I didn't do it, sir...I didn't do it...

76 INT. CLUBROOM - NIGHT - MED. SHOT

As the men file in, silently, still a little shocked. Elwood moves to the wall and begins to take out his pipe. His hands shake nervously. Captain Barney goes to him. CAMERA MOVES IN on them.

> BARNEY
> The boy's just trying to absolve himself, John. Pay no heed.

> ELWOOD
> Of course...of course.

Elwood nods, fills his pipe from a pouch and puts it in his mouth.

77 REVERSE SHOT

PANNING some of the members as they watch Elwood curiously. CAMERA HOLDS on Logan at end of pan.

78 MED. CLOSE SHOT - ELWOOD

Trying to light his pipe. His hand shakes as though with the ague. He finally controls the shaking with his other hand and lights his pipe.

79 MED. CLOSE SHOT - LOGAN

His eyes narrowing suspiciously.

WIPE TO:

80 INT. DINING ROOM - NIGHT - MED. SHOT

Richardson and Jesse, helped by the 2nd Serving Boy, have the table all set and ready.

> RICHARDSON
> (to Jesse)
> Now get out. Both of you!

The boys back up. Jesse is frightened and looks at the table as though it were haunted. Richardson waits until they have gone through the kitchen door, then he goes to the clubroom door, never turning his back on the table, watching it carefully.

36.

81   ANGLE ON THE DOOR

Richardson opens it, still looking at the table.

                    RICHARDSON
          You may come now, Gentlemen.

Richardson walks upstage, behind the table, keeping away from it. The men come into the room slowly. Elwood is the last to file in. They all stare at the table hesitantly.

82   ANOTHER ANGLE

Only half the table in the shot.

                    RICHARDSON
          The boy did it, gentlemen.

The men seem to relax suddenly and equally as suddenly the cloth is pulled from the table and the food thrown to the floor with a SHATTERING of china.

83   MED. CLOSE SHOT - ELWOOD

Staring transfixed, eyes wide with fear.

                    BARNEY'S VOICE (o.s.)
          The Saints preserve us!

                    LOGAN'S VOICE (o.s.)
          Her ghost! Her ghost!

Other ad libs simultaneously: "The table's haunted!" "Why has she come?"

                    ELWOOD
                    (shouting)
          No! No!

84   ANOTHER ANGLE

Including most of group, Elwood prominent. He rushes to the fallen food, points to it.

                    ELWOOD
          The cloth slipped! Are you all
          fools, frightened by a super-
          stitious serving boy?

He begins to pick the food and dishes up in a frenzy.

                                        (CONTINUED)

84   CONTINUED:

                    ELWOOD
                  (continuing)
             I'll show you! Logan!
             Barney! Help me!

Logan and Barney look at one another, then come forward and
begin to help Elwood pick up the fallen things. They are
put on the table without the cloth.

                    ELWOOD
                  (continuing)
             Leave off the cloth!
                  (as he works)
             Can you be such fools?

85   ANGLE ON RICHARDSON AND CLUB MEMBERS

Watching. They are ready to believe the worst, but common
sense makes them wait and see if Elwood is right.

86   ANGLE ON TABLE

As it is piled with messy food and scattered dishes by
the frenzied Elwood and the slower working Barney and Logan.

                    ELWOOD
             There now! The cloth slipped!
             I'll prove it to you.

He puts his hands on the table and watches as do they all.
For a moment, nothing happens, then from the clubroom comes
a weird, moaning CRY, like a woman in distress far away.
They all freeze and look to the clubroom. The cry is re-
peated. Elwood is the first to make a run for the room.
The men all turn to look into the room.

87   GROUP SHOT - THE MEN

At the door, behind them comes the crash of dishes and the
thump of the table. They all whirl, CAMERA PANS to reveal
the table again on its side, the food scattered.

88   ANGLE ON ELWOOD AND LOGAN

Others in b.g. watching.

                    ELWOOD
                  (hysterically)
             This is some kind of trick!
             Logan! You're trying to trick
             me!

                                             (CONTINUED)

88   CONTINUED:

                    LOGAN
               (he knows, or
               suspects the
               truth)
          Trick ya into what, Captain?

                    ELWOOD
          You think I killed her! You're
          trying to trick me into saying
          I killed her!

Logan points his finger at the cringing Elwood.

                    LOGAN
          It's her ghost come for re-
          venge. Only the ghosts of the
          murdered return!

                    ELWOOD
          No! I didn't! I <u>didn't</u>!

He looks at the accusing faces of his friends, then at the table and suddenly turns, with a helpless cry and runs from the room. As the men look at one another, then at the table we HEAR the eerie, moaning cry again as we:

                              DISSOLVE TO:

89   EXT. BUILDING - DAY - CLOSE SHOT - SIGN (SILENT)

Reading: NEW ENGLAND SHIPPING CO. CAMERA PANS away to where two men are talking somberly.

                    KARLOFF'S VOICE
          The suspicion of murder caused
          Captain Elwood to be ostracized
          by the people of Gloucester.

They look o.s. One leaves the scene, the other man goes to the door next to the sign and enters the building as Elwood enters shot and goes to the door, which is closed in his face. HOLD ON Elwood staring at door.

                    KARLOFF'S VOICE
               (continuing)
          No reputable company would hire
          him. In despair, he took the
          Captaincy of an old hulk, with
          a long record of bad luck.

90   SCHOONER BEING TOSSED ABOUT IN VIOLENT STORM - STOCK SHOT

> KARLOFF'S VOICE
> (continuing)
> Two days out, the ship was
> caught in a gale and sank.
> All hands were saved except
> Captain John Elwood.

WIPE TO:

91   INT. MARINER'S CLUBROOM - DAY - CLOSE SHOT - LOGAN

> LOGAN
> Aye, every man jack of 'em
> 'cept Elwood.

CAMERA PULLS BACK to reveal Logan is talking to the members of the club.

> LOGAN
> (continuing)
> It's retribution, I say.
> The devil's claimed his own.

Behind them the door opens and Richardson enters.

> RICHARDSON
> Gentlemen, the food is on the
> table.

Suddenly they all turn, Richardson does too and looks out into the dining room. The men smile at one another and as they troop toward the dining room:

FADE OUT.

THE END

PROD. NO. 9206

"THE RETURN OF MME. VERNOY"

Teleplay by

STANLEY SILVERMAN

THE VEIL

Created by

FRANK P. BIBAS

HAL ROACH STUDIOS

PRODUCER: FRANK P. BIBAS

"THE RETURN OF MME. VERNOY"

CAST

SANTHA NAIDU .... 14-15, a youthful, introspective Hindu "Madonna".

RAMA MUKERJEE .... 26, Hindu, fairly well-educated, more mature than his American counterparts.

MME. NAIDU .... 34-40, gentle, devoutly religious Hindu widow.

ARMAND VERNOY .... 55-60, French archaeologist and long-time resident of India.

KRISHNA VERNOY .... 17, Armand's son by a Hindu mother. Intelligent, assertive, devoted to his father.

CHARLES GONCOURT .... 55-60, professor of mathematics at the Sorbonne in Paris. Old friend of Armand.

Street Beggar

Train Passengers (at Station)

SETS

EXTERIORS:

Section of street or alley outside Naidu garden wall

Section of wall, simulating Ext. of Muttra R.R. station

Facade and garden area in front of Vernoy house

INTERIORS:

Naidu sitting room

Armand's living room-study

Native-type hotel room

"THE RETURN OF MME. VERNOY"

FADE IN:

1   DOWN ANGLE SHOT - MAP OF INDIA - SPECIAL OPTICAL - DAY   1

SHOWING entire country. CAMERA MOVES DOWN to MED. CLOSE on top part of map, to area including MUTTRA, DELHI and JUMNA RIVER, as:

>   KARLOFF'S VOICE
>   (over)
>   This is a tale of two cities in
>   the heartland of India, on the
>   holy River Jumna...

CAMERA in CLOSE, clearly showing "Muttra" (bot. of FRAME) and "Delhi" (near top), each located on wavy vertical line indicating RIVER JUMNA.

>   KARLOFF'S VOICE
>   (over)
>   Here, in the city of Muttra --
>   stronghold of the ancient Hindu
>   faith --

Word "Muttra" on map now POPS OUT into:

2   SHOT - CITY OF MUTTRA, INDIA - DAY (STOCK)   2

INCLUDING the river. Shot should feature some temple, or some religious scene or ceremony.

>   KARLOFF'S VOICE
>   (over)
>   -- a beautiful young woman died
>   -- in August of 1927. Her name
>   was Sita Vernoy.

DISSOLVE:

3   SERIES OF SHOTS - CITY OF DELHI, INDIA - DAY (STOCK)   3

SHOTS INCLUDE:

A. View of Delhi along river's edge.   A

B. One of Delhi's distinctive Hindu temples.   B

C. Street scene in residential "native" area.   C

(CONTINUED)

3	CONTINUED:	3

                  KARLOFF'S VOICE
                     (over)
      Ninety miles up the river from
      Muttra -- in the capital city
      of Delhi -- a beautiful baby
      girl was born... also in August,
      in the following year, 1928.
      Her name: Santha Naidu.
           (beat)
      This is her story. It is based
      on documented facts. We call
      it "The Return of Mme. Verney".

                                            DISSOLVE:

4	SHOT - DELHI, INDIA - DAY (STOCK)	4

emphasizing "modernity" of city -- and also, if possible, a parade of "native" troops. Over this, SUPER: DELHI, APRIL 1943.

                                            DISSOLVE:

5	EXT. STREETSIDE OF NAIDU GARDEN WALL - ANGLE ON BEGGAR - DAY	5

seated against the wall, begging-bowl on his knees. RAMA (white legging-like trousers, black knee-length coat) strides by, pausing briefly to drop some coins in the bowl. CAMERA PANS WITH HIM to entrance to garden.

6	INT. NAIDU SITTING ROOM - CLOSE SHOT - MME. NAIDU - DAY	6

who is working at a table, packing food into jars and small containers. She looks up and o.s. at the SOUND of a LIGHT KNOCK on the door.

7	ANGLE TOWARD DOOR	7

to include Rama at the open door. Mme. Naidu reacts with pleasure.

                    MME. NAIDU
      Rama... come in.

                    RAMA
      Forgive me, Mme. Naidy... but
      ... I would like to talk to
      you. About Santha.

                                            (CONTINUED)

7   CONTINUED:

Mme. Naidu reacts very slightly, as though she is somewhat leery of what Rama will have to say.

> MME. NAIDU
> Of course, Rama. Sit down.
> May I get you something cold
> to drink?

Rama is preoccupied with what he has in mind. He is a little too nervous to sit.

> RAMA
> No, thank you.
> (beat)
> Mme. Naidu... you must know
> how I feel about Santha...

> MME. NAIDU
> And she of you. You are one
> of her oldest friends.

> RAMA
> (slight smile,
> reminiscing)
> I remember when your son Kala
> first brought me here... may
> his soul be at peace...

> MME. NAIDU
> Santha was just a baby.
> (beat)
> Since Kala's death, she has regarded you as her older brother.

Rama's smile vanishes. This is the crux of the matter.

> RAMA
> That is what I wish to discuss.
> (beat)
> I have watched Santha grow from
> a child to a young lady, and
> you know I would do anything to
> make her happy.

Mme. Naidu now knows for sure what he's driving at, and her face gets sadder, but she lets him continue.

> RAMA
> (continuing)
> I am not the wealthiest man in
> Delhi, but my prospects are
> good, and...
> (MORE)

(CONTINUED)

7   CONTINUED - (2):   7

                    RAMA (cont'd)
               (stops abruptly,
                beat)
          Mme. Naidu... I would like your
          permission to marry Santha!

Downcast, Mme. Naidu is forced to turn away. Rama
watches, first with surprise at this reception, then with
worry.

                    RAMA
               (continuing)
          Have I said something wrong?

                    MME. NAIDU
               (turns back)
          Rama... this is a day I have
          prayed for -- yet feared would
          come.

                    RAMA
          I do not understand...

                    MME. NAIDU
          Since Kala died you have been my
          son. I have watched your in-
          terest in Santha grow, as she
          grew, and hoped that someday...
               (stops, shakes her
                head sadly)
          You should have been told...

                    RAMA
               (growing frantic)
          Told what?!

                    MME. NAIDU
               (beat)
          Rama... if I were to say to you
          ... Santha is already married.
          With a son...

                    RAMA
          You mock me!!

                    MME. NAIDU
          Not in this life. In a pre-
          vious one.
               (as he stares)
          Are we not taught to believe it
          is only the body that dies at
          death? That the true self is
          in time, reborn?

                                                    (CONTINUED)

7   CONTINUED - (3):

                    RAMA
               (still stunned)
          Of course...

                    MME. NAIDU
          Once in a very great while it
          is said one is born with memory
          of a previous incarnation.
               (beat)
          I am afraid that Santha is such
          a one...
               (beat)
          And the love she bore for her
          husband and son remains as
          strong as ever.

                    RAMA
          To remember another life...!
          How can this happen?!

                    MME. NAIDU
          Who is to say?
               (beat)
          Perhaps it is proof that Nirvana
          is within reach of all.

                    RAMA
               (beat)
          Why was I not told of this be-
          fore?

                    MME. NAIDU
          It is not something one speaks
          of freely... even to one as
          close as you.

Rama takes a long beat as he tries to assimilate this
information. Then he shakes his head violently.

                    MME. NAIDU
               (continuing)
          Rama... listen to me, my son...
          For her fifth birthday, I made
          her a little cloak... the color
          of flame. She cried when I put
          it on her. Why?
               (shakes her head)
          Because, she said... because
          her husband wished her to wear
          only blue.

                    RAMA
          A five-year old child?!

                                        (CONTINUED)

7   CONTINUED - (4):

                    MME. NAIDU
                      (nodding)
                I put the cloak away, Rama...
                and then I cried...
                      (beat)
                For I knew that naught but sor-
                row would come of this...

                    RAMA
                Are you saying she knew all
                this even then?!!

                    MME. NAIDU
                Not all... it came slowly...
                      (beat)
                She recalled his face... their
                home... Muttra, where they lived
                ... her son...
                      (beat)
                And yesterday... the name...
                      (beat)
                Vernoy... Armand Vernoy.

                    RAMA
                And now... ? What happens now?

                    MME. NAIDU
                      (indicating prepara-
                       tions)
                I am preparing now. Tomorrow
                we leave for Muttra. If there
                is an Armand Vernoy...
                      (beat)
                Well... we shall see.

    They stare at each other for a moment, troubled, which
    is broken by their reaction to:

                    SANTHA'S VOICE
                      (cheery delight)
                Rama!!!

8   CLOSE SHOT - SANTHA

    poised in the doorway. Now she rushes to Rama and throws
    her arms around him, kissing him sisterly on the cheek.

                    SANTHA
                      (continuing)
                I did not know you were here!

                                              (CONTINUED)

8   CONTINUED:

                    RAMA
           I wished to speak with your
           mother.

Now Santha steps back, looking from one to the other, noting their troubled expressions.

                    SANTHA
           What is wrong?

                    MME. NAIDU
           Santha... Rama has come to ask
           for your hand in marriage.

Santha's expression turns to one of dismay.

                    SANTHA
                 (sadly)
           Oh, Rama...
                 (to mother)
           Have you... told him?

Mme. Naidu nods silently.

                    RAMA
           Santha...! You cannot really
           believe all this!!

                    SANTHA
                 (gently)
           It is true, Rama... I have a
           husband and son.

                    RAMA
           But... but even if it *is* true!
           Your husband will be an old
           man by now! And your son! He
           could be older than you are!!

                    SANTHA
           It will be as you say... I
           have been away too long.

                    RAMA
           Nothing can come of this but
           tragedy, Santha!

                    SANTHA
           It is the will of our Lord,
           Krishna... and my name is Santha
           no longer... I am Madame Sita
           Vernoy... and my husband has
           need of me.
                    (MORE)

                                        (CONTINUED)

8.

8   CONTINUED - (2):   8

                        SANTHA (cont'd)
                  (beat)
             Forgive me, Rama... I must make
             ready for my journey.

    She takes a beat, then leans over and kisses his cheek.
    As he stares after her, she exits. Another beat, then
    Rama turns to Mme. Naidu.

                        RAMA
             Madame Naidu... this will be no
             journey for two women alone...

                        MME. NAIDU
                  (beat)
             You love her so much?

    He nods.

                        MME. NAIDU
             We would welcome your company.

    He bows gravely.

                                             DISSOLVE:

9
thru   (OMITTED)   (OMITTED)   9
17   thru
                                                                 17

18 EXT. DELHI, INDIA, RAILROAD STATION - DAY (STOCK)   18

    SHOWING mixed "native" crowd boarding a "native-type"
    train. Train pulls out of station.

                                             DISSOLVE:

19 SERIES OF SHOTS - TRAIN THROUGH INDIAN COUNTRYSIDE -   19
    DAY (STOCK)

    Same type of train as in PREVIOUS STOCK SHOTS.

                                             DISSOLVE:

20 EXT. MUTTRA, INDIA, RAILROAD STATION - DAY (STOCK)   20

    SHOWING arrival of train (same type as in PREVIOUS STOCK
    SHOTS). Passengers disembark pell-mell.

                                             DISSOLVE:

21   EXT. SECTION OF WALL OF STATION BUILDING - MED. SHOT -   21
     DAY

Rama and the two women are "swept up" against wall by hurrying crowd of train passengers (with same type of luggage and bundles as in STOCK SHOTS). As the passengers scurry by --

     RAMA
Wait here -- I'll get a carriage.

     SANTHA
There's no need. My husband's house is not far.

     RAMA
You know -- exactly where it is?

     SANTHA
      (patiently)
Of course -- the first house beyond the Curzon Museum, on High Street. Armand chose it himself -- to be near his work.

     MME. NAIDU
Santha --

     SANTHA
Yes, Mother?

     MME. NAIDU
I would like first to give thanks for our safe arrival in Muttra -- and to pray that all goes well with you now.

     SANTHA
      (agreeably)
Very well. The Temple of Dwarkashish is on the way -- in the Street of the Silversmiths.
      (pleasurable
       memory)
I prayed there every day for months -- to Lord Krishna -- that he might send me a son. And he answered me.

     RAMA
      (wonderingly)
Your son -- what is his name?

       (CONTINUED)

21   CONTINUED: 21

                           SANTHA
                        (smiling)
                   What a question, Rama! How
                   else could I thank him than
                   to give his name to my child?

Rama nods -- then steps aside, for Santha to lead the
way.

                                              DISSOLVE:

22   EXT. ARMAND VERNOY'S HOUSE - FULL SHOT - DAY (STOCK)   22

     The house is large -- fairly imposing, if possible -- of
     white stone, in Hindu architecture. It's pleasantly
     landscaped, with gardens in front, and perhaps a fence
     with a gate.

                                              DISSOLVE:

23   INT. ARMAND'S LIVINGROOM-STUDY - ANGLE ON KRISHNA - DAY 23

     Listening to CHARLES GONCOURT reading a letter to him.
     His father, ARMAND VERNOY, stands nearby. The room re-
     flects Vernoy's profession and interests -- archaeology
     -- with various Hindu antiquities on random display.
     On one wall is a pair of framed portraits -- one, of
     Sita Vernoy, looking vaguely like Santha (but clearly
     NOT Santha); the other, of Armand, painted some 20
     years earlier -- slender, dashing, and with a moustache
     he now does NOT wear. Charles does wear a moustache,
     and a Van Dyke beard.

                           CHARLES
                   Now, here's the important part,
                   Krishna. Listen:
                        (reading aloud)
                   "... Therefore, my dear Pro-
                   fessor Goncourt, we are pleased
                   to accept Krishna Vernoy as a
                   member of the Class of 1947 at
                   Columbia College... !"

                           KRISHNA
                        (overjoyed)
                   Oh thank you -- thank you, Pro-
                   fessor!
                        (turning to Armand)
                   Isn't that wonderful, father?

24   CLOSE SHOT - ARMAND   24

disturbed -- trying not to show it.

                    ARMAND
          Yes, my son.

25   CLOSE SHOT - CHARLES   25

registering reaction to Armand's forced enthusiasm. He shrugs, and resumes with the letter.

                    CHARLES
               (reading aloud)
          "Please let us know when you ex-
          pext to arrive in New York with
          him" -- et cetera, et cetera.
               (explaining)
          We are old friends, the Dean
          and I.

26   THREE SHOT - ARMAND, CHARLES AND KRISHNA   26

                    KRISHNA
          Very good ones, it seems. When
          will we leave for America?

                    CHARLES
          In about two weeks, I should
          think.

                    KRISHNA
          How will we get there? I don't
          suppose we can go by way of the
          Pacific -- because of the
          Japanese --

                    ARMAND
          Krishna...

                    KRISHNA
          Yes, my father?

                    ARMAND
          Professor Goncourt has just
          arrived in Muttra. He wished
          you to have this -- this news
          -- at once. But now --

                    KRISHNA
          Forgive me, my father -- and
          you, Professor. I know you
          must have much to say to each
          other. If you will excuse me --

                                                    (CONTINUED)

26   CONTINUED: 26

                        ARMAND
              Thank you, my son.

                        KRISHNA
              You will permit me to join you
              again -- later? I have so
              many questions...

                        ARMAND
              Of course. A bientot.

     Krishna smiles pleasantly, and exits. Charles looks
     after him, then turns to Armand.

27   TWO SHOT - CHARLES AND ARMAND   27

                        CHARLIES
              Armand, mon vieux -- what is
              the matter?

                        ARMAND
              Nothing.

                        CHARLES
              It is not like you -- to greet
              such good news with so little
              pleasure...

                        ARMAND
              I did not expect you so soon.
              I thought it would be another
              few weeks -- a month perhaps...

                        CHARLES
              Is it because you will be send-
              ing him so far away -- ?

                        ARMAND
                   (deeply unhappy)
              I can't do it, Charles. I can't
              send him anywhere.

                        CHARLES
              Come, Armand -- he is no longer
              a child.

                        ARMAND
              You don't understand. I can't
              send him to America with you
              because I don't have the money.

                                              (CONTINUED)

THE VEIL #9206 - Rev. 11/24/58   13.

27   CONTINUED: 27

                    CHARLES
               (dismayed)
          Armand...!

                    ARMAND
          I made certain investments.
          Bad ones.
               (wry grin)
          I didn't have Sita to advise
          me, as in the old days.

     He looks wistfully toward the portraits on the wall.

                    ARMAND
               (continuing)
          She knew how to manage things,
          that one...

28   SHOT - PORTRAITS ON THE WALL   28

     FAVORING Sita's portrait.

                    ARMAND'S VOICE
               (continuing; over)
          If she'd lived, there'd be
          money now, and to spare.

                    CHARLES' VOICE
               (over)
          She was a wise woman. Wise --
          and very beautiful.

29   BACK TO TWO SHOT - CHARLES AND ARMAND   29

     Both are looking at the portraits. They turn away, as:

                    ARMAND
          And as frugal as I was extrava-
          gant.
               (ruefully)
          Charles -- Charles -- when I
          think of the money I've spent!
               (shaking his
                head)
          I could have paid for Krishna's
          education three times over!

                    CHARLES
               (beat)
          If only I could help...
               (beat)
          Well, I won't be leaving for the
          States for two weeks, Armand.
          Perhaps in that time...

                                                    (CONTINUED)

THE VEIL #9206 - Rev. 11/24/58   14.
29   CONTINUED: 29

                        ARMAND
            We are both men of science.
            We neither of us believe in
            miracles.
                (beat; heavily)
            Krishna will have to discontinue
            his studies for a time. And I
            shall have to tell him so.

                        CHARLES
            It will break his heart.

                        ARMAND
            And mine.

                        CHARLES
            Armand -- would you like me to
            help you tell him?

                        ARMAND
                (nodding)
            You are very kind, mon vieux.

He gets up -- as does Charles.

                                              (CONTINUED)

29 CONTINUED - (2):   29

>   ARMAND
>   (continuing)
>   We shall ask him to walk with us
>   through the Temple garden -- it
>   is a favorite place with him.
>   We will tell him there.

Charles nods. Armand takes his arm -- they start from the room together.

>   DISSOLVE:

30 EXT. ARMAND'S HOUSE - ANGLE ON SANTHA - DAY   30

crossing to gate in fence, in f.g., with Rama and Mme. Naidu close behind. (In b.g., back to CAMERA, Krishna is practicing with a field-hockey stick -- like a golfer with a golf-club). Her hand on the gate, Santha stares at the house, thirstily. Then, half-turning to Mme. Naidu and Rama:

>   SANTHA
>   Thank you, Mother -- and you,
>   Rama -- for bringing me home.
>
>   RAMA
>   You are certain that this is
>   the house?
>
>   SANTHA
>   Of course... but how badly the
>   walls need whitening!

She shakes her head, ruefully. In b.g., Krishna turns -- and sees the group at the gate. He starts down toward them.

>   SANTHA
>   (continuing)
>   Armand has let things go
>   dreadfully. I'm afraid I
>   shall have to scold him.
>
>   MME. NAIDU
>   Still, it is a fine house.
>
>   SANTHA
>   I was very happy here.

31 FULL SHOT - KRISHNA, MME. NAIDU, RAMA AND SANTHA   31

as he comes down to the gate, hockey-stick in hand -- his

                                                    (CONTINUED)

31 CONTINUED: 31

    face set in the smiling, polite greeting that is Hindu custom.

                          KRISHNA
    Namaskar, my friends.

                   RAMA and MME. NAIDU
    Namaskar.

                          SANTHA
          (studying Krishna's
           face)
    Namaskar. Can you -- can you be
    <u>Krishna</u>?

                          KRISHNA
          (pleasantly)
    That is my name.

                          SANTHA
          (with deep emo-
           tion)
    Oh, my son, my son! Krishna,
    my son!

                          KRISHNA
    I beg your pardon... ?

                          SANTHA
    You are all that I prayed for
    to the Lord Krishna -- all and
    more!

                          KRISHNA
          (uncertainly)
    Thank you -- you do me such
    honor -- but --

                          SANTHA
    You will understand, my son --
    your father will help me to
    tell you.

                          KRISHNA
    Tell me what? Forgive me, please
    -- I don't mean to be discourteous
    -- but who are you?

                          SANTHA
    I -- I had hoped you might know.
    But -- how could you? You were
    not two weeks old when I left
    you, my son.

                                       (CONTINUED)

31   CONTINUED - (2):   31

>   KRISHNA
>   (sharply)
>   Don't call me that, please!
>
>   RAMA
>   (bristling)
>   This young lady has come all
>   the way from Delhi to speak to
>   Mister Armand Vernoy.
>
>   KRISHNA
>   Very well -- I shall take her
>   to him.
>   (to Santha)
>   But I still must ask you not
>   to call me your son! It --
>   it's ridiculous! I'm sure I'm
>   older than you are.
>
>   SANTHA
>   (with a smile)
>   Are you?
>
>   KRISHNA
>   I'll be eighteen in August!
>
>   SANTHA
>   (nodding)
>   On the 14th day of August.
>
>   KRISHNA
>   (slightly startled)
>   How did you know?
>
>   SANTHA
>   (quietly)
>   I gave you life, my son.
>
>   KRISHNA
>   (outraged)
>   Do you mean to say -- are you
>   trying to tell me that you're
>   my _mother_?!
>
>   SANTHA
>   I am.

Krishna glares at her, then opens the gate abruptly.

>   KRISHNA
>   I will take you to my father
>   at once --
>   (MORE)

(CONTINUED)

31 CONTINUED - (3):   31

                    KRISHNA (cont'd)
                 (glaring at Rama)
            -- all of you. He will know
            how to deal with you.

    Santha nods serenely -- and moves through the gate onto
    the path that leads to the house. Rama and Mme. Naidu
    follow.

32 PAN SHOT - THE GROUP   32

    going up the path. CAMERA PANS PAST THEM, to front en-
    trance. Armand and Charles come through entrance, onto
    path, arm-in-arm.

33 CLOSE SHOT - SANTHA   33

    stopping short, as she sees Armand and Charles. (Rama
    and Mme. Naidu are seen behind her.) Her face becomes
    radiant with joy.

                    SANTHA
            Armand. Armand!

34 TWO SHOT - ARMAND AND CHARLES   34

    Armand is astonished, Charles curious, at sight of this
    "perfect stranger".

                    ARMAND
            Yes -- young lady?

35 FULL SHOT - THE GROUP   35

    as Santha hurries forward to them, expectantly -- Krishna
    accompanying her. Rama and Mme. Naidu come up behind
    them, hesitantly.

                    SANTHA
            My husband -- it is I -- Sita.

                    ARMAND
                 (shocked)
            What?

                    SANTHA
            I have come home to you.

    She starts toward him, to embrace and be embraced -- and
    then stands stunned, heartbroken -- as she sees him
    shake his head, frowning angrily.

36   TWO SHOT - ARMAND AND KRISHNA   36

                    ARMAND
          Krishna -- this -- this is not
          some silly schoolboy joke?

                    KRISHNA
          It is no joke of _my_ making!
          She says she is my mother.

37   (OMITTED)   (OMITTED)   37

38   FULL SHOT - THE GROUP   38

                    ARMAND
                 (to Santha)
          No -- no -- his mother died
          when he was born.

                    SANTHA
          Yes. Seven days later -- my
          body _did_ die.

                    ARMAND
                 (taken aback)
          It _was_ -- seven days... Charles,
          I don't understand this -- I
          don't like it!

                    CHARLES
                 (soothingly)
          Just a moment, old friend.
                 (to Santha)
          If I may be permitted a ques-
          tion?

                    SANTHA
          Surely, Professor Goncourt.

                    CHARLES
                 (to Krishna)
          You told her my name?

                    KRISHNA
                 (puzzled)
          No, sir.

                    CHARLES
          Then how --
                 (breaks off, then:)
          No matter.
                 (to Santha)
          Tell me, please -- on what date
          did you -- did your _body_ -- die?

                              (CONTINUED)

38   CONTINUED: 38

> SANTHA
> I thought you would remember.
> You were visiting us then. I
> gave you the blue bedroom --
> no, it was the pink one -- you
> complained that the blue was
> too drafty.

Charles is almost literally staggered -- as is Armand.
Charles "recovers" first, with:

> CHARLES
> What -- what was the date of
> your -- death?

> SANTHA
> August the 21st, 1927.

Charles darts a glance at Armand -- who stands almost
open-mouthed, and nodding confirmation.

> SANTHA
> (continuing)
> But Braham permitted me to be
> born again -- and to come back
> now to my husband and son.

39   CLOSE SHOT - KRISHNA   39

> KRISHNA
> No. I do not believe it!

40   CLOSE SHOT - SANTHA   40

> SANTHA
> My son -- your father's heart
> knows that I speak the truth.

41   GROUP SHOT - FAVORING ARMAND   41

> ARMAND
> (troubled)
> I don't know anything of the
> kind.

> SANTHA
> Do not be angry with me,
> Armand. I returned as soon
> as Brahma permitted me to
> remember.

(CONTINUED)

41   CONTINUED: 41

                             ARMAND
                   To remember -- me?

                             SANTHA
                   Your name. I remembered your
                   face always -- how you
                   crinkled your eyes when you
                   smiled -- how your mouth --
                        (breaks off, dis-
                        mayed)
                   Oh, my husband -- you should
                   not have done it!

                             ARMAND
                   Done what?

                             SANTHA
                   You should not have shaved off
                   your moustache!

Involuntarily, Armand claps his hand to his mouth. He
exchanges a startled glance with Charles... as the CAMERA
ZOOMS into CLOSE UP of Armand.

                                              FADE OUT.

                    (MIDDLE COMMERCIAL)

22.

ACT TWO

FADE IN:

42   INT. ARMAND'S LIVING ROOM - STUDY - PAN SHOT - DAY   42

STARTING with Mme. Naidu, resigned and patient -- moving on to Rama, seated nearby, concerned -- then to Charles Goncourt, seated across from them -- then to Krishna, glancing toward entrance to room.

43   MED. SHOT - ENTRANCE TO ROOM - SANTHA AND ARMAND   43

as they enter. He has been showing her through the house. She is bubbling over with excitement; he is still bewildered, wary.

> SANTHA
> (looking around)
> ... Armand -- you've changed this room all around also!
> (smiling)
> You never let *me* move one of your ash-trays!

> ARMAND
> In what way has *this* room been changed?

> SANTHA
> Why, the settee was in the corner --
> (he nods, surprised)
> -- and the table -- let's see -- it was against that wall.

Armand looks at Charles, and shakes his head wonderingly.

44   FULL SHOT - THE GROUP   44

> ARMAND
> It is so, Santha. As you say.

> SANTHA
> You still will not call me Sita?

> ARMAND
> Sita is not your name. Is it, Madame Naidu?

(CONTINUED)

44   CONTINUED: 44

>   MME. NAIDU
>   No, Mister Vernoy. But ever
>   since she was a little girl,
>   again and again she said she
>   had another name.

>   SANTHA
>   Of course.

>   RAMA
>   And a few days ago -- she re-
>   membered it. She remembered
>   everything.

Mme. Naidu nods gravely. Armand looks at her and at Rama
-- searchingly.

45   THREE SHOT - SANTHA, ARMAND AND MME. NAIDU   45

>   ARMAND
>   Madame Naidu -- when was she
>   born?

>   MME. NAIDU
>   On August 31st, 1928.

>   ARMAND
>   A year and ten days after Sita
>   died.
>   (beat)
>   It -- it cannot be!

>   SANTHA
>   It is, Armand! I have been re-
>   born.

>   ARMAND
>   (slowly)
>   I loved my wife very much. I --
>   would _like_ it to be as you say,
>   but -- _you_ -- you're a child!

>   SANTHA
>   I am Sita!

>   ARMAND
>   No. You are not.

46   CLOSE SHOT - KRISHNA   46

CAMERA PANS him into group.

                                              (CONTINUED)

46   CONTINUED: 46

                    KRISHNA
               My father -- please tell her to
               go.

                    SANTHA
                    (pleading)
               Krishna, my son --

                    KRISHNA
                    (very strongly)
               I'm not your son!

   Rama springs to his feet, goes to Santha, who is shaken
   by Krishna's outburst.

                    SANTHA
                    (brokenly, to Rama)
               What must I say -- what must I
               do -- to convince them?

   She begins sobbing. Armand is deeply moved by her cry.
   He goes to her, Rama stepping back.

47   TWO SHOT - ARMAND AND SANTHA   47

                    ARMAND
                    (taking her hand)
               Listen, ma petite --

   Santha looks up, smiling a little through the tears.

                    SANTHA
               Oiseau. Ma petite oiseau.

                    ARMAND
                    (stunned)
               What?

                    SANTHA
               Petite oiseau. You used to call
               me that. Your little bird.

                    ARMAND
               I did. I _did_...!

   He looks at her, almost beside himself now with confusion
   and shock -- then comes abruptly to a decision.

48   FULL SHOT - THE GROUP   48

                    ARMAND
               Go now, child -- go, with your
               mother and your friend. There
               is a hotel on Agra Street --
               Krishna will guide you...

                                                        (CONTINUED)

48   CONTINUED:

                    SANTHA
           Oh, it's much too expensive.
           We will go to the inn on the
           Drovers Road.

                    ARMAND
           No -- the hotel -- I will pay...

                    SANTHA
                 (tenderly)
           My dear husband -- extravagant
           as always.

Charles darts a glance at Armand -- who shrugs ruefully.

                    ARMAND
                 (to Krishna)
           Go with them now, son.

                    KRISHNA
                 (stiffly)
           Yes, my father.

Rama helps Mme. Naidu to her feet.

                    SANTHA
                 (pathetically)
           This -- this is not goodbye,
           Armand?

                    ARMAND
                 (gentle head-shake)
           Au 'voir. Until tomorrow.

She smiles hopefully, starts out with Krishna.

                                        DISSOLVE:

49   EXT. UPPER-CLASS NATIVE-INDIAN HOTEL - DAY - (STOCK)   49

     SHOWING street traffic.

                                        DISSOLVE:

50   INT. NATIVE-INDIAN HOTEL ROOM - FULL SHOT - DAY   50

     SHOWING a pleasant room -- with archways leading off to
     other rooms in the suite. Santha and Mme. Naidu are
     seated, Rama standing nearby. Kriskna is taking leave of
     them.

                                        (CONTINUED)

50   CONTINUED: 50

                    KRISHNA
          I trust you will find these
          rooms comfortable. May you rest
          well.

                    SANTHA
          I am sure that we shall. Thank
          you, my son.

                    KRISHNA
          Not at all, Miss Naidu.
              (addressing the
               others)
          Madame Naidu -- Mister Mukerjee
          -- good day.

                    MME. NAIDU
          Good day, Mister Vernoy.

Rama nods stiffly to Krishna. Krishna returns the nod,
bows slightly to the women, and exits. Rama glares after
him.

51   THREE SHOT - SANTHA, RAMA, MME. NAIDU   51

                    SANTHA
          Rama -- do not be angry with
          him.

                    RAMA
          He thinks you are trying to
          play some kind of a trick...!

                    SANTHA
          You did not believe me at first.
          Now you have opened your heart
          to the truth.

                    RAMA
          He won't.

                    SANTHA
              (quietly confident)
          When Armand accepts me, Krishna
          will also.

Rama looks challengingly at Mme. Naidu -- she nods, in
agreement with him.

                    MME. NAIDU
          Mister Vernoy is not of our faith,
          my child. He may not be willing
          to believe.

                                              (CONTINUED)

51 CONTINUED: 51

                    SANTHA
          He will -- I know this!

                    RAMA
          Even if it means that his son
          would turn his face from him?
          I do not think so.

                    SANTHA
          In the morning, Armand will
          greet me again as his wife.

                    RAMA
          In the morning, he will turn
          you away!

                    SANTHA
          We shall see.

                    RAMA
          I don't wish you to see it!
          Let us return to Delhi tonight.

                    SANTHA
               (gently)
          My life is in Muttra now. With
          my husband and my son.

                    MME. NAIDU
          A woman has no husband who puts
          her aside. A woman has no son
          who denies her.

Santha looks at her a long moment -- then, at point of
tears, gets up.

                    SANTHA
          I -- I am very tired. With your
          permission...

Mme. Naidu nods, understandingly. Santha starts toward
one of the inner rooms.

                                                DISSOLVE:

52   INT. ARMAND'S LIVING ROOM - STUDY - CLOSE ANGLE -   52
     CHARLES - CLOSE ANGLE

Shaking his head -- as he looks at Armand (SEEN in pro-
file) who is standing, looking at the wall portraits.
Charles is seated at table, on which a reading lamp --
only source of light in room -- is lit. CAMERA PULLS
BACK.

                                              (CONTINUED)

52   CONTINUED:

                    ARMAND
          She has Sita's voice. The same
          music -- the same swift rise and
          fall...

                    CHARLES
          You only imagine that.

                    ARMAND
          "Ma petite oiseau"? I did not
          imagine that.

                    CHARLES
               (shrugging)
          A common endearment.

                    ARMAND
          In French, Charles. The girl
          speaks no French.

                    CHARLES
          She could have heard the phrase
          somewhere.
               (beat)
          I tell you -- there is a ra-
          tional explanation...!

53   TWO SHOT - CHARLES AND ARMAND

     Armand comes forward now, seats himself across from
     Charles, with:

                    ARMAND
          She has never been in Muttra
          before. She knew you -- your
          face, your name -- and you have
          not come to this house since
          Sita died. She knew the room
          Sita gave you!

                    CHARLES
          You sound as though you <u>want</u>
          to believe her!

                    ARMAND
          Whether I want to or not, Charles
          ... how can you explain a child
          her age knowing these intimate
          details?!

                    CHARLES
               (slightly sarcastic)
          Like your moustache?

                                            (CONTINUED)

53 CONTINUED:
53

> ARMAND
> Yes, my moustache -- and the furniture in all the rooms -- and the names of servants Sita kept twenty years ago!
>
> CHARLES
> (a bit sharply)
> Look, Armand -- unless you are prepared to believe in reincarnation after all --
>
> ARMAND
> I'm not.
>
> CHARLES
> Then you must seek an explanation elsewhere.
>
> ARMAND
> If there is one.
>
> CHARLES
> We'll find one!
>
> ARMAND
> And if we don't -- ?
>
> CHARLES
> We shall.
>
> ARMAND
> Charles -- listen to me. If we *can't* find an explanation -- and the girl persists in her belief that she is Sita, reborn -- what am I do do?
>
> CHARLES
> (slowly)
> You are not -- you cannot be thinking of accepting her as your wife?

Armand gets up abruptly, turns away.

> ARMAND
> I don't know. I don't know...

54 FULL SHOT - FEATURING THE DOOR
54

as Krishna enters the room. He stands waiting respectfully.

(CONTINUED)

54 CONTINUED: 54

                    ARMAND
               (looking up)
          Yes, my son?

                    KRISHNA
          Have you decided what you will
          do? What you will say to this
          girl from Delhi?

                    ARMAND
          Professor Goncourt and I have
          been talking about it.

                    KRISHNA
               (almost curtly)
          But you have not decided?

                    ARMAND
          No.

                    KRISHNA
          I have decided.
               (beat)
          I am sorry, my father, but I
          cannot accept as a mother a girl
          no older than I am! If you take
          her into this house, I will not
          stay. Not even for the two weeks
          remaining.

                    ARMAND
          Two weeks?

                    KRISHNA
          Until I leave for America.

                    CHARLES
               (realizing the boy
                doesn't know)
          Krishna...

                    KRISHNA
               (sensing trouble)
          That is when we are going, you
          said.

Charles and Armand exchange uncomfortable glances.

                    CHARLES
          That was my plan. But now --
          your father feels that perhaps...
               (giving up)
          Armand...

                                              (CONTINUED)

54   CONTINUED (2):

                    ARMAND
               (to Krishna)
          My son -- you may not be able
          to leave Muttra for a time.

                    KRISHNA
          Because of this foolish girl?
          You would want me to stay --
          to please her?

                    ARMAND
               (shaking his head)
          It is something that happened
          before she came. Months before.
          I did not know how to tell you...

                    KRISHNA
          There -- there is not enough
          money -- ?

                    ARMAND
          I -- I invested my savings --
          unwisely. The war has ruined
          me.

                    KRISHNA
          So -- I shall remain here in
          Muttra.

                    ARMAND
          Perhaps not for long. I may
          be able to devise some way...
               (trailing off;
                then)
          I'm sorry, my son.

                    KRISHNA
          It -- it's all right. I won-
          dered how you would arrange it
          -- I knew things were not well
          with us...

                    ARMAND
          When the war is over -- you will
          see -- we will make up for the
          lost time.

                    KRISHNA
               (cutting him short)
          Of course, my father. But now?
               (Armand looks at
                him question-
                ingly)
          What will you do with the girl?

                                        (CONTINUED)

54   CONTINUED (3):   54

                         ARMAND
                    (long pause)
               I will send her away.

Krishna nods with satisfaction.

                                                      DISSOLVE:

55   INT. THE HOTEL ROOM - CLOSE - RAMA - DAY   55

     in fresh clothes, looking rested. He is addressing
     Santha (o.s.).

                         RAMA
               Please, Santha -- it's for
               your good. Let us return to
               Delhi.

     CAMERA BACK to INCLUDE Santha. She shakes her head.

                         SANTHA
               My husband needs me.

                         RAMA
               He is old -- he doesn't love
               you.

                         SANTHA
               He is my husband. Come -- you
               will see me to my house?

                         RAMA
                    (painfully)
               Yes -- and I will wait outside
               the door for you. I will wait
               for you all the rest of my life,
               is that is the will of Brahma.

                         SANTHA
                    (distressed)
               Rama --

                         RAMA
                    (simply)
               I love you. I know that you
               are of another time and place --
               but I shall always love you.

                         SANTHA
                    (deeply moved)
               Rama -- let us go now!

     She turns to leave -- Rama taking her arm.

                                                      DISSOLVE:

33.

56 INT. ARMAND'S LIVING ROOM-STUDY - TWO SHOT - ARMAND AND 56
    CHARLES - DAY

    seated slightly behind him (for "moral support"). Armand
    is deeply upset -- and deeply regretful. He has told
    Santha the "bad news", and is anguished at her reception
    of it.

57 CLOSE SHOT - SANTHA   57

    seated across from Armand, a low coffee-table between them.
    She looks down, away from Armand.

                    SANTHA
          I -- I thought I would be wel-
          comed -- with gladness and joy...

58 FULL SHOT - THE GROUP   58

                    ARMAND
          You are welcome, my child. I
          -- I cannot bring myself to
          believe you are Sita --

                    SANTHA
               (raising her eyes
                to his)
          I am, my husband. I am!

                    ARMAND
          It's no use, my child. Even if
          I could bring myself to believe
          ... there is Krishna -- he never
          could believe.

                    SANTHA
          In time, perhaps -- ?

                    ARMAND
               (painfully)
          No. I have hurt him enough.

                    SANTHA
          You, my husband?

                    ARMAND
          Only last night we had to tell
          him -- Professor Goncourt and
          I...
               (beat)
          Krishna was to go to America
          with him -- to continue his
          studies at a great university...

                                              (CONTINUED)

58   CONTINUED: 58

                         CHARLES
               He is a fine scholar, you see --
                    (she smiles, proudly)
               -- a genius, perhaps.

                         ARMAND
               But I can't send him to America.
               I don't have enough money.

59   CLOSE SHOT - SANTHA   59

smiling -- now she claps her hands, delightedly.

                         SANTHA
               That then is why Brahma has sent
               me! I knew that I was needed...

60   PREVIOUS ANGLE   60

Both Armand and Charles look bewildered.

                         ARMAND
               I don't understand...

                         SANTHA
               So that together, we might help
               our son.

                         ARMAND
               How?

                         SANTHA
               You have forgotten your gifts
               to your bride? The jewels a
               maharanee would have been proud
               to wear?

                         ARMAND
                    (slowly)
               Those -- those were Sita's words.
               She wept when I gave them to her.

                         SANTHA
               For joy, Armand.
                    (beat)
               To have such riches against an
               evil day.

                         ARMAND
                    (nodding; then)
               But they are gone -- as if they
               had never been. When Sita left
               me --

                                                          (CONTINUED)

60   CONTINUED: 60

                            SANTHA
              The jewels remained, my husband
              -- in this room.

        He stares at her. She smiles, reassuringly.

61   ANOTHER ANGLE   61

        Santha goes to corner of room (or elsewhere -- set-
        designer's option), where a heavy piece of furniture has
        been placed. She tries and fails to move it -- Armand
        helps her, successfully. This exposes the rich Indian-
        style rug. Santha pulls it back, exposing the wooden
        flooring. She kneels, and removes a skillfully set-in
        piece of flooring -- and lifts out from the receptacle
        below it, a japanned-metal box. She hands Armand the
        box. He opens it.

62   CLOSE SHOT - JEWELS IN BOX   62

        glittering -- looking like a small treasure-trove.

63   CLOSE SHOT - ARMAND   63

        overcome with joy and with almost superstitious amaze-
        ment.

64   CLOSE SHOT - CHARLES   64

        "rocked" in his skepticism by this inexplicable develop-
        ment.

65   CLOSE SHOT - SANTHA   65

        pleased -- but "remote".

66   TWO SHOT - ARMAND AND SANTHA   66

                            ARMAND
              What -- what can I say to you?

                            SANTHA
              Only what is in your heart.

                                                          (CONTINUED)

66   CONTINUED: 66

                              ARMAND
                        (long pause; then)
                   No one but Sita could know the
                   jewels were there. No one but
                   Sita could know what you know
                   of me...

                              SANTHA
                   But -- you still do not believe..?

          Armand would like to be forthright, unequivocal -- but
          cannot.

                              ARMAND
                   My house is yours. I would
                   like you to stay here -- as
                   long as you wish.

          Santha looks at him gravely -- then smiles slightly.

                              SANTHA
                   You always looked so -- when
                   you were trying to keep the
                   truth from me.

          Suddenly, she reaches up and kisses him on the cheek.

                              SANTHA
                        (continuing)
                   May Brahma watch over you and
                   our son.

                              ARMAND
                   You -- you will not stay?

                              SANTHA
                        (shakes her head)
                   Had it been Brahma's will --
                   he would have opened your heart
                   to me.

          With her fingertips, she touches his forehead, his cheeks,
          his mouth. Then she turns -- and exits the room. Armand
          looks after her -- tears in his eyes. Charles comes to
          him, puts an arm around his shoulders, comfortingly.

67   TWO SHOT - ARMAND AND CHARLES   67

          as, a moment later, Krishna enters the room -- in some
          excitement. He crosses down to Armand and Charles.

                                                      (CONTINUED)

67   CONTINUED: 67

                         KRISHNA
               I just saw the girl -- leaving
               with her friend.

                         CHARLES
               Yes. She is returning to Delhi.

                         ARMAND
                    (to Krishna)
               And you are going to America,
               my son, with Professor Goncourt.

                         KRISHNA
               What? But how? You said that
               you have no money...

                         CHARLES
               He was wrong.
                    (indicating the
                     jewels)
               Your mother just proved it.

     Krishna looks at him, startled -- then at his father,
     who nods. This stuns Krishna still further. He looks at
     the jewels -- then back at Armand, who nods again. On
     Krishna's face -- on which belief is beginning to dawn --

                                           FADE OUT.

                         - THE END -

Appendix 1
Additional Scripts Unveiled!
By Tom Weaver

At least six *Veil* scripts were written and, to the best of my knowledge, never filmed: "The Tumbled Coffins," "The Bottled Ghost," "The Indian Key," "The Warning," "Model Ghost" and "The Signal."

"The Tumbled Coffins"
by Sidney Morse, Production No. 9201, 31 pages, dated September 25, 1958

Synopsis: Wentworth, an Englishman, is the cruel and arrogant master of Balmaine, a plantation in the Paladores [*sic*] that employs slave labor. Tala, an attractive teenage slave girl, is serving him coffee one morning when he yells and scares her and she spills the coffee. With his riding crop, Wentworth beats her until she drops to the floor dead. His son Richard enters and sees what's happened, but Wentworth is unrepentant: "It's impossible to train these people properly."

Later, in the plantation fields, Richard tells his father that his (Richard's) pregnant wife Anne is sick and should be taken back to England before the baby is born. Wentworth: "Nonsense! Try being a man for once! This is your home and your place is here! And your wife's place is with you!" He goes on:

> Some day this [the plantation] will all be yours! Can you understand that? Thousands of acres of the best land in the world! The man who rules here is a king! With the power of life and death over hundreds of slaves! Stiffen your spine, Richard! Learn to use that power!

Richard, weak and shy, gives in.

At night, in the jungle, to the beat of voodoo drums, natives are performing a ceremony over the body of Tala. When Wentworth storms into the clearing with his house slave Jethro, the natives and the voodoo priestess flee. Wentworth tells Jethro this "voodoo nonsense" must stop "or I'll have your hide," and orders him to bury Tala.

One day Jethro enters the Wentworth crypt and then dashes out, panic-stricken. He fetches Wentworth and Richard, who come to the crypt and see that the coffins have been moved around. To prevent this from happening again, Wentworth has slaves slide a tremendous rock in front of the crypt entrance. Then he gathers all the slaves and, when no one will admit responsibility, he randomly picks three for some unspecified but no doubt severe – or lethal – punishment.

Richard meets with the islands' English governor, who asks about Balmaine's high slave death rate. Richard can't bring himself to spill what's going on even though Wentworth's brutality is making slaves revert to their drum-beating voodoo ways. The governor visits Wentworth to talk about the situation, and asks about Anne. Wentworth: "According to Richard, she's a delicate flower who should be in a hothouse. ...I've seen native women have their children and be back in the fields an hour later." On the slave issue, Wentworth stands by his attitude of the law of the lash. Richard enters, his face a lifeless mask, and announces that Anne has died. "My father and I … we did it," he tells the governor. "We killed my wife."

Native pallbearers cart Anne's coffin to the crypt as the huge rock is moved aside. Inside, the coffins are again in disarray, one even standing on end. "Voodoo…" mumbles Jethro. After the funeral, Wentworth is determined to flay every slave until he finds the man responsible, but the governor tells him that there'll be no further use of the whip because it will incite a voodoo uprising. The governor has the crypt entrance cemented and bricked-up.

Some time later, in his library, Wentworth tries a kinder, gentler approach, telling Jethro that if he learns who's been desecrating the crypt, he (Wentworth) will reward him with any woman he wants. When Jethro finally answers "Tala," an almost-screaming Wentworth orders him out. An argument between Wentworth and Richard ends with Wentworth slashing his son across the face with his riding crop. Richard stalks out and goes for a wild ride on his horse. He's killed in a fall, and a dazed Wentworth orders the re-opening of the crypt. Participating in Richard's funeral procession, Wentworth looks old and beaten. As they enter the crypt, their eyes adjust to the darkness and then all see that the coffins have yet again been tossed around as though by a giant hand. Jethro yells in terror "Voodoo!!!" and the six pallbearers drop the coffin and flee. Finally a wild-eyed Wentworth does too: "Jethro!! Jethro, wait!! Richard! Help me!! Somebody help me!!"

The plantation fields are empty and Wentworth's house is silent when the governor arrives. He and a guard don't like what they see and cautiously enter the house, where Wentworth sits in the library, now completely mindless. In his closing comments, Karloff mentions that Wentworth died in an asylum; with his death came the end of the Wentworth line.

Notes: "The Tumbled Coffins" and "The Indian Key" (see below) are my favorites of the unmade *Veil* scripts. With its too-bad-to-be-true Wentworth and his comic-book-level racist dialogue ("[Our slaves] are tools! Nothing more! They're here to be used!"), the "Tumbled Coffins" script reads like an old *Creepy* or *Eerie* horror comic adapted for TV. But, just like "Indian Key," the last few pages are a disappointment. After all the build-up, there's no twist or climactic shock, just a gander of the gone-mad Wentworth to satisfy TV's need for a "Justice is served" ending. Wentworth is described as 55 and the governor as 55 or 60, so Karloff could have played either role. If Karloff had played Wentworth, it would have been fun to see how he stacked up against similar cinematic tyrants such as Charles Laughton (*White Woman*, 1933), Peter Lorre (*Island of Doomed Men*, 1940), etc.

"The Bottled Ghost"
by Jack Laird, Production No. 9208, 37 pages, dated September 30, 1958

Synopsis: The story begins in 1585, in a wooden glen in the Scottish Highlands. Pushing through the brush under cover of night are Lady Anne Dalrymple ("a handsome, blonde piece of baggage in her late 'teens") and Clyde MacPhail ("a handsome, stalwart youth of 20-odd, with dark curly hair and beard"). They're lovers; her father has pledged her hand to a member of the nobility, a "twittering fop," so she and Clyde are running away together. Suddenly the father, Laird Dalrymple of Gowrie Castle, "a grim, towering, bewhiskered bear of a man," steps out of the bushes. Two of his armed servants overpower Clyde. As the servants drag him away to behead him, Clyde places a curse on the Dalrymples.

We jump ahead to the present, 1958, where the current versions of Anne and Clyde ("portrayed by the same actors who interpreted their ancestral namesakes") are seen in the same spot (the wooded glen at night) and the samer pickle: Their love is frowned upon by her father because of the 373-year clannish feud between the Dalrymples and the MacPhails. Her short and squat dad (the script calls him Laird Dalrymple II) enters the clearing and instructs his companion, his aged manservant Ian, to escort Anne back to their castle. Then Laird tells Clyde that Anne has too much family loyalty to marry without his (Laird's) consent, and permanently banishes him from the vicinity of Gowrie Castle.

Clyde goes home to MacPhail Hall and broods. His manservant Malcolm ("a spry, weazened [sic], sparrow-boned little man [with] mischievous eyes") tells him something he never knew, that the original Clyde (from here on, Master Clyde) placed a curse on the Dalrymples—and suggestively describes what would happen if Master Clyde's ghost created havoc at Gowrie Castle: "[I]n no time atall, he'd have Laird Dalrymple on his knees, *begging* ya to marry his daughter!"

Later, at Gowrie Castle, Laird is insisting to Anne that she'll never marry Clyde when he hears the sound of bagpipes; Anne and even Ian claim *not* to hear the music. After Laird goes to bed, he's wakened by a moan that builds to a shriek. He notices that wet footprints lead up to the door of his bedchamber and orders Ian and other servants to follow the trail and find the intruder. Ian returns to report that the trail ends at the edge of the castle's quicksand-like moat, where the beheaded Master Clyde was dumped in 1585.

Laird thinks it's suspicious that his run-in with Clyde was closely followed by the reappearance of Master Clyde, so he has six rifle-bearing servants guard the castle. Despite this precaution, a ghostly silhouette makes a middle-of-the-night appearance in his bedchamber, then disappears. The "ghost" *is* Clyde in a black hooded cape, and everything is going according to his plan: Laird calls in the gnarled, white-bearded Black Angus, who diagnoses that there is a ghost afoot and recommends that Murdock of Galt be summoned to exorcise it. Black Angus says that another necessary step is for Laird to make up with Clyde, but Laird refuses to "knuckle to a MacPhail." Later, in the wooded glen, Clyde pays off Black Angus, who looks apologetic and says he tried his best.

That night, after Laird goes to bed, Ian is cleaning when he hears a shriek and a gunshot. Laird comes running down the stairs, saying that the ghost grabbed him by the neck, shook him like a rag doll and didn't react when Laird shot him point blank. "He had no head! [laughing hysterically] D'ye ken, Ian? *No head*!!" When Anne appears, he tells her, "Ye may marry your MacPhail. A *dozen* if ye like. An' what's left over, *I'll* marry myself, if only the ghost will leave me in peace…!"

Now that Laird has agreed to the marriage, Murdock of Galt is called in to subdue the ghost. He tells Laird he will do so with a bottle and a piece of chalk.

> LAIRD II
> (incredulous)
> Just *those* – that's all – ??!
>
> MURDOCK
> Would ya rather I impress ye – or the Ghost?

Murdock draws a large chalk circle on the floor, sets the bottle in the center of it and begins chalking in the magic design (see illustration to the right) After Laird leaves the room, Murdock drops the hood from his head and reveals himself as Clyde's manservant Malcolm. We next see the bottle on the fireplace mantle at MacPhail Hall – where Anne tells Clyde that her conscience has forced her to tell her father that they've hoodwinked him. Laird unexpectedly enters, saying, "On the one hand, 'tis relieved I am to learn the whole thing was nothing but a hoax. Yet on the other—" He pauses and then, smiling a generous smile, adds, "No. I'll go the full distance. 'Tis relieved I am all around." Glad to forget about the Dalrymple grudge against the MacPhails, he shakes Clyde's hand. Regarding the previous night's appearance of the headless ghost, Laird asks Clyde how he managed it. Clyde is confused at first, and then solemnly swears, "Word o' honor. I never went near the castle last night. *I was right here all evening.*"

All eyes go to the bottle on the mantle. When Malcolm picks it up gingerly, Laird says, "Make sure the cork's in tight."

Notes: It's hard to be sure, just from reading the script, but this story was probably intended as a comedy; the right kind of acting and the right kind of music could easily have turned it into one. Writer Jack Laird reveals that he's in a whimsical mood with a line of his script: He calls for a stock shot of Gowrie Castle at night, adding underneath, "Everything is quiet except those goddamn crickets." Perhaps Laird was also being mischievous when he named the main character Laird. He went on to script the occult thriller *Dark Intruder* (1965) and to produce (and sometimes write and direct) the Rod Serling-hosted teleseries *Night Gallery* (1969-73). It occurred to me that Laird might not have wanted his "Bottled Ghost" script to go to waste and could have adapted it for *Night Gallery*, so I went to the go-to guy on that series Scott Skelton, co-author of the four-star book *Rod Serling's* Night Gallery*: An After-Hours Tour*. He told me that no, there was no *Night Gallery* episode that resembled "Bottled Ghost." The closest *Night Gallery* came was "The Ghost of Sorworth Place" (1972) with Richard Kiley and Jill Ireland, set in

Jack Laird's script "The Bottled Ghost" came complete with artwork of the huge magic circle that, in the story, Murdock was to draw in chalk on the floor.

Scotland and featuring the ghost of Ireland's husband. Eerily effective, with moments reminiscent of the ghost sightings in *The Innocents* (1961), it's light years from the silly "Bottled Ghost."

Laird took the trouble to include in the "Bottled Ghost" dialogue scores of phonetic spellings to make the characters sound Scottish: noo (now), doona (do not), doesna (does not), willna (will not), canna (cannot), d'ye (do you), wi' (with), etc. A real ghost taking the place of a "pretend" ghost is meant to be a surprise ending, but it willna be a surprise to anyone who's read "Banquo's Chair" or seen its *Alfred Hitchcock Presents* adaptation; you can see that twist coming from halfway to Aberdeen.

If Karloff had appeared in this episode, he might have played Ian, Black Angus or even Malcolm. Black Angus would be my guess.

"The Indian Key"
by Bernie Schoenfeld, Production No. 9211, 29 pages, dated September 25, 1958

Synopsis: In 1857, Paul Travers and John Davis are surveying and mapping an unexplored section of the Dakota Territory for the Department of the Interior. Sitting at their campfire at night, John, a science buff and Mr. Fix-It, repairs a piece of surveying equipment. A ferocious-looking Indian chief, almost nude, appears out of the dark thicket, followed by a half-dozen braves. Captives, Paul and John spend the next three days and nights being transported over rugged territory to an Indian village — where they hear Beethoven being played on a piano. In a teepee, the chief is about to begin torturing them. An Indian girl objects and runs and fetches "The Man": a white man, "[t]all, lean, 45. Dressed in buckskin hunting togs of the period. But when he speaks it is in the precise tones of the educated gentleman." He apologizes to Paul and John for the treatment they have received from "these savages," somehow knows their names, and escorts them to his home: a white, clapboard, painted, shuttered cottage complete with lawn, bushes, white fence and brick chimney. Inside are the Man's sofa, mahogany table, fine prints on papered walls and grand piano, "giv[ing] the room the feeling of a Boston salon awaiting afternoon tea." The Man, who has been avoiding all their questions, will not say how the materials for the house and its furnishings were transported to this nearly inaccessible mountainous spot.

The Man changes into clothes that make him look like an imposing banker and serves them Portuguese wine. He indicates that somewhere nearby is a possession, a small part of which is damaged, and he wants Paul to repair it (he somehow knows that Paul is clever with anything mechanical). He brings Paul a metallic box about three feet square, with wires and gears, and expects him to fix it without knowing its function. When Paul bristles at the Man's demanding attitude, the Man reminds his "guests" that he can turn them over to the Indians, who despise white strangers. Paul points out that the chief doesn't seem to dislike the Man, a comment which makes the Man smile: "You're wrong. He detests me. But he *fears* me. He *fears* this house. But he doesn't fear either of you, so if I give the word..."

As the Man pounds more Beethoven out of the piano, Paul disassembles the contents of the box and becomes filled with excitement at the challenge of repairing "[a] product of technological skill beyond his knowledge." When he finishes, the Man takes it outside, into the woods, to re-attach it to his possession, which (we get the impression) will enable him to escape his "life among the savages" which he abhors. Paul and John want to follow, but the doors are locked and the window won't budge. The Indian girl, the Man's servant, brings them a key and urges them to flee, but instead they search for the Man. The sound of the girl's scream brings them running back to the cottage, where they find her strangled to death. The chief's men grab Paul and John and bring them inside, where the Man is again playing the piano. "Wherever you're from, whoever you are – you're worse than these savages!" John says when it becomes clear the Man is going to hand them over to the Indians. After the Man leaves, Paul and John begin brawling with the Indians and manage to escape from the house. The Man, who left just seconds ahead of them, has vanished. Paul is shot by an Indian, but John half-carries him away and they elude their Indian pursuers.

Lost and without food and water, the men appear to be doomed, but along comes an Army lieutenant and his men. Paul and John tell him their fantastic story and lead him to the village — where there *is* no village. Or Indian or cottage or anything else. The lieutenant, angry and disgusted, can't decide if the men are suffering from delirium or hoodwinking him, and he's not impressed by the discovery of a section of a piano keyboard and the Indian girl's key. Now Paul and John can hear Beethoven being played tempestuously on a piano, but the lieutenant can't: "I hear nothing! Nothing but your lies!"

John: "Come Paul, let's ride back ... we'll never prove it to him now..."

Notes: Karloff narration tells us at the outset that "The Indian Key" is based on the accounts of "several credible reporters" but I'd be surprised if this wild tale had even an iota of a basis in anything that was actually ever reported. What reporter would bother to chronicle the tall tale of delirious, lost-in-the-wilderness men, especially after the Indian village and cottage proved to be non-existent?

That said, however, "The Indian Key" is a real page-turner of a script – until the disappointing non-ending, anyway. Maybe it's the Monster Kid in me but I got the impression that writer Bernard C. Schoenfeld (*Phantom Lady, The Dark Corner, The Space Children, The Magic Sword*) wanted to create the impression that the Man came from another planet, perhaps stuck on Earth as a result of some vehicular breakdown like the *It Came from Outer Space* (1953) Globs. The scenes in which Paul is tasked with assembling a technological, perhaps futuristic gizmo evokes memories of Cal and the interociter in *This Island Earth* (1955). I found it weirdly appealing to find these whiffs of sci-fi in a bizarre Western. Needless to say, I pictured Karloff as the coolly cruel Man as I read the script, and then recalled that according to the up-front list of character descriptions, the Man was 45. But the only other part he could have played was the half-nude chief, and I don't want to even *try* to envision a 1959 Karloff as the Least of the Mohicans. Speaking of the script, it describes the Indian girl as "very young. If possible, 'Sex-in-Buffalo-Hide, à la *Vogue* Magazine' should be avoided."

The Karloff outro ends with our host saying, "This is Boris Karloff bidding you – good night." The *Veil* host identifies himself as Karloff in no episode.

"The Warning"
by Robert Bloomfield and Jerry D. Lewis, Production No. 9221, 39 pages, dated February 12, 1959

Synopsis: At Phipps College for Women, attractive, impulsive 20-year-old Diane Harper has a crush on her tutor, art class teacher Andy Charlevoix. Phipps' Professor of Fine Arts and Archaeology, Milo Woodford, an engaging Englishman, "somewhat mid-Victorian in dress and manner," secretly watches a spat between the two.

That night, on his house on a tree-lined street in the college town, Diane's uncle and guardian Douglas Harper tells visitor Andy that he knows Diane has a crush on him ("Every time I hire a tutor, Diane falls in love"). Before coming to Phipps, Andy worked at another college until one of his girl students made some serious (and false) charges about him showing affection to her. Andy was innocent (and everyone knew it) but he quit and came to Phipps—and now someone has anonymously written to the Phipps dean about that incident in Andy's past. After Andy leaves, Uncle Douglas tells Diane that – to get out of the awkward pupil-teacher romance that Diane has instigated – Andy might have written the letter himself. At the college the next day, Prof. Woodford vaguely conveys to Andy that Diane reminds him of Virginia, a now-dead woman he knew in Italy more than 20 years ago.

Andy's next headache: The Phipps dean gave him the anonymous letter, and he can tell that it was typed on the same typewriter as Diane's term notes. Andy thinks Uncle Douglas wrote it, so Diane confronts him. He denies it, and raises the possibility that Andy wrote it on her typewriter—or that Diane herself wrote it ("You chased him. He rejected you. You wanted revenge, so you…"). Later that night, Diane breaks into a wall cabinet in Uncle Douglas' work shop and takes a locket and then, her eyes glazed over, she sits at a desk and writes; it's as if "some uncontrollable force has seized her hand." After the spell passes, she looks at what she's written and screams.

On the paper, not in her handwriting, is the word etadab. She's certain it means something, so with Andy she visits professors of French, Spanish, Greek, Latin and Oriental languages and they're stumped. At last she visits an expert on *dead* languages, Prof. Woodford, who tells her about Virginia, the American girl he loved in Italy. He describes her as a girl who did everything intensely, including learning and speaking Italian. ("I don't think I ever heard her speak English again, not even to her husband – and he was from Pittsburgh.") He adds that she and her husband were later murdered. Diane says that she's been told that her parents disappeared in the wilds of Canada when she was a baby. Woodford now notices that Diane's locket looks like one Virginia wore.

The subject turns to etadeb, the word Diane wrote in her trance. Woodford calls it a case of automatic writing and, looking at the paper in a mirror, says that Diane really wrote bedate, the Italian word for beware. Woodford also says it looks like Virginia's handwriting.

Diane quietly returns home and, doodling while using the phone, writes **Bedate di Char** before Uncle Douglas enters and she snaps out of her spell. *Bedate di* means **Beware of**, and Char may be the start of Charlevoix, Andy's last name. But Diane starts to look at Uncle Douglas suspiciously when she learns that he's made plans for them to move to Seattle the next morning without telling her. (He also keeps calling her "my little girl.")

Woodford tells Andy about Diane's visit and mentions that she was wearing a locket that looked like Virginia's

— a locket she got from "a man she was afraid of. He followed her…even after she was married. …A man she was afraid of." Meanwhile, the tense confrontation between Diane and Uncle Douglas continues, Diane accusing him of putting her in a new school every year so that she'd have no friends or boyfriends: "You don't want to love me, you want to own me!" Eventually it becomes clear that Uncle Douglas was the stalker of Virginia in Italy — and the killer of Virginia and her husband — and that he stole their baby, who grew up to be Diane. Crazy Uncle Douglas now starts acting like Diane *is* Virginia, and he's about to strangle her, when Andy bursts in. Crazy Uncle Douglas becomes himself again and resigns himself to his fate: "Go ahead. Call the police. I'll wait." Woodford walks into the house and immediately recognizes him as Virginia's stalker, **Char**les Richards.

Notes: Awful, isn't it?

"Model Ghost"
by Eustace Cockrell and Jerry D. Lewis, Production No. 9223, 41 pages); no date

Synopsis: Stock footage establishes a remodeled old brownstone in New York City's Gramercy Park. Its superintendent (i.e., janitor) Adam Briscoe, a distinguished-looking gent in his 60s, is obviously living in reduced circumstances. He appears to take an intense interest in tenant Lillian Todd, a tall young beauty "who could be one of the top models in New York if she had more competitive drive"; she intends to model only until she marries. Lill tells Adam that she's expecting a friend named Anne Barret; Adam promises that when she arrives, he'll send her up. But when Anne knocks on his door and introduces herself—and mentions that *she* wants to be a model — Adam regards her warily and lies that Lill is out of town. At this point, the script calls for a fade to black, a commercial and *then* the Karloff narration.

On the roof of the building are the studio and darkroom of Lill's fiancé Paul Monroe, a resourceful but not yet successful photographer. He's excited to have been invited to submit a girl's photo in a competition that will decide the next Rainbow Girl (who will then be New York's most famous model); Lill will be the photographic subject. That night, as Anne is walking across Lill's apartment, a framed ad featuring Lill falls from the mantel and the glass breaks.

The next morning, as Paul is on the roof preparing for the photo shoot, Adam visits Lill's apartment and, showing *too* much interest, tells her that this is her chance to become a big star. "I'd just as soon stay in bed…and let [Anne] do it," says Lill. That idea is repellent to Adam. When Anne walks near the edge of the roof, Adam watches her closely, and when she looks down into the empty elevator shaft, he rushes up behind her and grabs her. Anne screams, but Adam claims he was only preventing her from falling in. As Paul prepares to take pictures of Lill (dressed as a Musketeer, complete with foil), Anne tells Lill her left cheek is shiny. Lill avails herself of Anne's compact. After Paul takes his pictures, Lill and Anne go back to the apartment, where Lill says it feels like her left cheek is burning. Fireplace tools inexplicably fall to the floor, including an andiron poker with an end shaped like an eidelweiss (a European plant). Paul develops the Musketeer photos and sees that there's an inexplicable smudge on Lill's cheek (identical to the end of the poker).

Paul prepares to take new photos while Adam plants in his head the idea that Anne had trick powder in her compact, burning Lill's face so that she (Anne) would be photographed instead. In Adam's apartment, Anne peruses a scrapbook full of clippings and sees that Adam once tried to produce a play starring his wife (now deceased). Adam catches her and they quibble, with Anne saying she'll move out after Lill and Paul's wedding. Adam, now wide-eyed, didn't know they were marrying. When Adam goes to Lill's apartment to fix a faucet, he tells her that marriage will ruin her career: "You've got to live for the theater." He also lies to her that Paul promised to marry every regular model he ever had. An angry Lill tells him to fix the faucet.

Adam is stunned when he sees the photos of Lill with the eidelweiss mark on her cheek. Lill and Paul argue and make up; Adam gets into the elevator with Anne and stops it between floors as Anne cowers. Eventually Adam comes clean: He reveals that he and his beautiful wife once occupied the whole building; he wanted her to become a big star but she didn't; and that he slaved to produce a stage vehicle for her. But just before opening night, she fainted while fixing the fire in what is now Lill's apartment, and fell against the red-hot eidelweiss poker, marking her left cheek. As for the recent strange events: "Liza must have been telling me not to try to make another unwilling star. And she's right…" He also says that he's avoided putting his wife's portrait (now hanging in Lill's apartment) in his room because "I've been too proud to let her see me as a superin… [he hesitates; then, smiling] As a janitor." But now he intends to move it into his room.

In Lill's apartment, Adam stares at the portrait. As he begins to leave without it, fireplace tools fall from their brackets. After a bit more hesitation, Adam smiles and returns for the portrait.

Notes: In the script, the name of Adam's wife starts out as Mary but later becomes Liza. The role of the haunted-by-the-past janitor would have fit Karloff like a Craftsman socket wrench.

"The Signal"
by Ellis Marcus, Production No. 9225, 39 pages, no date

Synopsis: Jeff Bradford, captain of the freighter *Greta Wilson* (or the *Pacific Star*; the name alternates) is sailing back to the U.S. after two years in the Orient. The script calls him a vigorous man just past 60, so this has to be the Karloff character. One night when the ship is about 75 miles from the California coast, Jeff feels compelled to turn on the ham radio set in his cabin and hears a distress call from the fishing boat *Magnetta*, which (according to the voice on the radio) is burning and sinking at Selby's Cove. Jeff calls the radio shack, but they can't pick up the signal. Neither did any of the authorities on shore.

Later, as the berthed freighter is being unloaded, Jeff feels a strange sensation that compels him to turn on the radio. Again the voice is heard, this time adding, "This was no accident. Someone must have…" before static drowns it out. Jeff has tape-recorded it this time, and now he rewinds and listens to the tape and recognizes the voice as that of Carl Reimers, who was once his radio operator.

Jeff tries to find Selby's Cove but instead finds a blonde sitting on a rise. She turns out to be Barbara Dean, Carl's fiancée – who tells him that Carl died over a year ago, when his boat the *Magnetta* caught fire and sank. Big, boyish, well-dressed Larry Barnes shows up looking for Barbara, and introduces himself to Jeff as Carl's best friend. He mentions that Carl had invented a new type of magnet for radio receivers and had gotten rich off of it. When Jeff talks about receiving a distress call from a burning, sinking boat and says the voice sounded like Carl's, Barbara and Larry look at him askance. Back on his freighter, Jeff learns from his first mate Mike that the ship owners are also looking at him askance: Concerned that Jeff apparently imagined a distress call, they're thinking about making Mike the skipper and putting Jeff out to pasture. Bud Reimers, Carl's intense 19- or 20-year-old brother (and sole heir), shows up to hear the tape-recorded SOS, but the tape is blank. Jeff is sure someone … maybe Bud? … erased it. On the pier, a heavy section of concrete pipe comes rolling at Jeff, and now he thinks someone is trying to erase *him*.

Convinced that Carl's death was no accident, Jeff now looks with great suspicion on Larry (who would have liked having Barbara as *his* girl), Bud (who inherited Carl's wealth) and first mate Mike (who perhaps wants to take over as skipper). Jeff senses that there'll be another distress call that night at nine and wants others to hear it with him at that hour. Meanwhile, an unseen, shadowy figure sneaks into Jeff's cabin and attaches an electric blasting cap to the ham radio.

Barbara, Larry and Bud are all in the cabin that night at nine when Larry asks to look inside the radio, notices wires that shouldn't be there and finds the concealed bomb, which is built into a hot rod tailpipe extension. This causes all eyes to go to car-lovin' speed-crazy Bud, but in the ensuing argument, Larry slips up and says something that only Carl's killer could know. When he pulls a gun, Bud backhands him and belts him twice and takes charge of the situation. A voice comes over the radio, startling everyone, but it's just first mate Mike, who says that their bosses are letting Jeff remain skipper of his freighter and giving Mike his own boat to command.

Notes: The premise of a man being supernaturally made aware of a murder stirs *Veil* memories of "Summer Heat" (Paige getting a preview of an upcoming murder), "Vision of Crime" (George seeing a vision of an in-progress murder) and even "Jack the Ripper" (Jack's dastardly deeds are "livestreamed" to Walter). The only difference is that "The Signal"'s Jeff learns about the murder through his ears, not his eyes.

As I read this script, I kept forgetting that Jeff had to be played by Karloff. The story, an offbeat mystery stocked with young people (including a lovely, wistful blonde), an oceanside setting and Jeff zipping back and forth between meetings with suspects, reads more like an episode of *Surfside 6* or *77 Sunset Strip* than a *Veil*. After Hal Roach Studios and *The Veil* went belly-up, scripter Ellis Marcus could have transformed "The Signal" into an episode of an action show, with (say) Troy Donahue or Roger Smith playing the Karloff role, without having to change as much as one word of dialogue. Well, at one point Jeff *does* call the late Carl a boy, but then later in the script, Carl's fiancée Barbara does too. When the concrete pipe rolls toward Jeff and he pushes a crate into its path to stop it, I could almost hear the blare of the jazzy William Lava-Warner Brothers TV action music. Karloff, Karloff, lend me your comb!

Appendix 2

The Monster Was Very, Very Good to Me
By Martin Varno

When I was 21, I was the youngest head of a story department on any studio lot in Hollywood. I had a real nice office with an immense glass front, and almost any time of day you could walk past and see me back there laboring over my typewriter on a screen property.

What you wouldn't know was that those scripts all belonged to me. The studio, sadly on the verge of receivership, couldn't afford to make any of them their own. While they were desperately attempting to impress potential investors by allowing them to peek in on their in-house "boy genius" story department honcho (the entire department consisting of me and Diane, my secretary), I was hustling to sell a screenplay to somebody, anybody who would buy with negotiable currency, first come first served.

Actually, I didn't really need a great deal in those days. I was very much in love with Diane. I had just written my first produced movie, *Night of the Blood Beast* for American International, and I was attached to one of the most historic motion picture lots in the entire existence of the film business, Hal Roach Studios. My office was on Mack Sennett Avenue, just across the parking area from Lake Laurel and Hardy. It was the best of times!

Hal Roach Studios was on its last legs in those days; anyone could see that, but if you walked its dingy passways late at night, out beyond the ancient brick sound stages, back where Fatty Arbuckle Boulevard petered out and became the Western street; when the night mist began to condense and become wet, and the high, overlooking security lights bounced against anything shiny and flat, you started to see things…from another time. In those moments, everything was brand new again and just beginning.

You knew the Keystone Cops were out there, every last one of 'em, shaking those ridiculous rubber billy clubs and splashing through every mud puddle they encountered. Oh, you couldn't see them straight on, but if you looked real quick, they were always dodging behind something just past the corner of your eye where the shadows were deepest.

That empty barrel over there … wasn't that the one Chester Conklin stuffed full of dynamite? Then Harry Langdon came along and sat on it 'til Mae Busch talked him into catching the streetcar for the beach just in the nick of time, and he didn't get blown to bits after all (whew!).

And over there; only a pile of plywood and broken plaster now, but then, when was it, 1919?, 1920?, it was the bank Charley Chase wrecked when he accidentally drove that school bus through the front door.

Diane, my lovely lady, and I, pretending we were leaving the lot for home at the end of the day, would start the car, hers, a large, rather impressive Cadillac (important in those days; also very comfortable if spending much time inside with the seats down!). We'd drive right past the main gate making our way to the Hong Kong Street on the back lot, where we would park in the now-drained harbor in front of the wharf where Harold Lloyd was waylaid by the evil Asian White Slavers in an epic (the name of which I'll probably never be able to recall) which I remember seeing at the old Silent Movie Theater on Fairfax Avenue.

I'd kill the engine and turn off our headlights; she'd open the ice chest, give a bounce to the mai tai shaker; we'd unwrap the chicken salad sandwiches, and neck for hours.

Several hours later we'd zoom past the little wooden house at the main gate on our way home, she wearing my button-down shirt, and I in her pink blouse, hopefully confusing the hell out of Mickey the guard. Sometimes, to really do it up good, I'd even wear a bright orange fright wig, and she, a huge bushy black mustache we'd stashed in the glove compartment for just that purpose!

Poor Mickey! But he never let on. Always a big smile and a snappy salute as we passed. The guy had a lotta class! He also knew our car, and he would have rather died than let us know we'd gotten to him!

Though on the verge of dismantlement, our illustrious lot at the same time was host to some of the classic examples of early filmed episodic television production.

Remember *The Gale Storm Show*, headlined for some strange reason by a lady named Gale Storm? Made right over there on Stage 12.

That's My Bob starring Bob Cummings? Those plaster walls over on the left were what used to be his photo studio. Last I heard, the show is still pulling in a nice syndicated profit.

Then there was *The Veil*, starring Boris Karloff, perhaps the gentlest giant in our business. What's that? You don't recall it? Well, there was probably a very good reason for that.

See, in those days of the mid-50s when TV was just entering its early adolescence, nobody bought any show, much less put it on the air, unless it came in lots of 13, that figure representing one of four yearly television seasons. They had just finished the tenth *Veil* segment when a battalion of U.S. marshals came riding through the main gate one Friday afternoon, pulling the plug on our wondrous nickelodeon for good. Something to do with not honoring a government banking regulation as I recall, but I don't really know for sure.

At any rate, everyone was told to go home and come back the following Monday for their checks, which would, by then, be government issue…and good.

It was a very sad day. Diane and I drove out to say goodbye to Hong Kong and love each other in our favorite spot one last time. We also looked out the windshield like two scared children, trying not to think of this magic place being transformed into a parking lot for a shopping mall, which is what eventually happened.

It was also upon this land that William Henry Pratt, aka Boris Karloff, filmed his television series *The Veil*, as in: "I don't know, ma'am, but I believe there are things out there that human beings were never meant to fool with. Things that lie … behind the Veil."

Mr. Karloff was the host and always played a pivotal role. In the fact that it afforded him a different personality to portray each week, it was a performer's dream, and one of the best things he ever did. Above all, the man was a superb actor!

He once chewed a line, and you would have thought the world had come to an end. He apologized to every-

Karloff and his wife Evie, his constant companion on many of his TV and movie sets. (Photo courtesy John Antosiewicz)

one from the director to the cameraman to the script girl to the guy who sweeps up the horse plop after the posse comes in, *every*body got an apology. Such things just didn't happen to a correctly trained English Actor. It was unheard of!

Always, just behind the action, very much like Madame Defarge in *A Tale of Two Cities*, there sat a small, often blanket-wrapped, cheerful little English lady knitting away like mad. Mrs. Karloff was a most important part of this set.

Mr. Karloff was immediately by her side the moment a take was printed and he wasn't required on stage any more. It appeared that they rather liked each other. Devoted would be the word, and it was a very nice thing to watch.

There was one unbreakable rule on a Karloff set. At exactly four o'clock in the afternoon, unless rolling in the very middle of a shot, Mr. and Mrs. Karloff sat down together and took tea.

The key grip had set up the hotplate, the best boy had strung the cable, the chief electrician plugged the connector into an adapter and then into one of the huge "busses" that fed enough juice onto the stage to run a small town, and as the time approached, Mrs. K. would boil the first water which was used to heat the pot that held the second water, into which the aromatic black leaves, now snug within their silver "tea ball," would be submerged for precisely the right length of time as dictated by tradition. And by God, there would always be an England!

They sipped from Wedgwood cups for exactly 15 minutes, discussing the news of the day as any married couple on the plain of Salisbury might enjoy a break in their labor. Everybody loved it, and everybody loved them. they were exceptionally nice people!

Over the months it took to film the ten segments, I became acquainted with them both. He, as an Actor, was of course a hero to me, and had been from the first time I watched the Monster take a drag off that stogie and begin to syncopate to the vibes of the Blind Hermit's fiddle. Actually, that occurred in the second Monster film, *Bride of Frankenstein*, but it just so happens that I saw that one first.

I remember the last time I ever saw him. It was on a variety show if I'm not mistaken, and there, upon a bare stage, in a single key light, sitting at the edge of an overstuffed chair, Mr. Boris Karloff spoke the words to the delightful "September Song" from Sherwood Anderson's musical play *Knickerbocker Holiday*, while "Youth," a young woman in a cloud-like, diaphanous white gown, danced solo adagio just out of reach in the shadows of his memory. As I sat at home bawling my stupid head off at the sight of this beautiful old man, dressed in a smoking jacket, a glass of brandy in his hand, I knew he was saying goodbye. It was, I've been told, the last performance he ever gave. He died a few weeks later. A dignified, proud and gentle soul.

During his final weeks, Mr. Karloff gave an interview to a young reporter. A fellow who, obviously lacking the experience to couch his questions in any kind of tact, kept over-bluntly pushing an image of the Great Man exchanging his artistic backbone for the American Buck; his words ending in inquiry as to how Karloff, trained from early years for the stage, felt about being relegated to playing in Hollywood horror movies instead of areas of his craft that would probably have been more to his liking.

Karloff took a deep breath, leaned slowly back in his chair, his eyes sweeping the heavens over the younger man's head almost as if in his own mind's eye he could recall all the moments, magic and otherwise, adding up to his long and distinguished career. He smiled very wide, very warm, as if remembering an old and close friend.

"It was all right," he spoke quietly, patiently explaining. "Oh, probably I would have enjoyed more Shakespeare and less Poe, but I'm very content. You see, the Monster gave me so much more than most players ever experience. After I made that film, I was never 'at liberty,' never out of work, not even for one day."

And he stretched happily. "Yes, indeed," he said. "The Monster was very, very good to me."

> Martin Varno was the son of Roland Varno, an actor Monster Kids will remember from 1943's *The Return of the Vampire*, playing Nina Foch's orchestra conductor fiancé. (Martin: "Oh, God, Father was horrible in that!") Martin wore many hats in the movie-TV business, from screenwriter to makeup artist, sound effects editor and more. In 1958, he received his first on-screen credit for writing the screenplay of Roger Corman's *Night of the Blood Beast* at age 21. He died in 2014.

Appendix 3

Forgotten, Rejected, Unseen, Vilified, Finally Acclaimed... and then Lost Again:

The Downs and Ups of Boris Karloff as Television Series Host

By Dr. Robert J. Kiss

Almost all of the original generation of "horror movie stars" from the 1930s and 1940s – whether preeminent genre names such as Bela Lugosi, Boris Karloff and Lon Chaney Jr., occasional lead performers including Fredric March, Claude Rains, Charles Laughton, Peter Lorre, John Carradine, Vincent Price, George Zucco and Gale Sondergaard, or standout supporting players like Maria Ouspenskaya and Lionel Atwill – were really, of course, *multimedia* stars, whose work extended beyond the motion picture screen into the realms of theater, radio, spoken word recordings, advertising and, for those who lived long enough, television. Even "Britain's horror man" Tod Slaughter could be seen on the DuMont Network during 1953-54, playing lip-smacking archvillain Terence Riley in all 13 episodes of the contemporary crime series *Inspector Morley of Scotland Yard*, shot in England for syndication in the U.S.[1]

American television had been swift to embrace the notion of employing a host to introduce drama anthology series, thus bringing a degree of continuity to such shows' otherwise disparate weekly offerings. Perhaps the most significant of the early series hosts was silent-era leading man and former president of the Actors' Equity Association Bert Lytell, who served as host, narrator and occasional performer on NBC's *The Philco Television Playhouse* from its inaugural episode on October 3, 1948. Indeed, the prestigious Advertising Club of Baltimore would name Lytell "TV's Most Outstanding Personality of 1948" when handing out awards for broadcasting excellence in March 1949.[2] Presenting a live hour-long adaptation of a different literary or dramatic work each Sunday night between 9 and 10 p.m. ET, the Lytell-hosted *Philco Television Playhouse* also demonstrated the new medium's readiness to engage with tales of horror and the supernatural, with Daphne Du Maurier's *Rebecca* selected for its second episode on October 10, 1948; J.B. Priestley's *An Inspector Calls* for November 21, 1948; and Charles Dickens' *A Christmas Carol* for December 19, 1948.

Lytell commented in March 1949 that acting on television "really gets back to the stock company idea. We do a different play each week and we build new sets for each of these hour-long plays. We have to get actors who are quick studies."[3] This viewpoint was keenly shared by Boris Karloff as he dove headlong into the realm of live television drama during the first half of 1949. Of course, Karloff was already well-established as a radio performer: Ronald L. Smith in his 2010 book *Horror Stars on Radio: The Broadcast Histories of 29 Chilling Hollywood Voices* enumerates some 85 confirmed radio appearances by the actor between 1933 and 1948. These include over 30 leading roles in the high-rating mystery drama series *Inner Sanctum*, *Lights Out* and *Suspense*, as well as repeat "guest star" turns on hugely popular variety and comedy shows such as *The Charlie McCarthy Show*, *The Eddie Cantor Show* and *The Fred Allen Show*.[4]

Karloff made his television acting debut alongside Dennis King and Vicki Cummings in the psychological drama "Expert Opinion," the February 9, 1949, episode of NBC's anthology series *The Chevrolet Tele-Theatre*. Adapted from a radio play by True Boardman originally performed in that medium as the April 16, 1939, installment of CBS's *The Silver Theater* in which Robert Montgomery had played the lead, "Expert Opinion" offered Karloff the opportunity to showcase his dual-personality acting credentials in the role of Gerald Conway, a con man who attempts to convince doctors that he's insane.[5] Karloff returned to *Chevrolet Tele-Theatre* in another psychological drama on May 9, 1949, portraying the sinister, universally rejected Ralph Walkes in an adaptation of Ellis St. Joseph's "A Passenger to Bali."[6]

On CBS, meanwhile, Karloff starred three times in quick succession on the network's television evolution of its hit radio mystery series *Suspense*. On April 26, 1949, he took the lead in an adaptation of Lord Dunsany's 1911 one-act play about a jewel stolen from an Indian idol, "A Night at the Inn." His subsequent two appearances were likewise stagings of Old World horror tales: on May 17, 1949, W.W. Jacobs' 1902 short story about an unlucky Indian charm, "The Monkey's Paw," and on June 7, 1949, Thomas Burke's 1921 piece of Limehouse Grand Guignol, "The Yellow Scarf." The level of exposure afforded by these appearances should not be underestimated. Back when Karloff had headlined on the radio version of *Suspense* (in the January 25, 1945, amnesia-themed episode "Drury's Bones" and the December 19, 1947, adaptation of John Collier's story of murder and British social mores "Wet Saturday"[7]), market research studies already advised that it was teenage listeners' favorite mystery show.[8] In October 1949, the Advertest Research Company interviewed 534 television viewers in New York and New Jersey and found *Suspense* to be the second most popular television drama, watched regularly by 53.2 percent of respondents and surpassed only by another CBS show, Gertrude Berg's radio-to-television domestic comedy triumph *The Goldbergs*, at 57.3 percent.[9]

Prior to *Suspense*, Karloff had already given a standout performance on the April 11, 1949, episode of CBS's dramatic anthology series *Ford Theatre*: an hour-long adaptation of *Arsenic and Old Lace* in which he reprised his Broadway role as Jonathan Brewster alongside Josephine Hull (likewise from the original Broadway cast) as Abby Brewster. The show had been broadcasting from New York since October 18, 1948, but this was the first occasion on which it could be seen in Chicago, with the horror-comedy consequently generating particular interest in the Windy City.[10] Even before the show aired, though, entertainment reporter Erskine Johnson announced in his April 5, 1949, syndicated column, "Boris Karloff has his Beverly Hills home up for sale and is telling pals he'll move to New York for good. He'll concentrate on radio and television and commute to Hollywood when a film role turns up."

In view of all the above, it seems as though Karloff ought to have been a shoo-in for assuming hosting duties on some television drama anthology series or another, in particular one that played to his notoriety in the fields of horror, mystery and suspense. And indeed, the actor *would* go on to receive tremendous critical acclaim and fan adulation as the host of NBC's *Thriller* at the beginning of the 1960s. However, as must already be evident to anyone reading this volume on *The Veil*, Karloff's career as television series host was not all plain sailing. What follows, then, is a show-by-show voyage across the decidedly choppy seas that our indefatigable host would traverse between 1949 and 1962, leaving him variously forgotten, rejected, unseen, vilified, finally acclaimed…and then lost again!

1. Forgotten: *Starring Boris Karloff* (1949, ABC)

In fact, early television executives could hardly wait to put Karloff to work on a series of his own. In a news item dated July 9, 1949, the trade journal *The Billboard* announced, "Horror thesp Boris Karloff was signed this week by the American Broadcasting Company (ABC) to do a TV series in September. The program, tentatively titled *Conflict*, will have Karloff portraying a different role each week."[11] Actually, the deal was a little more complicated than that since *Conflict* had been commissioned for 13 episodes as a so-called "dual media" show, meaning that each half-hour episode would be broadcast first on radio on Wednesday nights at 9 p.m. ET, and then performed live in a revised version for television on Thursdays at 8:30 p.m. ET. This "doubling of radio shows in television" was a common practice during the fall 1949 season, as networks adjusted to increased television ownership and availability while at the same time seeking to ensure that popular and new programs continued to reach radio listeners.[12]

Needless to say, learning lines for two different versions of the same script each week was hard work, but Karloff absolutely relished the experience, writing to his brother Sir John Pratt after the show's seventh episode, "The television series goes on, and in combination with a radio show really keeps me hopping which I like."[13] Speaking to Sonia Stein of *The Washington Post* about performing the show live, he added, "The clock is ticking and there's no stopping it. If your head falls off at five minutes to nine, you have to find a way to screw it back on. It's a hideous kind of excitement, a terrific stimulus."[14]

By the time he spoke to Stein ahead of the final episode, the show was no longer called *Conflict*, although that title had stayed with it throughout advance publicity and was changed to *Starring Boris Karloff* so late in the day that some newspaper listings columns still referred to it as *Conflict* for its debut broadcast. Presumably Karloff must also have called it *Conflict* when he joined moderator Conrad Nagel and regular panelists Ilka Chase and John Daly (still five months away from

Starring Boris Karloff on radio and TV, *Detroit (MI) Free Press*, September 21, 1949.

making his debut on *What's My Line?*) on the September 4, 1949, edition of ABC's television game show *Celebrity Time* in order to publicize the imminent arrival of his drama on the air. To confuse matters further, stations in some parts of the country would only start to carry *Starring Boris Karloff* from the first week of November and employed the more straightforward titles *Boris Karloff Mystery Theater* and *Boris Karloff Mystery Playhouse* for these abridged runs.

Since Karloff introduced each episode of *Starring Boris Karloff* as himself before stepping into character, it represented his first instance of hosting a drama anthology series for television. This wasn't the only "first" relating to cast and crew: it was also the first time that 34-year-old producer-director (and future Emmy winner) Alex Segal had helmed an entire TV series. The 13 episodes which aired were:

1. "Five Golden Guineas," September 22, 1949
2. "The Mask," September 29, 1949
3. "Mungahara," October 6, 1949
4. "Mad Illusion," October 13, 1949
5. "Perchance to Dream," October 20, 1949
6. "The Devil Takes a Wife," October 27, 1949
7. "The Moving Finger," November 3, 1949
8. "The Twisted Path," November 10, 1949
9. "False Face," November 17, 1949
10. "Cranky Bill," November 24, 1949
11. "Three O'Clock," December 1, 1949
12. "The Shop at Sly Corner," December 8, 1949
13. "The Night Reveals," December 15, 1949

As those titles make clear, the scripts selected for *Starring Boris Karloff* were certainly in keeping with the horror-mystery reputation of its eponymous host and star. While Karloff himself referred to the show simply as presenting "exciting, offbeat stories," advance press publicity was singularly free from such British understatement.[15] The *Olean Times Herald* promised "the screen's best known menace" would be "[d]ramatizing strange stories of the super-natural," while the *Des Moines Register* anticipated "the master of the macabre in a penetrating psychological melodrama." *Kokomo Tribune* columnist Charlene Brown told readers to look forward to "mystery classics and tales of suspense and horror," which *The Battle Creek Enquirer and News* felt sure would benefit from Karloff's "gift for interpreting the nuances of psychological melodrama." As *The Anniston Star* concluded: "[I]f Mr. K. runs true to form, there will probably be no holds barred when he endeavors to scare the dickens out of us this evening."[16]

Alas, each and every one of the above examples (and many more besides) referred solely to the *radio* version of *Starring Boris Karloff*. The show's television presentation, by contrast, merited barely a word in the press. While large graphic ads for *Starring Boris Karloff* on radio showed Karloff alongside dangling spiders and creepy crawlers, even simple text-based ads for the television incarnation remained few and far between. This was in part because radio still massively outperformed television in terms of coverage and set ownership.

But also, it was due to the television version lacking a presentational context. On radio, *Starring Boris Karloff* constituted part of a special two-hour block of suspense and thriller programming for the fall-winter season billed collectively as ABC's "Night of Mystery."[17] This line-up included crime drama *The Amazing Mr. Malone*, adapted from Craig Rice's John Malone mystery novels, in addition to two further half-hour shows that made their debut alongside *Starring Boris Karloff*: the Milton Geiger-scripted supernatural-themed *The Croupier*

ABC's "Night of Mystery" line-up, *Alexandria* (LA) *Town Talk*, September 28, 1949.

which in its opening episode featured Vincent Price as a Roman soldier doomed to walk the Earth forever unless a woman falls in love with him; and *The Adventures of Sherlock Holmes* with Ben Wright as Holmes and Eric Snowden as Watson. As an ad in the *Burlington Free Press* enticed: "Mystery lovers, Wednesday night is your night to stay at home with the lights burning low and your radio tuned."[18]

On television, the live and fairly intense *Starring Boris Karloff* wound up playing alongside a variety of ill-matched filmed fare ranging from (the sublime) World War II documentary series *Crusade in Europe*, based on Dwight D. Eisenhower's best-selling memoirs, to (the ridiculous) Charlie Ruggles Hollywood-lensed family sitcom *The Ruggles*. Only the programmers at a number of ABC-TV stations in California that came late to *Starring Boris Karloff* in November appear to have spotted this shortcoming and reworked their schedules to create what Los Angeles-based KECA-TV (now KABC-TV) described as "a full schedule of chillers and who-dun-its."[19] Thus, on these stations, *Starring Boris Karloff* went out sandwiched between the courtroom re-enactment series based on real cases, *Your Witness*, and the crime drama *Photocrime* adapted from *Look* magazine's murder mystery photo-stories of the same name.

Even with some care being given to the presentational context of *Starring Boris Karloff*, critic Jerry Franken of *The Billboard* felt that the ABC drama would "face tough competition" from CBS and NBC on radio and television alike.[20] On Wednesdays, it was up against the new *Bing Crosby Show* on CBS and long-established popular crime drama *Mr. District Attorney* on NBC, while its Thursday small-screen broadcast clashed with Olsen and Johnson's hour-long variety show *Fireball Fun-for-All* on NBC-TV. The sixth episode of *Starring Boris Karloff*, "The Devil Takes a Wife," somewhat ironically went head to head against the (extant) Halloween episode of *Fireball Fun-for-All* featuring a Universal-inspired Frankenstein Monster in a sequence that draws heavily on *Abbott and Costello Meet Frankenstein* (1948).

Despite such reservations, Jerry Franken was the only contemporary critic to publish a detailed review of *Starring Boris Karloff* – or at least, its debut episode – which serves to confirm the show's credentials as a work of all-out psychological horror and to highlight that the revisions to the television version could extend as far as changes to the actual story if these would deliver a powerful pictorial effect (in the case of the opening episode, the spectacle of Karloff approaching the gallows):

> "Five Golden Guineas" was the title and the story is a morbid, implausible, malodorous item about a man with a psychotic compulsion to be a hangman and who eventually hangs his own son. In his lust to hang he destroys a letter proving the son's innocence. The endings differed in the two media. In radio the hangman destroys himself when he is told by his wife – who left him before the child was born when appraised of his calling – what he has done. In the TV version he kills his wife in a frenzied rage and in turn walks to the gallows where he himself officiated for so many years.[21]

As much as Franken expresses unambiguous disdain for the Robert Stephen Brode script, writing that "a more distressing vehicle for the dual premiere couldn't be imagined," he nevertheless praises a number of elements of the television adaptation. Although finding director Charles Warburton's radio presentation "dull, unimaginative and plodding, burdened by an overdose of narration," Franken thought that Alex Segal's television version, "while essentially static, was effectively lighted and directed and maintained, in general, a satisfactory fluidity."[22] Incidentally, the hangman's wife in "Five Golden Guineas" was portrayed by Mildred Natwick, a future Martha Brewster opposite Karloff and Tony Randall in the 1962 *Hallmark Hall of Fame* television rendition of *Arsenic and Old Lace*.

Aside from Jerry Franken, it's also fair to assume that writer and humorist William Ritt (the co-creator with artist Clarence Gray of the comic strip *Brick Bradford*) was paying at least a modicum of attention to the presence of *Starring Boris Karloff* on television. On September 20, 1949, archaeologists at the American Museum of Natural History in New York had generated copious nationwide newspaper and newsreel coverage when they unwrapped a Peruvian mummy.[23] Quipped Ritt in his September 27 column for the *Los Angeles Times*: "Now that Boris Karloff has become a video star, he might find a job for the defunct Inca in his TV cast."[24]

A copy of the radio version of "Five Golden Guineas" is preserved in the collection of the Paley Center for Media. However, not a single episode of the television version is believed to have survived. This means that it is impossible for us to envisage exactly what form Karloff's opening hosting may have taken. Given that it was a live presentation, it might well have been staged on one of the sets that would later be seen in the episode, just as was the case for Karloff's final television anthology series hosting gig in 1962 on *Out of This World* for British commercial television. Whether the actor's approach was earnestly prosaic, merely introducing the story and players, or a little more playful, abstract or bombastic, we may never know.

It is possible, though, to glean some insight into the subject matter of individual episodes and to thereby gain a better idea of just how horror-tinged the series as a whole may have been. A contemporary synopsis reveals that in "Mad Illusion," Karloff appeared as an escapee from the Devil's Island penal colony, hell-bent on exacting revenge on those who caused him to be incarcerated there. A playful teaser line for the show described the episode as being "set on Devil's Island and in a French boudoir."[25] In "False Face" meanwhile, Karloff portrayed a matinee idol whose looks are destroyed in a car crash; after unsuccessfully resorting to plastic surgery, the one-time star goes insane.[26] The Halloween episode "The Devil Takes a Wife" was described in a teaser as "a half hour with ghouls and guns."[27] In fact, it was an adaptation of an existing radio play by Gibson Scott Fox, previously produced as the December 8, 1946, installment of the Mutual Broadcasting System series *The Shadow*, in which a phony haunting in a Louisiana bayou serves as a cover for crime and murder. "Mungahara," as the title was rendered in all radio and television listings, was promoted as "a story of voodoo,

Starring Boris Karloff's radio version, *Wilkes-Barre* (PA) *Evening News*, October 12, 1949.

Karloff and Julie Harris brought their Broadway play *The Lark* to NBC-TV on Sunday, February 10, 1957 – and were shellacked ratings-wise by that night's CBS lineup, including *Alfred Hitchcock Presents*.

pearl divers and gold mining."[28] Actually it was just a curious respelling (or misspelling) of "Munghara," an existing radio play by Arch Oboler that had originally been performed on September 2, 1939, before being used as the October 27, 1942, episode of NBC's *Lights Out* with Oboler hosting. This time Karloff played a greedy English adventurer who steals a valuable pearl from a diver. The latter incants a voodoo curse, according to which the adventurer will die three days after he reaches London; this duly occurs, albeit with a strong indication that nothing more than the power of suggestion was at work.[29] If nothing else, all of these roles would surely have afforded Karloff the opportunity for some fervorous, emotionally charged enactments of psychological collapse, despair and delusion.

As for the last-but-one episode of *Starring Boris Karloff*, "The Shop at Sly Corner," it was a cut-down version of Edward Percy's stage play about a seemingly respectable Frenchman in London, Desciuss Heiss, who operates an antique shop as a front for his criminal and underworld activities. The play had run for two years in London's West End from 1945, and was brought to the U.S. in late 1948, with Karloff taking on the Heiss role.

As he had related to Hedda Hopper in her December 1, 1948, column: "I play the part of an old Alsatian fence for thieves. The man commits a few murders, but he's such a nice old dear that you just can't help hoping that he gets away with it all." Following a two-week tryout at Boston's Wilbur Theatre commencing on Christmas Day 1948, the production moved to Broadway's Booth Theatre where it played for precisely seven performances between January 18 and 22, 1949. Perhaps aimed a little too strongly at British tastes and mores, *The Shop at Sly Corner* had proved a terrible flop.[30] Yet as its inclusion in *Starring Boris Karloff* indicates, Brit abroad Karloff apparently still believed in its worth as late as December 1949.

When its commissioned 13-week run came to an end, *Starring Boris Karloff*'s slot in the ABC-TV schedule was quietly taken over by Wendy Barrie's celebrity talk show *Photoplay Time*. There was no public or press outcry; like so many ephemeral endeavors in early television, it was forgotten almost as soon as it was no longer on the screen. And throughout the course of Karloff's subsequent engagements as a television series host, neither he nor anyone else would refer back to this initial experience of working in that capacity.

2. Rejected: *Tales of Frankenstein* (1957-58, ABC/Screen Gems)

As the 1950s dawned, Karloff remained a regular and welcome face on television. He continued to undertake guest turns on variety and entertainment shows that were at the absolute zenith of their popularity, making repeat appearances on *The Milton Berle Show* and *The Ernie Kovacs Show* for NBC, and on *Frankie Laine Time* and *The Red Skelton Show* for CBS. The actor starred on CBS's *Suspense* a further three times, in the Yuletide mystery "The Lonely Place" on December 25, 1951; as Rasputin in the March 17, 1953, episode "The Black Robe"; and in the ghostly Charles Dickens adaptation "The Signal-Man" on June 23, 1953. The considerable number of other drama anthology series on which he appeared included CBS's *Climax!* hosted by William Lundigan and ABC's science fiction-focused *Tales of Tomorrow*. He also memorably headlined on the latter network's *The Elgin TV Hour*, in the killer bee-themed February 22, 1955, episode "The Sting of Death," adapted from H.F. Heard's 1941 novel *A Taste of Honey*. But Karloff additionally essayed roles in a significant body of dramas that fell well outside the realm of horror, mystery or suspense. On NBC these included both the experimental blank-verse western "Even the Weariest River," broadcast as the April 15, 1956, episode of *The Alcoa Hour*, and a *Hallmark Hall of Fame* reprisal of his Tony Award-nominated role as Cauchon alongside Julie Harris' Joan of Arc in French playwright Jean Anouilh's "The Lark," broadcast on February 10, 1957.[31]

Karloff furthermore starred in a half-hour filmed drama series of his own, *Colonel March of Scotland Yard*, produced by Fountain Films in England under American producer Hannah Weinstein. Categorizing the 26-episode series as "drama/mystery," Official Films offered it for syndication in the U.S. as early as October 5, 1953,[32] with the show debuting on DuMont Network affiliate WDTV (now KDKA-TV) in Pittsburgh on January 27, 1954, before also joining the line-up on ABC-affiliated WKBK (now WLS-TV) in Chicago from February 18, and on about-to-turn-independent[33] station KTTV in Los Angeles from March 6. The program's title led several entertainment journalists to assume that it would be a straightforward detective show. A letter from one "W.L. of Buffalo" to Steven H. Scheuer's "TV Key" column of December 4, 1953, enquired of Karloff's "TV series on film": "Is it going to be a horror show? I hope so. I love a good murder." The punning response read: "Sorry to disappoint you, fiend – er, friend – but Boris will be on the right side of the law in this one, playing *Colonel March of Scotland Yard*. Better luck next crime."[34] Eve Starr, in her syndicated "Inside TV" column of January 26, 1954 – published the day before the series made its debut in Pittsburgh – meanwhile pondered whether if mightn't be better for Karloff to "scare up a few shivers as narrator on a horror show."

In fact, *Colonel March of Scotland Yard* was a paranormal-themed series, with Karloff embodying noted mystery writer John Dickson Carr's title character as a frankly unconventional, eyepatch-wearing precursor to *The X-Files*' Mulder and Scully.

Employed by D3, Scotland Yard's Department of Queer Complaints, March went up against locked-room mysteries, an apparent Abominable Snowman and other such supernatural-tinged matters as ghosts and sorcery in the course of his duties. Advertising on stations that picked up the show early referred to its star as "the new Boris Karloff," implying a break from the old-dark-house and monster movie aesthetics of earlier times (in the actor's career) and a move toward

"The new Boris Karloff," *Pittsburgh* (PA) *Post-Gazette*, January 27, 1954.

the contemporary and a rational, science-based approach to the seemingly unexplainable. This shift from "old school" scares to modern-day metaphysics would find its articulation even more strongly in Karloff's participation as host and performer on *The Veil*.

However, before that could happen, "the old Boris Karloff" suddenly returned with a vengeance ahead of the fall 1957 television season when Screen Gems released its "Shock!" package of 52 pre-1948 Universal horror movies including *Frankenstein* (1931), *The Mummy* (1932) and *The Raven* (1935). Sales to major metropolitan stations such as WABC-TV in New York, WCAU-TV in Philadelphia, KTLA in Los Angeles and KRON-TV in San Francisco proved rapid and profitable.[35] Associated Artists Productions quickly jumped aboard with its own "Horrors" package of 52 lesser (and previously-seen-on-TV) features comprising such fare as Monogram's *The Ape* (1940) starring Karloff. From early October 1957, these tens of vintage horrors started to be rolled out in special slots, giving rise to the whole "Shock Theater," Monster Kid and horror host phenomenon on a nationwide scale. The trade magazine *Broadcasting•Telecasting* commented, "Boris Karloff and Bela Lugosi, 'horror' twins of the movies some years ago, may be headed for second stardom via tv features."[36] Perhaps such a remark offers some insight into why Karloff was initially far from enthused to see his old pictures revived on the small screen. Throughout his career following World War II in particular, he had consistently striven to embrace new media, to select projects that offered new approaches to subjects and situations, and above all to remain current.[37] These old Universal films provided audiences with a view of Karloff that was 20 or more years out of alignment with his self-image and his sense of accomplishment, with the barely disguised implication that this all constituted a comeback for the actor essentially effacing his entire prolific postwar output. And associating himself with these revived movies in the here and now of 1957 could only represent a backward step.

At the same time, the horror genre was garnering further attention thanks to Britain's Hammer Films, whose Eastmancolor *The Curse of Frankenstein* with Peter Cushing and Christopher Lee had been released in the United States by Warner Bros. on June 25, 1957.[38]

Various parties considered how they might be able to utilize Karloff in order to ride this "horror wave," as *Television Digest* dubbed the phenomenon in its October 26, 1957 edition.[39] Producers Richard Gordon and Charles Vetter Jr. briefly toyed with the idea of starring Karloff in a new color CinemaScope production of *Dracula*, tentatively titled *Dracula's Revenge*. Larry Wolters, in his September 7, 1957, "TV Ticker" column for the *Chicago Daily Tribune*, linked the project directly to the "Shock!" package: "There are three *Dracula* pictures in the group of 'horror' films just released for TV by Screen Gems: the original 1931 production with **Bela Lugosi**; *Dracula's Daughter*, produced in 1936; and *Son of Dracula* with **Lon Chaney**, vintage 1943. And **Boris Karloff** is about to come back in a screen remake, *Dracula's Revenge*." Erskine Johnson's syndicated "Hollywood Today" column of September 12, 1957, likewise managed to convey the impression that the project represented both a comeback and a return to decades-old past glories for its star, under the rubric "Boris Karloff returning to his first love – horror movies." As Richard Gordon later related, Karloff was actually only interested in *Dracula's Revenge* so long as it offered a faithful interpretation of its literary source, presenting "the story more or less as it was in the Bram Stoker novel."[40] Copyright issues with Universal sunk the project anyway, with Vetter and Gordon instead starring Karloff in *Corridors of Blood*, whose realist, science-focused approach to its nevertheless horror-themed depiction of events surrounding the discovery of modern medical anesthesia proved much more in line with "the new Boris Karloff." Indeed, the ever-focused-on-the-present actor would declare it his favorite film role to date in a January 1959 interview with James Bacon of the Associated Press.[41]

The unleasher of the "Shock!" package, Screen Gems, meanwhile approached Karloff with a proposal to undertake the second television anthology drama series hosting engagement of his career on a 39-episode compendium of horror tales to be co-produced with Hammer Films and titled *Tales of Frankenstein*. The announcement of Karloff's participation was widely reported in specialist and mainstream publications alike during the final two weeks of September 1957, although there was some confusion about whether he was to "serve as host but…not act in the new teleseries," as maintained by columnist Mike Connolly of *The Pasadena Independent* and in TV trade journal *Sponsor*[42], or else "host and occasionally star," as asserted by columnist Ann Wardell Saunders of the *San Bernardino Sun-Telegram* and in *The Billboard* and *Broadcasting•Telecasting*.[43]

Either way, all these publications were dealing merely in hypotheticals, since Karloff flat-out rejected the notion of working on *Tales of Frankenstein*, unimpressed by Screen Gems' clichéd (and ultimately decidedly vague) planned approach to presenting half-hour "stories of the supernatural, demonology and imagination mystery, all within the framework of the concept represented by the name of 'Frankenstein.'"[44] Story suggestions involving 'mutations, voodoo and cryogenics' drawn up for Hammer by Jimmy Sangster which might have helped modernize the show in a way that appealed to 'the new Boris Karloff,' were meanwhile dismissed out of hand by Screen Gems[45] even though Hammer had originally been lined up to shoot 19 episodes at Bray Studios.[46]

Whatever pent-up ire Karloff may have been harboring at this point rose to the surface – after a very decent, British fashion, of course – in an interview he gave to Marie Torres for her syndicated *New York Herald Tribune* television column of December 16, 1957:

> I'm afraid that the men pushing the thrillers are in for a rude awakening. The Frankensteins and the Draculas were all right in their day, but now they're rather old-fashioned, just a curiosity. We've all moved ahead since the Frankenstein era. While television finds that out for itself, I'll go along my merry way in motion pictures… I think there could be a place in television today for horror shows if they were brought up to date and done in a proper vein. But, if I know the television people, they will try and play it safe, as they usually do, and make those shows an exact copy of the old movies. Just recently, there was some discussion about my appearing in a TV series called *Tales of Frankenstein*. It didn't appeal to me very much. I rejected it because I failed to see where it had a future. It would have been just another anthology series, and I would not do a series just for the sake of doing

one. One has to have, you know, responsibility to oneself as well as to the viewer… I have four motion pictures lined up from January on. By the time I finish with them, I imagine television will have had its fill of those so-called horror shows.

Reader Dick Cole was distinctly unimpressed by Karloff's remarks and shot off a response to television columnist Harry Harris of *The Philadelphia Inquirer*:

> Boris Karloff fails to see a future for the horror pix and states, "We've moved ahead since the Frankenstein era." Yet Mr. Karloff will star in the movie *Frankenstein 1960*. If he feels the monsters are old-fashioned and out of date, why is he making this picture? Mr. K. should stick to his specialty, horror, and not guest-haunting on TV programs.[47]

Don Megowan in *Tales of Frankenstein, Sponsor*, July 1958

Evidently Dick Cole wasn't particularly sensitive to the nuanced distinctions between retreading past successes ("the old Boris Karloff") and embracing more contemporary, more science-fictional propositions such as Aubrey Schenck and Howard W. Koch's *Frankenstein 1960*, ultimately released as the even more futuristic-sounding *Frankenstein 1970* (1958) with "the new Boris Karloff" reassuringly billed on posters as "The One… The Only KING OF THE MONSTERS as the new demon of the atomic age!" However, Cole had one final zinger left for Karloff: "As for *Tales of Frankenstein*, if Screen Gems is still looking for a star, how about Roland – a natch for the job!"[48] It had only been a couple of months since local horror host Roland, embodied by John Zacherle, had first been stationed in his studio crypt at WCAU-TV in Philadelphia to present movies from the "Shock!" package, and already Cole considered him to be more than a match for Karloff's quarter-century tenure in the horror genre. As discussed later, the eye-rolling, tongue-in-cheek approach of TV horror hosts would go on to impact on Karloff's most successful engagement as television anthology series host on NBC's *Thriller*; and no matter how unintentionally and obliquely, Philly's Dick Cole was the first to imply that the presenting style of local horror hosts might have some repercussions for established genre actors.

Meanwhile, with much-reduced input from Hammer, Screen Gems plowed on with producing an $80,000 pilot for *Tales of Frankenstein* in Hollywood titled "The Face in the Tombstone Mirror." With a script by Henry Kuttner (co-author with his wife Catherine Lucille Moore of the 1942 science fiction short story "The Twonky"), the pilot was directed by former 1940s Universal screenwriter Curt Siodmak and starred Anton Diffring as Baron Frankenstein and Don Megowan as the Monster. In Erskine Johnson's syndicated "In Hollywood" column for Valentine's Day 1958 – bearing the unduly optimistic headline "*Tales of Frankenstein* Heads for Home Screens" – Siodmak surely didn't appear to be penning a love note to Karloff when he declared that the show's monster "[i]s going to be more human and less horrible than the old Boris Karloff characterization."

The comment proved rather ironic, since in the finished product Megowan's Monster strongly resembles the old Universal conceptualization. Just as Karloff had feared, "The Face in the Tombstone Mirror" offered up an unoriginal and uninspired Frankenstein tale that seemed to be stuck in the 1940s; perhaps that was precisely what Screen Gems had hoped for, to emulate the style of the movies in its "Shock!" package. As for the show's host, "he" was now an unholy hybrid of stock footage of David Hoffman as "The Spirit of the Inner Sanctum" lifted from Universal's 1940s Inner Sanctum movie series and new, unsynchronized narration. As late as April 1958, *Tales of Frankenstein* was still being vaunted as a fall release that would air on ABC at 10 p.m. on Saturdays.[49] After it failed to materialize, the official line was that the series "couldn't find a sponsor"[50]. In reality, Screen Gems simply lacked a cohesive strategy for developing the show and proved unable to reach any kind of agreement with Hammer's creative

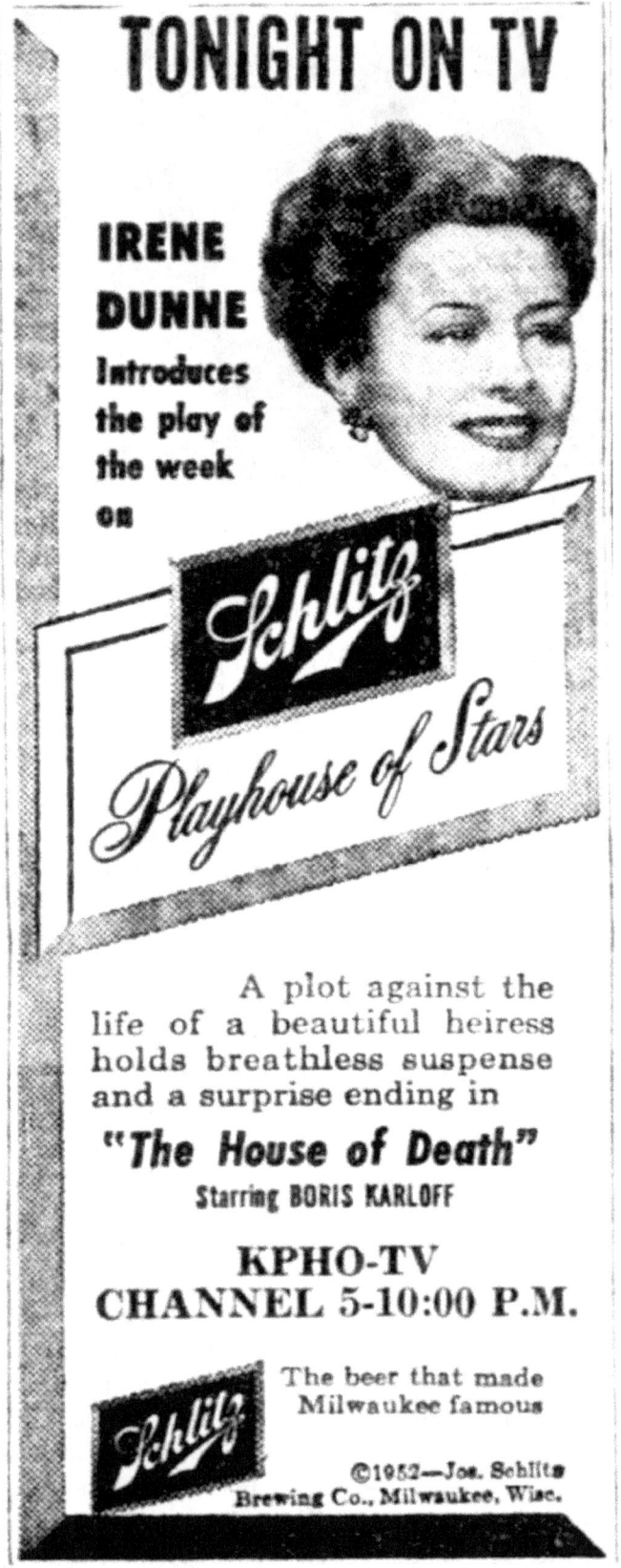

Karloff on *Schlitz Playhouse of Stars*, *The Arizona Republic* (Phoenix AZ), July 8, 1952.

team.[51] The pilot was eventually broadcast with no fanfare whatsoever as the November 16, 1960, episode in the third season of Screen Gems' *The Award Theater* drama anthology series.

3. Unseen: *The Veil* (1958-59, Hal Roach Studios/Guild Films)

In Marie Torres' December 16, 1957, column in which Karloff politely but firmly distanced himself from the ongoing small-screen horror wave, she commented:

> In the television frenzy to snare Karloff for anything that smacks of the eerie, he was approached to front a series having to do with psychic phenomena. But that, too, he dismissed because it was to be nothing more than the same old horror fare.

This may be a reference to a proposed filmed half-hour docudrama show by producer Martha Rountree that was to have Karloff narrate the histories of "authentic haunted houses" in the United States and Europe.[52] However, it might equally well refer to Frank P. Bibas' *The Veil*, indicating that the actor at that time had yet to be persuaded of the projected series' faithful, up-to-date and rationalist approach to presenting the purportedly authentic cases it would dramatize[53], in order for it to fall in line with the nuanced precepts of "the new Boris Karloff."[54]

If the latter is indeed the case, then Karloff must have been reassured extremely swiftly, since just two days after Torres' column was published, he signed a contract to host, narrate and perform in *The Veil* for Hal Roach Studios that would give him a paycheck of $2000 per half-hour episode plus a further $1000 per episode when the show was rerun in syndication.[55] Of course, if he had entertained even the vaguest notion of the precarious state of the studios' finances, he might have changed his mind again. As it was, Eve Starr declared in her April 3, 1958, "Inside TV" column that Karloff was "very much enthused over the project." When the actor subsequently stood in for Starr on her November 24, 1958 column[56], reproduced at the beginning of this volume, he expressed further excitement that "[f]or the first time in my life I'm acting as narrator and host of an entire series." A statement that was true insofar as he had not *narrated* the earlier *Starring Boris Karloff*.

Trade magazine *Sponsor* noted in its May 3, 1958, edition: "A recent Schwerin research study reports that a male host evoked a higher liking for a half-hour drama than did a female narrator for the same show."

A scant five inches down the page, the publication announced that Boris Karloff was to host "*The Veil*, a dramatic anthology of true mysteries."[57] Certainly there had always been a conspicuous gender imbalance in the area of drama anthology series hosting, with Karloff's name here appended to a male-led bastion that – in the years between 1950 and 1958 – also included Robert Montgomery (NBC's *Robert Montgomery Presents*), Ronald Reagan (CBS's *General Electric Theater*), Douglas Fairbanks Jr. (NBC's *Douglas Fairbanks Jr. Presents*), Adolphe Menjou (Ziv-TV's *Your Favorite Story* and the suspense-horror series *Target*), Gig Young (ABC's *Warner Bros. Presents*) and, widely regarded as head of the field, Alfred Hitchcock (CBS's *Alfred Hitchcock Presents*). There were some notable exceptions such as NBC's *The Loretta Young Show*, which would ultimately run for eight seasons from 1953 to 1961, picking up multiple Primetime Emmys and a Golden Globe along the way; and the same network's Primetime Emmy-nominated *Jane Wyman Presents: The Fireside Theatre*, running for three seasons from 1955 to 1958.

But other female hosts struggled to get – and then keep – their foot in the door. Karloff had signed up to appear on the Fourth of July 1952 suspense drama episode "The House of Death" for *Irene Dunne's Play of the Week*; by the time the show aired, Dunne's name had been expunged from the title, with the series now known as *Schlitz Playhouse of Stars*.[58] A proposed 1959 whodunit anthology series for ABC, *This Is Murder* with Ida Lupino as host, went unrealized.[59] And despite picking up a Primetime Emmy for "Outstanding Performance by an Actress in a Series," *The Barbara Stanwyck Show* would be promptly jettisoned by NBC after a single season running from the fall of 1960 through the summer of 1961…in order to make space in the schedule for a second season of the Karloff-hosted *Thriller*![60]

A further television drama-related "finding" disseminated by Horace Schwerin's market research company at this time involved the question of "What makes a good horror program?" Schwerin's published four-point outline in fact corresponded closely to the content, approach and subject matter of the imminently forthcoming paranormal-themed *The Veil*:

1) Plots in which **ordinary, likable people** get fouled up in supernatural situations are best received.

2) **Psychopathic characters don't go over very well.**

3) For maximum impact, the precise supernatural circumstances should **thread through the plot from start to finish** – not [be] sprung as a final surprise.

4) The supernatural elements should have **some connection with reality** – even if only the figments of someone's imagination. Yarns which turn out to be mere dreams or nightmares apparently strike the viewer as too weak or fraudulent.[61]

Production of *The Veil* would be beset from the start by cost-cutting measures. Although Eve Starr seemed elated to be able to report in her April 3, 1958, column that "Roach has already completed the first film of a new Boris Karloff series, *The Veil*," the supposed pilot episode in question, titled "The Vestris," was in reality nothing more than a repurposing of the February 25, 1958, episode of ABC's Roach-produced filmed anthology series *Telephone Time*, in which Karloff had guest-starred (to great effect) as a ghostly apparition aboard a ship at sea, warning of impending doom and causing the vessel to change course – only for it to then happen upon him as the survivor of a shipwreck. The original *Telephone Time* "Vestris" featured the era's favorite television educator, erudite and affable Dr. Frank Baxter; to turn the episode into the *Veil* pilot, the Baxter footage was discarded with the intention of inserting a new sequence with Karloff as host in its place. Astoundingly, 'The Vestris' would be repurposed *sans* Frank Baxter yet again as the August 15, 1958 episode of *Tales of E.S.P.*, a mind-boggling ABC summer replacement series hosted by Vincent Price that had debuted on July 11 under the title *E.S.P.* as a quiz show offering cash prizes to contestants who could demonstrate 'the sixth sense,' before transforming after four episodes into *Tales of E.S.P.*, showing repeats of paranormal-themed dramas – in which revised format it endured for precisely three more episodes through August 22.[62]

ABC's evanescent (*Tales of*) *E.S.P.* nevertheless points to the fact that *The Veil* wasn't the only TV production of 1958-59 to deal in the paranormal. Indeed, by addressing themes otherwise broached in the likes of Morey Bernstein's past life regression-themed bestseller *The Search for Bridey Murphy*, that book's movie adaptation by Paramount and the Universal-International variant *I've Lived Before* (all 1956), *The Veil* in many ways constituted part of a distinct strand of programming to that which was more directly inspired by the "Shock!" horror phenomenon, even though the latter also helped to fuel industry and audience interest in such excursions into the paranormal.

As the filming of regular episodes of *The Veil* commenced at Hal Roach Studios in October 1958 for an intended spring 1959 release, ABC was already lining up its paranormal drama series *One Step Beyond* created by writers Merwin Gerard and Larry Marcus, producer Collier Young and director John Newland, who would also serve as the series' host. Just like *The Veil*, *One Step Beyond* sought to eschew "old school" horror approaches in its dramatizations of authentic cases drawn from "the untapped field of psychic phenomena – telepathy and supernatural occurrences like possession." Entertainment journalist Charles Witbeck visited the creative team behind *One Step Beyond* ahead of his January 20, 1959, syndicated "TV Keynotes" column, published on the day of the series' premiere, and concluded, "Writers Gerard and Marcus have sufficient source material. Gerard estimates there are about 8000 books on psychic phenomena available." Gerard further informed Witbeck: "The stories we're using have been documented and checked. They aren't old wives' tales." Newland added: "We're going to play the stories straight. We're not going to scare with the mood, trick lighting or spider webs. We're endeavoring to show reality. We will never use Boris Karloff." In this latter statement, Newland – who would go on to direct four episodes of the Karloff-hosted *Thriller* during 1961-62, including the outstanding "Pigeons from Hell" – was clearly envisaging the actor exclusively in terms of "the old Boris Karloff," too synonymous with the pre-war Universal approach to the supernatural to be of any use to *One Step Beyond*. It must be said that Karloff's performances in *The Veil* – and indeed, *Colonel March of Scotland Yard* before it – indicate that "the new Boris Karloff" was far more deeply involved in the drive for realism and breaking away from spider webs than Newland gave him credit for on this occasion.

Meanwhile, on December 4, 1958, shooting also commenced on the pilot for Rod Serling's *The Twilight Zone*, with the series ultimately making its debut as part of the fall 1959 CBS roll-out. Early descriptions of the show's concept are couched in terms which seem essentially indistinguishable from those employed in outlining *The Veil*, with *The Twilight Zone* characterized as a collection of "dramas with a stranger-than-fiction theme" intended to explore "that area of man's experience which is startling, unpredictable and sometimes unexplainable."[63]

In his capacity as host of *The Veil*, Karloff does not simply appear as himself. Although he addresses the audience in the first person, he never identifies himself by name and seems rather to be equal parts Karloff and Colonel March, the embodiment of a paranormal researcher with years of experience in the field. At the end of "Girl on the Road," Karloff's host asserts, "In my pursuit of these strange and unusual happenings, I've come across several other such occurrences." At the beginning of "No Food on the Table," he informs us that the incidents depicted are "like many others which I've come across in the course of my research." And in "The Doctor," he concludes with: "Time and again in my research, I've encountered reports of cases of this kind." The host's professional status is further connoted by the sets on which he appears: an imposing, castle-like room where he clutches onto what might be a rare volume of arcane literature in the episodes produced by Bibas; and a well-appointed and somewhat quirky study and office in the final two episodes produced under Hal Roach executive Ben Fox. In portraying this not-quite-Karloff host, the actor's manner remains engaging and friendly enough but still quite appropriately conveys an impression that viewers are in the presence of a knowledgeable, authoritative yet slightly unconventional academic type. At the same time, the perpetually roaring flames of the fire in the hosting segments of the Bibas episodes hint at a certain otherworldliness.

Unbeknown to the outside world, by the time *The Veil* went before the cameras, Hal Roach Studios were positively hemorrhaging money, posting a net loss of $534,568 for the period from September 1 to December 20, 1958.[64] Some of the budgetary restrictions imposed on *The Veil* worked to its advantage. As would also be the case with *Thriller*, instead of big stars, it featured a cavalcade of (more affordable) up-and-coming talents and established character actors, including in the former category George Hamilton, Robert Hardy and Patrick Macnee, and in the latter Morris Ankrum, Whit Bissell, Myron Healey and Katherine Squire.

On occasion, though, the underlying cheapness – and associated frenetic pace of the shooting schedule – bled through onto the screen, not least in Karloff's hosting sequences whose uncorrected imperfections at times cause them to resemble a live presentation rather than anything created for a filmed series. During the opening of the Bibas episodes, when Karloff says "Tonight I'm going to tell you another strange and unusual story of the unexplainable which lies behind the Veil," a microphone creeps up into the shot in front of him; this piece of footage is nevertheless reused in eight different episodes. Karloff can also be seen momentarily looking down at something off-screen (perhaps a cue card) and then blinking uncontrollably as he asks viewers to "Please join me again for another journey into the world of the unexplainable which lies behind the Veil"; this substandard take is similarly employed at the

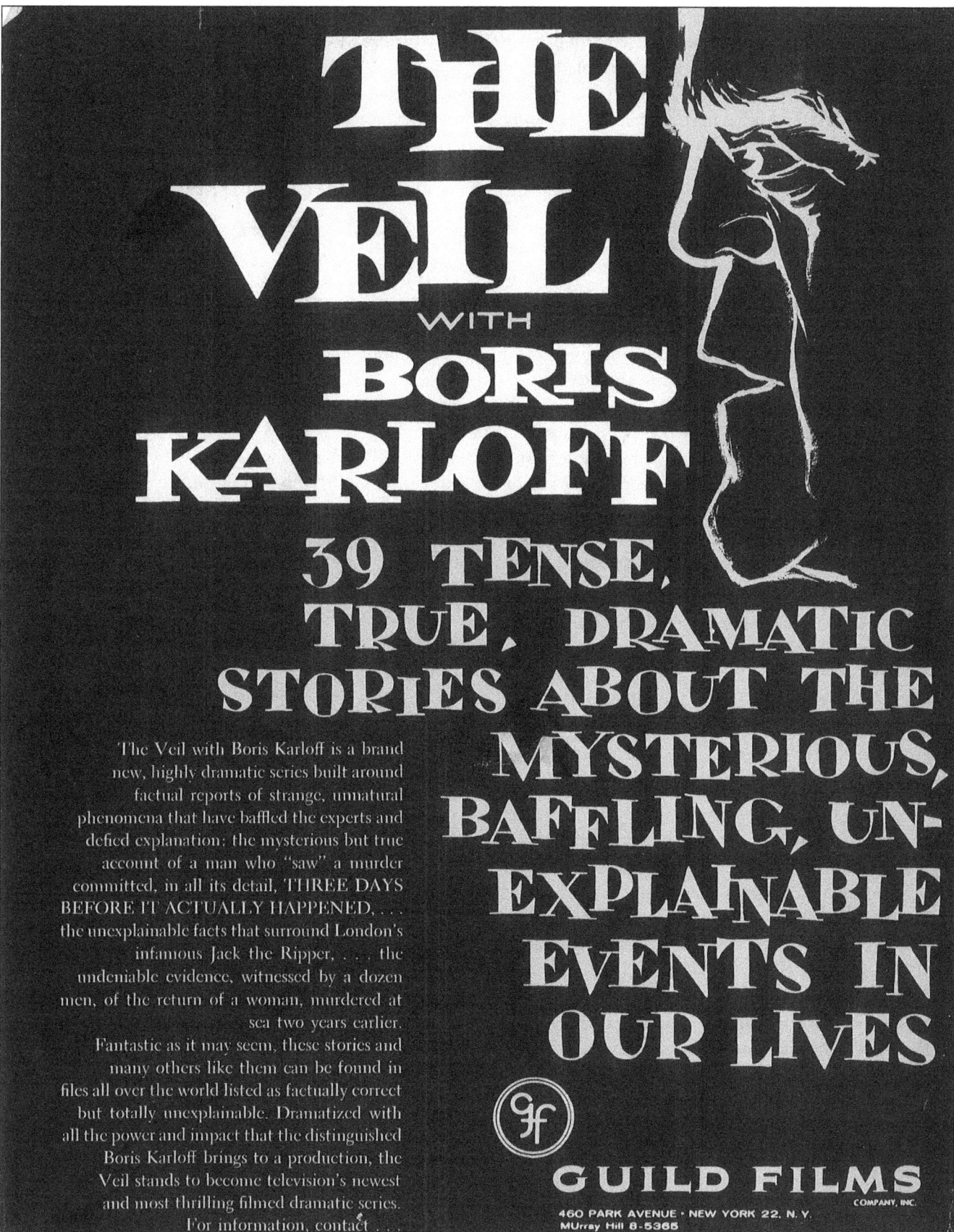

Guild Films trade flyer for *The Veil*, circa February–March 1959.

close of multiple episodes. The Bibas hosting sequences are furthermore shot from an extremely limited number of fixed, static camera positions; only in the Ben Fox episodes "Destination Nightmare" and "Peggy" is there a (welcome and relieving) shift to fluid, mobile camerawork in the host's office and study. In some of the Bibas installments, Karloff's hosting additionally seems to serve less to inform or entertain than to pad out an episode that had come in under length. While an average episode contains something in the region of one and a quarter minutes of Karloff actively hosting, in "The Doctor" he rattles on for three minutes and 18 seconds; and this in addition to the one minute and six seconds taken up by the standard opening and closing shots in which the camera dollies into and out of Karloff's fireplace-dominated hosting set.

After the demise of Hal Roach Studios caused the completed episodes to be vaulted, with Karloff unsuccessfully attempting to recoup the loss of tens of thousands of dollars of contractually agreed pay, a widely carried United Press International news item first published on May 13, 1959, summed up the sorry situation:

> Boris Karloff put in several weeks on a projected TV series that may never see the light. Ten half-hour dramatic films under the general title of *The Veil*, an extra-sensory perception series, were completed at the Hal Roach Studio in Hollywood. But then all work was stopped at the studio… Karloff has gone to his native England to establish a home but not to retire.[65]

Following this, *The Veil* would scarcely be mentioned again in mainstream, trade or fan publications. The unseen series quite unexpectedly resurfaced on TV – recut as three anthology features – at the end of the 1970s; up until then, the only place where Karloff's hosting of it could be glimpsed for a while was in the January 31, 1959, episode[66] of the Hal Roach Studios-produced half-hour comedy *The Gale Storm Show*, "It's Murder, My Dear," which continued to play in syndication until the end of the summer 1962 television season. Advance coverage of the episode by Erskine Johnson in his December 22, 1958, "Hollywood Today" column had described it as "a nice little plug for the new Karloff series." In "It's Murder, My Dear," Storm and ZaSu Pitts visit the Hal Roach Studios and watch the filming of one of Karloff's hosting sequences for *The Veil*, only for the actor to suddenly be incapacitated by an unhinged lookalike (Karloff in a Jonathan Brewster-tinged dual role) who feels that his own acting career has been held back by his resemblance to Karloff; the double now takes Karloff's place before *The Veil*'s cameras. Needless to say, the redoubtable Storm-Pitts comedy duo succeeds in restoring the real Karloff to his rightful position: a fictional happy ending for what had otherwise devolved into a disappointing fiasco within the actor's career as television series host.

4. Vilified: *Thriller* debuts (September 1960, NBC)

With *Starring Boris Karloff* forgotten and *The Veil* unseen, it is perhaps no wonder that Karloff's engagement as host of *Thriller*, a new Hubbell Robinson-produced hour-long crime-mystery-suspense anthology show for NBC's fall 1960 season, ended up being (mis)described in the press as "his first role as host of a TV series."[67]

Hubbell Robinson was an illustrious former program director at CBS, who had ultimately risen to executive vice-president at the network, producing such phenomenally popular, long-running and award-winning anthology series as *Studio One*, *Climax!* and *Playhouse 90*. (Karloff had appeared more than once on all three.) Robinson had stepped down in 1959 to form his own television company, Hubbell Robinson Productions.

News of Karloff's hosting role on the forthcoming *Thriller* was announced in mid-February 1960, just after the actor had delivered a forceful, "critically applauded" performance in the live February 10 installment of CBS's previously Robinson-produced *Playhouse 90*. In the World War I romantic drama "To the Sound of Trumpets," scripted by 1959 Academy Award nominee John Gay[68], Karloff had what he described to TV and radio writer Win Fanning of the *Pittsburgh Post-Gazette* as "a tough assignment" of "having to come on in the last act," declaring that live TV "keeps you on your toes."[69] The messy outcome to his hosting gig on *The Veil* and resettling in England clearly hadn't stilled the septuagenarian's appetite for a stateside acting challenge.

The motivation behind the production of *Thriller* – and the choice of Karloff as host – could be accounted for in two words: Alfred Hitchcock. NBC had made a deal to poach the high-rating *Alfred Hitchcock Presents* from CBS; news of this was likewise first announced in mid-February 1960.[70] Desiring a companion anthology series with which it could create a block of mystery-suspense drama programming to fill a single evening's line-up, NBC commissioned *Thriller*. Thanks to his well-regarded long association with the genre, his unmistakably British manner and perhaps also his age and white-haired appearance, the 72-year-old Karloff may have struck Robinson as an ideal match for the eponymous 60-year-old host of *Alfred Hitchcock Presents*, a kind of Hitchcock-with-less-avoirdupois. At any rate, a contract was swiftly signed: Karloff would "receive $2500 for each episode, above-the-title billing, plus an additional fee if he also featured in the drama."[71]

Hitchcock's "wry introductory and breaktime remarks" during his tongue-in-cheek hosting segments had become the stuff of telelegend almost as soon as the filmed half-hour show debuted in October 1955.[72] Some advance coverage had couched its descriptions of "Hollywood's master of suspense" in more or less horror movie-like terms, with *Motion Picture Daily* for example asserting that Hitchcock "will bring his eerie and dramatic talents to television" and that "Mr. Hitchcock has contracted for suspense, the macabre and the humorous."[73] By the time *TV Radio Mirror* handed out its tenth annual awards as chosen by readers for 1956-57, Hitchcock's "newcomer" show was able to secure a win in the "Favorite TV Mystery-Adventure Program" category on account of its "thrills and chills," with the publication noting, "It took viewers only one full season to discover that the most 'suspenseful' director of Hollywood movies was equally effective on CBS-TV screens."[74] In the lengthy and thoughtful article "The Horror 'Kick,'" published in the same magazine in May 1959, Charlotte Barclay argued that the playfully irreverent approach to murder and mayhem of Hitchcock-as-host, his inspired use of props and his very direct manner of addressing the audience and the whole televiewing experience, had effectively laid much of the groundwork for the manner and presentational style of such "Shock!"-induced horror hosts as WABC's New York-based Zacherley (John Zacherle) and KPTV's Portland, Oregon-based Tarantula Ghoul (Suzanne Waldron).[75] Even though there had been some earlier TV horror hosts, foremost among them the Los Angeles-based Vampira (Maila Nurmi), it was Hitchcock who had *popularized* such an impish and whimsical approach to hosting on the small screen.[76]

Karloff had a lot to measure up to, then, if he was going to come anywhere close to Hitchcock's towering accomplishments in the field of television hosting – which latter would now be seen immediately before his, with *Alfred Hitchcock Presents* scheduled for 8:30 p.m. and

Before Angelyne: Karloff-branded billboard for *Thriller*'s first season.

Thriller for 9 p.m. in the Tuesday night NBC schedule for fall 1960. There was also no doubt that just like *Alfred Hitchcock Presents*, *Thriller* would be marketed and publicized primarily on the strength of its host's name.

Once Karloff had been revealed as host of the forthcoming series, an assorted gaggle of journalists jumped in with assumptions of horror-type programming. "Boris Karloff will be host on the series, which should give you an idea of the type of entertainment involved," conjectured one syndicated story put out by United Press International.[77] "Wouldn't you call this perfect typecasting?" crowed Louella Parsons in her February 18, 1960, column. "K – K – Karloff," qu-qu-quivered the headline on the front cover of *The Daily Herald Weekly TV and Amusements Guide* in Provo, Utah, two weeks ahead of *Thriller*'s premiere, with a portrait of the actor looking sinister also adorning the page.[78] And even on the day that *Thriller* made its debut, Cecil Smith of *The Los Angeles Times* was still suggesting that viewers might require "an appetite for flesh-crawling," with NBC's Tuesday night rookie about "to give the nation the jitters" and "to put the country into a state of shock."[79]

There was only one problem: Horror simply wasn't part of *Thriller*'s brief. Instead, as Hubbell Robinson informed the *Pittsburgh Post-Gazette*'s Win Fanning, "We plan to produce quality thrillers picked for their entertainment value and their literary excellence." *Thriller* would feature "characters studied in depth" and scripts "which encompass creditability and a satisfying denouement involving normal people caught in terrifying circumstances." As for Karloff's hosting segments, these would "in a highly pictorial manner provid[e] a logical, even teasing, lead-in to the story." In respect of contemporary concerns about the possible effects of showing violence on television, the series would furthermore include "no pistol whippings, no unnecessary bloodshed, no basic violence."[80] Karloff expounded on this latter point in an interview with Aleene Barnes of the *Los Angeles Times* published two days ahead of *Thriller*'s premiere: "[O]ne thing you won't find on *Thriller* – violence for the sake of violence, shock for the sake of shock. The two skillful men who are in charge of this operation – Hubbell Robinson and Fletcher Markle – are going to prove that you can have all the suspense, mystery, adventure and excitement you could want without resorting to violence."[81]

As lofty as Robinson's concept may have sounded, his various statements were also riven by vagueness and ambiguity.[82] Behind the scenes, executive producer Robinson, producer Fletcher Markle and associate producer and story editor James P. Cavanagh couldn't agree on just what direction the program should take, with their divergent opinions still vacillating between crime, mystery, psychological thriller and suspense drama as episodes started to be filmed from late February 1960 onwards. *Thriller* had been commissioned without a pilot on the strength of Robinson's reputation[83]; and what was to follow perhaps serves as a useful object lesson on why it remains standard industry practice to shoot a pilot for prospective series, helping to sharpen and focus ideas and to identify individual elements that may or may not work. Karloff meanwhile remained a relative outsider to the show's production, since he was flown over from England to shoot all his initial hosting segments as a block in the space of a single day.

Regardless, publicity for what many entertainment journalists construed to be the "first major event of the new TV season"[84] continued to revolve almost exclusively around Karloff, with whom copious numbers of *Thriller*-focused interviews were conducted in various media. Dapper *Thriller*-branded promotional portraits of the actor ate up newspaper and magazine column inches from coast to coast and for the week of the show's premiere, the front cover of the *TV Times* supplement to the *Los Angeles Times* carried a sumptuous and striking full-page original sketch of Karloff, with an uncredited Natalie Trundy's eyes looming over him, by graphic artist Oliver French.[85] Even Karloff seems to have sensed a degree of overkill, emphasizing in an interview with Samuel L. Singer of *The Philadelphia Inquirer* that "the important thing is the television series. Talk about the thrillers, I'm just an incidental part of it." He could have saved his words, because when Singer's article on the show was published the day before the premiere, its headline soberly declared: "Boris Karloff to Host, Act in Thrill Series."[86]

One of the very few to signal any kind of apprehension ahead of *Thriller*'s debut was Bill Ladd of *The Courier-Journal* in Louisville, Kentucky, who expressed a cynical attitude toward anthology series hosts in general in the August 26, 1960, edition of his "TV Almanac" column:

> In most cases the host is just a name to draw a crowd. As an instance, there are already seven *Thriller* segments "in the can" for this fall. **Boris Karloff** is "host." He hasn't even gone to Hollywood to film his part yet!

Thriller's opening episode "The Twisted Image" went out at 9 p.m. on September 13, 1960. As it happened, *Alfred Hitchcock Presents* wouldn't join NBC's Tuesday evening line-up for another two weeks; while this meant that Karloff's hosting received a temporary reprieve from having to stand cheek to jowl with Hitchcock's, it left the series without a presentational context, a situation that had impacted negatively on the television version of *Starring Boris Karloff* 11 years earlier. Instead of forming part of a block of mystery-suspense drama programming, *Thriller* momentarily found itself dovetailing with such unpredictable fare as repeats of the cop show *M Squad* with Lee Marvin and a news (pronounced "snooze") special titled *Summary of U.N. Developments*.

Karloff's hosting segment at the beginning of "The Twisted Image" comprised 37 seconds of off-screen narration, followed by 58 seconds on screen – although for 20 seconds of this time, he rather alienatingly had his back turned to the audience at home, in particular while introducing the episode's lead players, "Mr. Leslie Nielsen, Mr. George Grizzard, Miss Natalie Trundy and Miss Dianne Foster." With Karloff's host appearing in front of footage from the drama to follow, the segment was technically flashy but didn't furnish him with much opportunity to communicate warmth or humor. A business suit and thick-rimmed spectacles that kept on reflecting the studio lighting likewise caused Karloff to come across as a little too staid and everyday. Or as radio-TV writer Dick Shippy of the *Akron Beacon Journal* put it: "Boris was togged out in his tailor-mades like a board chairman; and how – I ask you – can a man be sinister in hand-stitched lapels?"[87] The only real highlights of the hosting segment, as quoted by numerous reviewers, were the two catchphrases Karloff introduced: "as sure as my name is Boris Karloff" (as distinct from his not-quite-

Karloff host for *The Veil*) and "I promise you one thing – this is a *Thriller*," which latter line in fact constituted his only direct addressing of the audience ("you") on this night, with the remainder of his scripted dialogue relating squarely to the episode's story.

Unfortunately that story, adapted by James P. Cavanagh from the 1953 murder mystery novel *Doubles in Death* by William Grew (a pen name of William O'Farrell), proved to be weak – and slow-brewing – tea indeed. In fact, the manner in which "The Twisted Image" presents its tale of "ordinary guy" Alan Patterson (Nielsen) getting mixed up with psychopath Merle Jenkins (Grizzard) almost conveys the impression that – supernatural-ness aside – Cavanagh had made overzealous study of the opening point on Schwerin's previously referenced four-point outline for producing a "good horror program," namely:

> 1) Plots in which **ordinary, likable people** get fouled up in supernatural situations are best received.

United Press International's Fred Danzig wrote in his syndicated review column published the day after "The Twisted Image" aired: "I thought the show missed fire [*sic*] because it was preoccupied with depicting how a 'normal, everyday' guy like Mr. Patterson got into a jam. The real excitement and suspense came in watching Jenkins operate. He was the story. His was 'The Twisted Image.'"[88] Bob Foster of the *San Mateo Times* similarly opined: "The writers missed the point I felt, mainly because they bent over backward to prove that the hero, played by Leslie Nielsen, was absolutely normal. He was so normal he appeared abnormal."

Foster additionally observed: "This series is a full hour in length. This is its only difference, actually, from umpteen hundred other similar things done in a 30-minute version for the past ten years on television."[89] No less unimpressed, the *Pittsburgh Post-Gazette*'s Win Fanning concluded that "The Twisted Image" "seemed pale in comparison to a run-of-the-tube *Perry Mason*," and expressed concern that

> it is entirely possible that when Alfred Hitchcock's 30-minute *Presents* makes its debut on Tuesday, Sept. 27, starting at 8:30 on the same network, we shall be in serious danger of being served dessert before the main course… [U]nless a marked improvement is made in the Hubbell Robinson entry, even a left-handed effort by old Hitch is going to be dreadfully difficult to follow.[90]

"Karloff the All-Defining," *Sioux Falls* (SD) *Argus-Leader*, September 13, 1960.

In marked contrast to the sense of affection signified by the familiarism "old Hitch," many reviewers of "The Twisted Image" elected to vent their spleen at Karloff; after all, the new series had comprehensively been pro-

BORIS KARLOFF
Pretty cocky

Hedda Hopper takes aim, *Tucson* (AZ) *Daily Citizen*, October 8, 1960.

moted on the strength of his name and image, with the two catchphrases from his opening hosting segment further evincing his personal endorsement of the show. Harry Harris of *The Philadelphia Inquirer* took a decidedly personal swipe in his review published under the title "Karloff Wrong on *Thriller*":

> Boris Karloff announced, after roaming about in front of huge blowups of members of the evening's cast, "I promise you one thing – this is a *Thriller*." But what followed…was no great shakes in the gooseflesh department. So much for Karloff's promises! But then, what else can you expect of a guy who goes around saying things like "as sure as my name is Boris Karloff," when it's really William Henry Pratt?[91]

Ogden Dwight of the *Des Moines Register* also complained that Karloff's "opening sinisterism, 'I promise you one thing – this is a *Thriller*,' was revoltingly untrue." Charlie Wadsworth of the *Orlando Sentinel* meanwhile deemed Karloff's hosting to have been utterly nondescript: "Boris Karloff was the host, and that's just what he was – the host." UPI columnist Fred Danzig expressed a comparable sentiment while rather disparagingly referring to Karloff as "that kindly old monument to mirthlessness." And Fred Remington of the *Pittsburgh Press*, who found "The Twisted Image" variously "shabby, tedious, implausible" and "wretched," took things a step further by suggesting that the show could make do without Karloff entirely: "[W]hy do you require someone to introduce a show at all? Good ones don't need it and as last night's tedious affair proved, it can't help a bad one."[92] The few reviewers who found a kind word or two for "The Twisted Image" couldn't be relied upon to praise Karloff either. To quote the *Akron Beacon Journal*'s Dick Shippy: "*Thriller* is promising. But Karloff doesn't add much."[93]

Even before *Thriller* made its bow, though, there had already been an extremely subtle negative undercurrent directed toward Karloff in some columnists' writing about the series. Or rather, directed toward his perceived gloating about how much he was being paid for his work hosting the show. A first hint of this could be detected after Win Fanning breakfasted with Karloff on February 17, 1960, and came away thinking that the actor – for whom he had immense respect[94] – considered the hosting gig to be a "little work, big pay, job," as he reported to readers of his "Television & Radio News" column for the *Pittsburgh Post-Gazette* the following day. A suggestion of how Fanning might have reached such a conclusion can be pinpointed in Eve Starr's syndicated "Inside Television" column of September 15, 1960, in which she quoted the "beam[ing]" Karloff at length:

> "I'm quite pleased with the whole thing," he beams. "Why, last week they flew me all the way from London just to do one day's work and let me bring my wife with me. We did six of the host-narrator spots in the one day, and then they'll bring me back in October to do some more."

However, it was the hat-wearing queen of the veiled barb, Hedda Hopper, who most clearly insinuated the idea of "pride coming before a fall premiere" for the actor. In her September 13, 1960, column – dedicated exclusively to the subject of Karloff on the day of *Thriller*'s debut – she made the seemingly innocent observation: "He's now 73 and pretty cocky about it since he enjoys splendid health."[95] The phrase didn't look quite so innocent once certain key words from it had been lifted out of context – "Boris Karloff Pretty Cocky" – and employed as a caption for an accompanying *Thriller*-branded promotional photograph of the series' host. Hopper's paragraph relating specifically to *Thriller* likewise veered off toward a decidedly pointed conclusion:

> Karloff admits that in his 30 years of movie-making he never had a really good picture.[96] "I've been in so many bread and butter films, and not one of them is really distinguished. I've survived more bad pictures, and how it happened I don't know – it's incredible."

From this low ebb, it would, as Win Fanning averred, take "something radical"[97] to turn *Thriller* around.

5. Finally acclaimed: the re-formulated *Thriller* (October 1960 to April 1962, NBC)

Producer Fletcher Markle was dismissed with immediate effect. In his place, Hubbell Robinson brought in two new producers: William Frye, who had helmed such successful shows as the radio-to-television sitcom *The Halls of Ivy* starring Ronald Colman and Benita Hume and the drama anthology series *General Electric Theater*, both for CBS under Robinson's tenure at the network; and Maxwell Shane, fresh from producing the third season of the NBC police drama *M Squad*. The latter, whose remit was to focus on crime episodes, would stay with *Thriller* for only its initial two blocks of 13 episodes during the first season, as Frye increasingly steered the series in an entirely new direction: visceral, pulp-inspired supernatural horror.[98]

This shift was first attested in the show's October 25, 1960, episode "The Purple Room," written and directed by Douglas Heyes, who had just directed several standout episodes of the first season of *The Twilight Zone* including "The After Hours" and the Richard Matheson adaptation "And When the Sky Was Opened." "The Purple Room" commences in an old dark house with a volley of screams and bullets as an unseen limb-dragging someone-or-some*thing* approaches a woman (Joanna Heyes, the director's wife) in a four-poster bed; the episode then cuts to Karloff's host. With a filmed backdrop of a gothic mansion interior behind him, the segment seems like an organic continuation of the preceding action; in other words, there is a tangible connection between the story being presented in the episode and the hosting segment. Karloff's spectacles are gone, his suit and tie dark and somber, and his gaze fixed upon the viewers at home (that is to say, the camera), whom

Scott Merrill begins admiring Elizabeth Allen's contours "Braille style" with only a cursed portrait as witness in *Thriller*'s "The Grim Reaper."

he addresses directly with a wry smile and a lighthearted air of *faux* menace:

> Don't be alarmed! The woman who just screamed is perfectly quiet now, as sure as my name is Boris Karloff. You see, she's been dead for nearly a hundred years. Her bed is empty and whatever it was that frightened her so seems to be gone. *Seems to be!* But I can tell you this much: that bed won't be empty much longer – and other screams will soon be heard. Whose? Perhaps *yours*!

While memorable catchphrases remain (the segment also concluding with the words: "Let me assure you, my friends – this is a *Thriller*!"), everything else has been completely overhauled. Even Karloff's introduction of the cast takes on a playful air: "Mr. Rip Torn, Miss Patricia Barry, Mr. Richard Anderson and – well, it seems the rest of our cast cannot be raised!" No longer exuding the rather distant persona of some smartly, if conservatively, attired corporate exec, Karloff's host instead seems to be thoroughly enjoying himself – and enticing viewers to do the same – as he assumes something of the "murder with a grin"[99] approach of

Hitchcock and the horror hosts. The entire segment, with Karloff on screen throughout, lasts just 57 seconds. But this no more feels too short than the tale which follows it – about an heir to a will (Torn) who must move into the spooky mansion – feels too long. With writing for the show having been drastically tightened up, all aspects of the episode's content are richer and more engaging.

It swiftly became expected that Karloff's host would now address viewers – and the purported precariousness of their position perched in front of the TV set – directly. At the beginning of the January 3, 1961, episode "The Hungry Glass," adapted by Douglas Heyes from Robert Bloch's 1951 short story "The Hungry House," he assured them: "Oh, you'll be perfectly safe – that is, if you turn your own mirrors to the wall and make sure that your television screen casts no reflection!" After being brought a tray of tea by a butler during his segment for the following week's "The Poisoner," he sniffed at the beverage suspiciously while offering a piece of off-the-cuff advice: "Oh, by the way – if in the course of our story someone brings you a cup of tea or a spot of brandy, I suggest you let them take the first sip." By the time the closing episode of the first season came around (another Robert Bloch adaptation, "The Grim Reaper"), this type of content had been taken to a delicious extreme, with a scythe-wielding Karloff lurching forward and moving beyond the camera as he advises: "Oh-oh! Stay where you are! I'll join you as you wait and watch!" His host would again breach the bounds of the television screen in the second season episode "Portrait Without a Face," broadcast on Christmas Day 1961 – only this time by firing a crossbow bolt into the audience while furtively warning: "Oh, if you have a skylight, be sure to bolt it securely, otherwise you won't know that you're absolutely alone." The scream of some expiring *Thriller* viewer whose festive fun has just come to an end suddenly invades the soundtrack.

The use of carefully selected, synecdochic props such as the abovementioned scythe and crossbow – which helped to establish the mood and effectively sum up the stories that followed their appearance – was also characteristic of the new-style *Thriller* hosting segments. In yet a further Robert Bloch adaptation, "Yours Truly,

Karloff in "The Prediction," *Honolulu* (HI) *Star-Bulletin*, December 11, 1960.

Jack the Ripper" (April 11, 1961), Karloff was introduced while dropping a surgeon's scalpel into an old-fashioned doctor's bag, as he urged: "I suggest you viewers draw just a little closer together. The Ripper always struck down solitary victims, you know. It'd be a pity if a member of our audience became – dis-*member*-ed!" He set the horror-comedy tone for the second season episode "Masquerade," shown the day before Halloween 1961, by launching a rubber bat toward said audience. And as that season's December 18, 1961, installment "The Remarkable Mrs. Hawk" – directed by John Brahm and adapted by regular *Thriller* screenwriter Donald S. Sanford from Margaret St. Clair's 1950 short story "Mrs. Hawk" – pork-rolled into action, Karloff's host petted a "pampered piglet," proving that he didn't always need to hog the screen for himself.

At the same time, the hollow technical flashiness-for-its-own-sake of the original production team's hosting segments, which lacked any kind of narrative motivation, was transmuted into amusing displays of special effects trickery that related directly to the stories being presented. The faces of cast members being introduced by Karloff were, for example, superimposed into mirror frames for "The Hungry Glass," a bubbling cauldron for "Hay-Fork and Bill-Hook" (February 7, 1961), the lid of a teakwood chest for "The Terror in Teakwood" (May 16, 1961) and an executioner's basket from which Karloff could lift them as decapitated heads in the second show of the second season, "Guillotine" (September 26, 1961). A series of snappily edited tongue-in-cheek TV ads for *Thriller* also earned NBC the 1961 International Broadcasting Award for Best Promotional Program.[100]

Back when reviewer Harold A. Nichols had **BOMB**ed *Thriller*'s opening episode "The Twisted Image" under the self-explanatory headline "*Thriller* Didn't" in the *Rochester Democrat and Chronicle* of September 14, 1960, he had commented: "Somehow, one wished Boris was in there to get things straightened out with a shriek or two."[101] One of the very first things that the replacement production team set into motion following the departure of Fletcher Markle was the shooting of an episode that actually starred the performer with whose name and image all publicity for the show was branded. It had always been intended for Karloff to enact leading roles in the series, but the actor was still procrastinating about this when he spoke to Samuel L. Singer of *The Philadelphia Inquirer* ahead of the latter's September 12, 1960, column: "While he is host for each story, the ones he will act in depend on 'if they find the proper type of story... [T]here must be some compromise on both sides.'"[102] Under new producer William Frye, Karloff's first – and in fact, only – starring role of *Thriller*'s first season was already before the cameras by October 19.[103] Titled "The Prediction," written by Donald S. Sanford and with John Brahm directing, it presented Karloff as a nightclub mentalist who apparently gains the ability to really see the future. Truth be told, it was the kind of paranormal tale that wouldn't have been entirely out of place on *The Veil*. But *Thriller*'s five-day shooting schedule and budget of between $125,000 and $150,000 for each episode[104] ensured that "The Prediction" possessed – among other things – a level of style, gloss and scale that the earlier Hal Roach Studios show could never have hoped to attain. That said, appearance fees for actors hired to work on *Thriller* were capped at $2500.[105] As with *The Veil*, this resulted in the use of a number of rising talents including Ursula Andress, Bruce Dern, Richard Kiel, Mary Tyler Moore (twice), William Shatner (also twice), Robert Vaughn and (in separate episodes) a pre-*Bewitched* Elizabeth Montgomery and Dick York; as well as character actors such as Walter Burke (twice), Fifi D'Orsay, George Macready, Reggie Nalder (twice), Alan Napier (thrice), Vladimir Sokoloff (twice) and the disarmingly cadaverous Henry Daniell (no less than five times!)

(Delving briefly into the realm of the hypothetical: If *The Veil* **had** been released in 1959, then perhaps Hubbell Robinson would have been less interested in employing Karloff due to the latter having recently hosted a [cheap-looking] drama anthology show already; in which case *Thriller* as we know it might never have come about, in turn prompting a butterfly to flap around a recording studio endlessly reciting Rudyard Kipling's "The Boris Karloff That Stamped.")

Advance coverage of the November 22, 1960, broadcast of "The Prediction" highlighted *Thriller*'s move into horror territory, not least by way of references to host and star Karloff's (pre-war) achievements in the field of horror movies. The November 7, 1960, edition of Provo, Utah's *The Daily Herald* for instance described the reformulated *Thriller*'s intent "to mystify and just plain scare the viewer," while reproducing headshots of Karloff from three movies in the "Shock!" package, correctly identified for readers as *Frankenstein* (1931), *The Mummy* (1932) and *The Invisible Ray* (1936).[106]

The "new" *Thriller* swiftly won over former staunch critics of the show. Harry Harris of *The Philadelphia Inquirer* in his January 5, 1961, "Screening TV" column designated that week's Robert Bloch adaptation "The Hungry Glass" an "unabashed spook yarn" that "managed to raise a pretty good crop of goose-pimples." Indeed, he rated it more highly than the Robert Bloch-penned drama that had preceded it, the tick-tock nightmare "Changing Heart" on *Alfred Hitchcock Presents*.[107] Bob Foster of the *San Mateo Times* in turn enthused in his February 8, 1961, "TV Screenings" column following the broadcast of "Hay-Fork and Bill-Hook": "My, my, but *Thriller* the Tuesday night NBC drama can be thrilling at times... Throughout the weeks, *Thriller*, which has Boris Karloff on hand as narrator, has proved just that." In his February 16, 1961, column, Foster continued: "*Thriller*, a series of highly suspenseful shows presided over by that professional boogey man, Boris Karloff, has developed into a series of better filmed drama. In fact, fans of Alfred Hitchcock are finding *Thriller* a lot more thrilling... as it should be."

Other entertainment journalists concurred. Eunice Field observed in the January 1961 edition of *TV Radio Mirror*: "That sound heard around the TV sets these nights is not the power tube going but teeth chattering, and Boris Karloff's NBC *Thriller* show is to blame."[108] Cecil Smith, writing in the *Los Angeles Times* of February 21, 1961, found it admirable that the show "is without pretensions – it offers itself as a melodrama with Boris Karloff as host and it says it will attempt to curdle the marrow of your bones; that's all. Yet the shows have been skillfully written, directed, cast and produced – many have been brilliant."[109] By the time the second season beckoned – with an opening episode that was indeed titled "What Beckoning Ghost?" – Associated Press TV-radio writer Cynthia Lowry in her

(Text continues on page 216)

Ursula Andress, with witch Jeanette Nolan, in "La Strega"

Richard Kiel, with Fintan Meyler, in "Well of Doom"

Many an up-and-coming performer passed *Thriller*'s way in their young careers, among them...

George Kennedy (right), with John Anderson, in "The Innocent Bystanders"

Elizabeth Montgomery, with John Carradine, in "Masquerade"

Mary Tyler Moore in "Man of Mystery"

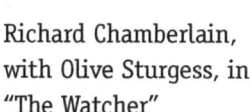

Richard Chamberlain, with Olive Sturgess, in "The Watcher"

(Continued from page 213)
September 7, 1961, column viewed Karloff as an "eminent practitioner" of the television hosting art with his "on-camera personality...of a tongue-in-cheek bogeyman." Just as Karloff had been held accountable by columnists, critics, reviewers and writers of angry letters to newspapers for the initial failure of the show branded in his name and image, so he was now accordingly placed on a pedestal as it met with success.

Lowry's column went on: "Karloff was busy the other day making a fall batch of introductions (13, to be exact) and was busily leering at the camera while inviting the public 'to a feast of fear and trembling.' ... He treats his host's role, he said, as a preliminary bit to set a mood of mock terror." With the show having now settled into its stride, these "preliminary bits" grew yet more playful and baroque as the second season unfolded. Karloff could, it seemed, out-Hitchcock Hitchcock with some of his merry monologues on murder. At the beginning of the New Year's Day 1962 episode "An Attractive Family," he blithely remarked: "There's nothing one could dislike about them – unless you object to the fact that they occasionally commit a casual murder. Of course, you really shouldn't object to that – after all, they only do it when it's *absolutely* necessary." Ahead of the eerie killer scarecrow episode "The Hollow Watcher" (February 12, 1962), he meanwhile inquired of his audience:

> I wonder how many of you have had the urge to ... to eliminate one of your in-laws. Oh, come now! Chances are it has occurred to you at least once, but ... after a moment's thought you decided against becoming a murderer. Of course, I wouldn't presume to ask if you made the *right* decision!

Karloff was also happy to poke fun at himself and his now-famous catchphrase on the show. In the second episode in which he also performed, the October 2, 1961, adaptation of Edgar Allan Poe's "The Premature Burial," he introduced each cast member while he or she was lying in a coffin. Upon reaching himself, he declared: "And as sure as *his* name is Boris Karloff, this is a *Thriller*." In the preamble to the John Brahm-directed "Cousin Tundifer" (February 19, 1962), he warned that the episode's story contained "turns and twists and such sudden byways that even my head reels. And for a moment – but only for a moment! – I cannot even be sure if my name *is* Boris Karloff!" When *Thriller* was preempted during the second season for the sole time in the show's run, the cause was only further indication of Karloff's prevailing popularity. On February 5, 1962,

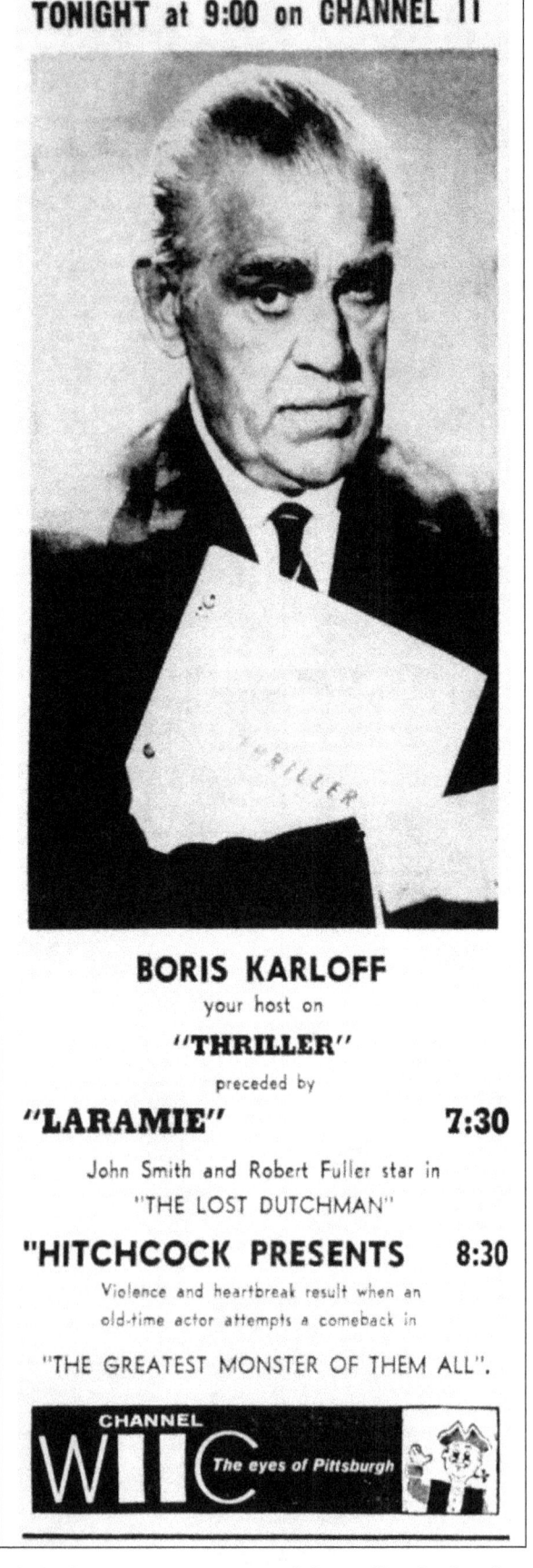

Who's the greatest monster of them all? *Pittsburgh (PA) Post-Gazette*, February 14, 1961

NBC instead aired a *Hallmark Hall of Fame* 90-minute color production of *Arsenic and Old Lace* featuring Karloff alongside Tony Randall, Dorothy Stickney, Tom Bosley and his one-time *Starring Boris Karloff* co-lead Mildred Natwick.[110] As the January 24, 1962, *Philadelphia Inquirer* succinctly put it: "Boris Karloff is preempting Boris Karloff."[111]

Finding success and acclaim by way of what was first and foremost a horror show may have mellowed Karloff a little in terms of reconciling himself with "the old Boris Karloff" and the horror expectations that this latter had continued to elicit throughout the actor's postwar career. Lunching with United Press International journalist Vernon Scott at the beginning of March 1961, he remarked: "I'm absolutely delighted that the show has been successful." And then, dispensing with his customary rejection of the term "horror": "A sly smile lighted on his face briefly, and he added, 'I'd hate to have someone offer me a really excellent horror picture. I might accept it.'"[112] It may not merely have been publicity puff when listings for Karloff's final acting appearance on *Thriller* in the Robert Florey-directed "The Incredible Doktor Markesan" (February 26, 1962) maintained that Karloff "once swore he would never again play a mad scientist. He goes back on that swear tonight."[113] One might ponder whether the positive experience of *Thriller* in turn led to Karloff's willingness to revisit his *Frankenstein* past in the much-loved October 26, 1962, episode of CBS's *Route 66*, "Lizard's Leg and Owlet's Wing." And from there, to make his big-screen horror comeback in the works of Roger Corman and his AIP cohorts from 1963.

It would be wrong, however, to suggest that the reformulated *Thriller* had pleased everyone. The show's increased popularity brought with it increased visibility and as the first season played out in an ever more scream-filled and visceral way, so the voices of anti-violence protesters began to rise up against it. Professional pot-stirrer Drew Pearson featured a portrait of Karloff under the headline "Viewers Protest to Sponsors" in the June 16, 1961, edition of his nationally syndicated "Washington Merry-Go-Round" column, in which he reported: "The public outcry against TV blood and thunder is beginning to shift to the sponsors who bring the bloodshed and horror into the nation's homes… One show that has drawn heavy protest is a chiller named *Thriller*, narrated by movie bogeyman Boris Karloff." A quoted report by the National Association for Better Radio and Television concerning the May 16, 1961, episode "The Terror in Teakwood" concluded: "Words cannot describe the utter terror of

No junk in this trunk, *Des Moines* (IA) *Register*, September 18, 1961

this film." Pearson then continued: "Hubbell Robinson, the producer, acknowledged to this column that he had received mail objecting to the *Thriller* shows. However, he insists that 85 pct. of the mail is favorable. 'The show isn't meant to be taken seriously,' he said." Some, such as Scripps-Howard staff writer Harriet Van Horne, countered that the real matter at hand was parental accountability for children's viewing habits, writing in her syndicated "Viewing TV" column of October 24, 1961:

> Every time conversation gets around to the question of what constitutes fit and proper viewing for children, the program usually cited as the most arguably [*sic*], the most appallingly unfit is *Thriller*… Boris Karloff, smacking his lips over hideous revelations to come, welcomes us each week… "*Thriller* leaves my children positively quaking," a young mother said to me at a recent dinner party. "Why are such programs permitted on the air, anyway?" "Why," one longed to ask, "are some children permitted to stay up so late?" Well, they're up late, I suspect to shudder along with mummy as she watches her favor-

ite program – *Thriller*. If anybody fancies these stories of the supernatural are aimed at an audience of elderly ghouls, he has only to look at the commercials. They speak directly to Mrs. Thrifty Shopper and they do not sell bat extermination kits or embalming fluid.

Thriller's producers were briefed by NBC on the subject of violence on the series prior to the start of its second season.[114] However, this didn't seem to make much, if any, difference to the show. And in fact, NBC had already decided on a solution of its own, way back in February 1961 when, rather than attempting to curtail the show's perceived excesses, it simply rescheduled it to appear in a later slot from the fall.[115] Commented critic-turned-fan of the series Bob Foster of the *San Mateo Times* in his October 4, 1961, column: "NBC moved the show to a time, 10 p.m. Mondays, when fewer youngsters would be looking in, and gave the producers their heads. What has resulted is a series of genuine thrillers, the most exciting on television."

Another party who wasn't too pleased with the extent of *Thriller*'s success was the man who had in effect prompted the series to be produced in the first place. As Alan Warren relates in his 2004 study *This Is a "Thriller": An Episode Guide, History and Analysis of the Classic 1960s Television Series*:

> For some time *Thriller* had been drawing consistently higher ratings than *Alfred Hitchcock Presents*… Hitchcock, irked by *Thriller*'s consistent high quality, issued an ultimatum: he wouldn't go on unless *Thriller* was withdrawn for one year. This was tantamount to cancellation; the network hesitated, but as [William] Frye ruefully recalls, "Hitchcock's clout at NBC was greater than Karloff's." The decision was made to axe the series.[116]

The sixty-seventh, and final, episode of *Thriller*, aired on April 30, 1962, was titled "The Specialists." Host Karloff appeared without props or horror styling in front of a plain black backdrop. What then followed was a pilot for a jaunty international crime caper made by another production team. It was a dull squib of a denouement as the show which had started out with no pilot of its own concluded by having someone else's foisted upon it.

Some six weeks prior to that final broadcast, it had been announced that Hubbell Robinson was returning to CBS as senior program vice-president – and it soon transpired he was taking Alfred Hitchcock with him. *Television Digest* of March 12, 1962, reported that this

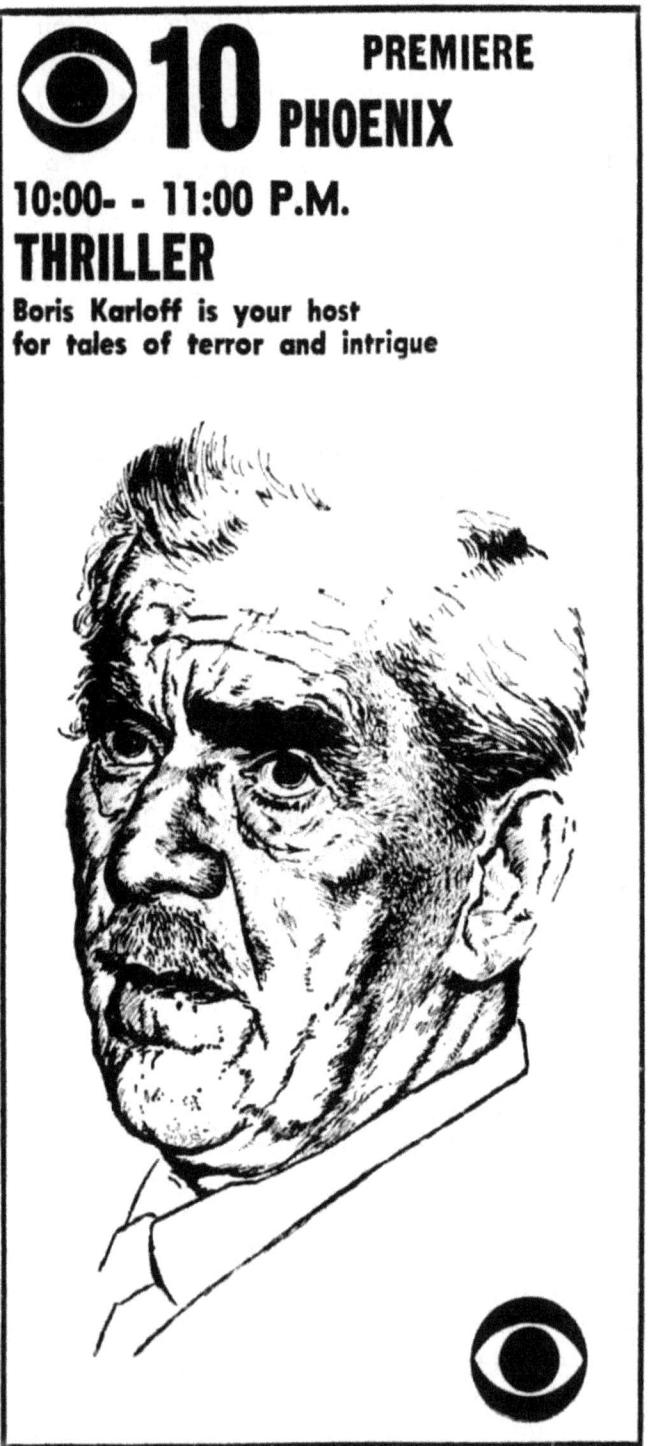

Syndicated *Thriller* on CBS, *The Arizona Republic* (Phoenix, AZ), September 29, 1962.

"is being viewed in network circles as part of an all-out effort on CBS-TV's part to capture lost leadership glories in program ratings & billings."[117] That same day, the entire back catalogue of *Thriller* episodes was made available in syndication through MCA[118], and it wasn't long before the former NBC hit started to turn up on CBS stations. Just as some elements of *Thriller* had benefited from becoming a little more "Hitchcockized," so

Hitchcock's addition to the CBS fall 1962 schedule, *The Alfred Hitchcock Hour*, adopted *Thriller*'s running time, started to deal in occasional horror-themed episodes and employed various writers, directors and other crew who had made sterling contributions to *Thriller*. In a pointed article published on May 16, 1962, Rick Du Brow of United Press International remarked:

> It is not a mere figure of speech to say that Alfred Hitchcock gets away with murder each week on his NBC-TV show... Hitchcock does it so well that he is not only returning next season – on another network, CBS – but having his air time extended from a half hour to an hour... It is interesting to note that NBC-TV's *Thriller* series, which was at least equal to the Hitchcock program in story respects, is going off, despite the excellence of its host, Boris Karloff.[119]

6. Lost Again: *Out of This World* (1962, ATV)

Two months to the day after the final episode of *Thriller* aired, Karloff could be seen hosting a new drama anthology series titled *Out of This World* – on British commercial television. Going out at 10 p.m. on Saturdays, the live hour-long program presented a different science fiction play each week over the course of 13 episodes:

1. "The Yellow Pill" (adaptation of Rog Phillips), June 30, 1962
2. "Little Lost Robot" (adaptation of Isaac Asimov), July 7, 1962
3. "Cold Equations" (adaptation of Tom Godwin), July 14, 1962
4. "Impostor" (adaptation of Philip K. Dick), July 21, 1962
5. "Botany Bay" (original story by Terry Nation), July 28, 1962
6. "Medicine Show" (adaptation of Robert Moore Williams), August 4, 1962
7. "Pictures Don't Lie" (adaptation of Katherine MacLean), August 11, 1962
8. "Vanishing Act" (original story by Richard Waring), August 18, 1962
9. "Divided We Fall" (adaptation of Raymond F. Jones), August 25, 1962
10. "The Dark Star" (adaptation of Frank Crisp's *The Ape of London*), September 1, 1962
11. "Immigrant" (adaptation of Clifford D. Simak), September 8, 1962
12. "Target Generation" (adaptation of Clifford D. Simak), September 15, 1962
13. "The Tycoons" (adaptation of Arthur Sellings), September 22, 1962

With no little irony, only the episode with the word "lost" in its title – "Little Lost Robot" – is known to survive today, together with a fan's off-air audio recordings of the next two episodes "Cold Equations" and "Impostor."[120] The rest of the series, like so much British TV output of the period, was lost to the insidious cost-cutting practice of discarding masters to save on storage fees and wiping videotapes for reuse.

Out of This World was a summer spin-off of *Armchair Theatre*, a popular dramatic anthology series that had been running since July 1956 on Britain's second (of two!) television stations, ITV, itself only on air since September 22, 1955. Produced by ATV (Associated Television) – the individual franchise tasked with supplying weekend programming content for the ITV network – the show had already launched one 13-episode spin-off focused on works of a specific genre by way of the 1960 summer replacement series *Armchair Mystery Theatre*, which had been hosted by Donald Pleasence. The use of anthology series hosts remained uncommon on British television but could nonetheless be encountered on a number of other programs such as the Harry Alan Towers-produced *Tales from Dickens*, a filmed half-hour series hosted by Fredric March who commenced each episode by selecting from his bookshelves the Charles Dickens work which was to be adapted that evening. At 5:20 p.m. on Sunday, June 24, 1962, this had been *David Copperfield* for the installment "David and Mr. Micawber," whose eponymous leads were played by child star Martin Stephens (Miles in *The Innocents* [1961]) and corpulent character actor Robert Morley (who would go on to embody one of the critics offed by Vincent Price and Diana Rigg in *Theatre of Blood* [1973; U.S.: *Theater of Blood*]). A little over five hours later, Karloff would pop up at the end of that night's 9:35 p.m. broadcast of *Armchair Theatre* which had featured an adaptation of John Wyndham's 1952 short story[121] "Dumb Martian," a sci-fi tale initially selected for inclusion on *Out of This World* but ultimately deployed by ATV's pioneering Canadian head of drama Sydney Newman as what the June 22, 1962, edition of the weekly viewing guide *TV Times* referred to as "a foretaste of the new series of science fiction plays."[122]

In a brief epilogue staged on one of the sets just seen in the live production of "Dumb Martian," a tuxedo-clad Karloff was to utilize a catchphrase that would

Front-page ad for *Out of This World*, TV Times, June 22, 1962.

surely have raised the eyebrows of American *Thriller* aficionados:

> Tonight's play has taken us to Jupiter 4-2, the second moon of Callisto! A mere pebble in space, about 40 miles across; 483 million miles out of this world. *Out of This World!* The first play next Saturday evening is called *The Yellow Pill*. If you do not find it a most unusual story, then my name isn't Boris Karloff.[123]

Though this – let us call it what it is – *knock-off* catchphrase wouldn't go on to feature in every installment of *Out of This World*, it certainly made a reappearance in Karloff's opening hosting segment for the fourth episode "Impostor" as the surviving off-air audio recording testifies:

> In tonight's play we look into a city of the future. A city beneath its own artificial sky, built to protect its people from destruction by the "outspace." A man lives here named Roger Carter and if his problem isn't the most amazing you've ever come across, then my name isn't Boris Karloff.

There should be no doubt that Newman, who had commissioned *Out of This World*, and various other members of its creative team were fully aware of *Thriller*, with the initial decision to engage Karloff as host indeed spurred by knowledge of his success with the NBC series. Karloff himself had long been an advocate of the U.S.-media-savvy approach of ITV's program makers, with the *Pittsburgh Post-Gazette*'s Win Fanning observing in his February 22, 1960, column:

> [Karloff] deplored the long-standing sloppy approach by the BBC in the producing and timing of its dramatic shows. "Nothing before has done the BBC so much good as have the commercial broadcasters," he said. He likes the "tight, precise manner of American producers and directors which British commercial stations have adopted."

The producer of *Out of This World*, Leonard White, had previously helmed the spin-off series *Armchair Mystery Theatre*, as well as a block of episodes for the 1960 police-medical procedural *Police Surgeon* and the gritty 1961 live opening season of *The Avengers*, both of which had starred Ian Hendry.[124] *Out of This World*'s story editor Irene Shubik had joined *Armchair Theatre* in 1960 following a stateside stint as scriptwriter at Encyclopædia Britannica Films in Chicago, where her brother Philippe was instructor in pathology at Northwestern

University.[125] An avid reader of science fiction literature, she had first approached Sydney Newman with the concept for *Out of This World* as a summer replacement show for 1961; however, a lengthy strike by members of British actors' union Equity disrupted these plans so that the series ultimately went out in 1962 not as a replacement show but rather as additional Saturday programming, with *Armchair Theatre* also still broadcasting on Sundays.

Shubik was assisted in selecting *Out of This World* stories by Edward John Carnell, editor of *New Worlds Science Fiction* magazine since the late 1940s[126]. Carnell promoted the ATV-produced series heavily within its pages, with the July 1962 edition employing a promotional shot of Karloff as host on its front cover. The same image adorned the cover of the June 22, 1962, issue of *TV Times*, showing the tuxedoed, black bow tie-wearing actor amid an array of vaguely futuristic-looking machinery and (in the foreground) a model of a domed city of the future, created for use in the episode "Impostor"; although on this occasion, Karloff had to share the limelight with photos of comedians Morecambe and Wise and of singer Cleo Laine, under the rather diffuse headline "NINE SUMMER SHOWS begin this week."

Out of This World's writers meanwhile included the prolific Clive Exton, who would latterly furnish the screenplays for big-screen adaptations of Emlyn Williams' *Night Must Fall* (1964) and Joe Orton's *Entertaining Mr. Sloane* (1970). Another *Out of This World* scribe, future *Doctor Who* luminary Terry Nation, cut his science fiction teeth on adaptations of Philip K. Dick's 1953 short story "Impostor" and Clifford D. Simak's 1954 tale "Immigrant," in addition to furnishing the original teleplay "Botany Bay" concerning a strange institute for the criminally insane whose inmates seem to be subject to alien mind control. In 1973, Exton and Nation collaborated on the whimsical old dark house feature *The House in Nightmare Park* (U.S.: *Crazy House*) starring tittersome comedian Frankie Howerd alongside a nonplussed Ray Milland.

Karloff's host would apparently also turn writer for *Out of This World*, with *TV Times* informing its readers: "Boris Karloff's name is synonymous with horror, suspense and mystery. Now he leaves horror fiction to introduce each week, both on screen and in *TV Times*, the Saturday… science-fiction series *Out of This World*." In his inaugural article for the publication, the actor offered up a viewpoint that epitomized the ever-current, realist-minded, science-focused outlook of "the new Boris Karloff":

> [W]ith projected journeys to other planets, satellites in space, and astronauts circling the Earth, science fiction is in touch with reality. And all the more frightening for it. This is why I think the stories in our series, which are admirably imaginative, but not too far-fetched, will be so effective.

While Karloff-as-magazine-host gazed forth toward this intriguing, if uncertain, future, the *TV Times* editors made sure to also direct readers' attention back toward "the old Boris Karloff" by placing the alert-like title "STAND BY FOR SHOCKS" above the piece in dark, attention-grabbing block capitals.[127] Although *TV Times* duly published a further 12 installments with Karloff's byline prominently featured, these were little more than synopses of individual episodes that exhibited little, if any, of the actor's usual writing style.

Out of This World episodes all commenced with the same filmed opening sequence featuring slightly unsettling macro-photographic stock footage of organic growth in nature (that cannot help but put one in mind of Irene Shubik's background at Encyclopædia Britannica Films), over which the text "BORIS KARLOFF introduces / OUT OF THIS WORLD" is superimposed. Karloff's tuxedo-wearing host would then appear on screen. In the surviving episode "Little Lost Robot," the opening hosting segment gets off to a slightly clumsy start, albeit one that is typical of live television, with Karloff looking off to the side for his cue as the camera cuts to him. As with *Thriller*, there is a tangible connection between hosting segment and main story, with an assortment of charts and technological paraphernalia filling the background; only much later in the episode does the audience get to see this set in full, representing the communications room of the outer space base. A further similarity to *Thriller* is the deployment of a single symbolic, mood-setting prop within the segment – in this case a cut rose which he lifts to sniff while delivering his opening monologue:

> Good evening. Tonight we meet Major General Kallner, in charge of Hyperbase 7 in the area of Saturn. His hobby is breeding oxygenated roses. As a matter of fact, this one was flown in to me this morning.

Speaking to Raymond E. Palmer of the Associated Press in London, Karloff maintained that for his *Out of This World* hosting role, "I will just play myself – a quiet, ordinary Englishman."[128] Producer Leonard White instead viewed Karloff's host "as Boris himself, with a touch of 'other worldliness.'"[129] Certainly his suggestion of having had a rose flown in from Hyperbase 7 indicates that the host is not merely Karloff but a little science-fictional too.

Out of This World looks a lot cheaper than *Thriller* for the simple reason that it was. The average above-the-line costs per episode were around £5000[130], corresponding at the time to roughly $14,000 or one-tenth the budget of a *Thriller*. As with all of Karloff's U.S. hosting engagements, the program was in black and white, with color television not introduced in Britain until the second half of 1967.[131] Just as with *The Veil* and *Thriller*, budgetary restrictions resulted in the series employing a mixture of up-and-coming talents and dependable character actors, with the former in this instance including a 16-year-old Jane Asher, Paul Eddington, Julian Glover and Pauline Yates; and the latter Maxine Audley, Maurice Denham and Clifford Evans.

It would be wrong to infer that *Out of This World* necessarily represented a step down for Karloff following a success on the magnitude of *Thriller*. In fact, the opening episode "The Yellow Pill" commanded an audience of over 11 million viewers[132] – when the United Kingdom's entire population numbered only 53 millions. Viewing figures remained high throughout the run with critics also praising the series; no mean feat in view of the fact that *Out of This World* was the third (and final) new science fiction series to hit British television screens during the summer 1962 season. The other two, both on the BBC, were the six-episode *The Big Pull*, a Cold War satire about an astronaut who unwittingly draws the Earth into a cosmic battle between two superpowers, which aired from 7:15 p.m. to 7:45 p.m. on Saturdays from June 9 to July 14, meaning that its final three installments went out on the same night as *Out of This World*; and *The Andromeda Breakthrough*, astronomer Fred Hoyle and screenwriter John Elliot's sequel to their alien intelligence-themed 1961 series *A for Andromeda*, with Susan Hampshire taking over from Julie Christie in the title role. The 45-minute show ran from June 28 to August 2, debuting just two days before *Out of This World*.

After the first four *Out of This World* episodes aired, H.F. Hall wrote in the *Yorkshire Evening Post* of July 25, 1962:

> If there is any handing out of prizes after the present crop of space-fiction series, the only question will be which of the BBC's two efforts, *The Andromeda Breakthrough* and *The Big Pull*, will come second to ITV's *Out of This World*, the most accomplished thing of its kind [British] TV has yet produced… In shape, form, lucid-

ity and sheer ingenuity it could not provide a greater contrast to *The Andromeda Breakthrough*, a tortuous tale which left me bewildered.

In the August 9, 1962, *Kinematograph Weekly*, Tony Gruner opined, "Leonard White, producer of the series, justifies an accolade for providing rich production values from what might appear to have been a limited budget… [T]he series is certainly the most intelligent and best written of its genre since *Quatermass*."[133] The latter reference points to the rich tradition of science fiction drama on early postwar British television, most famously characterized by the BBC's Nigel Kneale-scripted *The Quatermass Experiment* (1953) and its sequels *Quatermass II* (1955) and *Quatermass and the Pit* (1958), but also represented by the lost ATV "Saturday serials" *The Strange World of Planet X* (1956) – starring William Lucas, who likewise took the lead in *Armchair Theatre*'s adaptation of "The Dumb Martian" at the end of which Karloff's host for *Out of This World* was introduced – and *The Trollenberg Terror* (1956-57). All of these series were considered sufficiently interesting to be adapted into theatrical features, each of which in turn gained a release in the U.S.[134] What distinguishes *Out of This World* from all these other series – and perhaps helped to give it the upper hand in the summer 1962 television line-up – is the fact that it was anthology-based, rather than trying to sustain a single story across six or more episodes. This is not to say that audiences in Britain weren't exposed to other genre anthology series; in fact, the highest-rated American show on British TV at the beginning of 1962 was *One Step Beyond*.[135]

Some reviewers additionally felt that *Out of This World* had set new standards for both Saturday night and summer programming, with *The Times* commenting on August 4, 1962, "*Out of This World* may well help to banish forever the view of summer as a time when just anything will do," and the *Daily Mail*'s Peter Black adding on September 17, 1962: "The whole of this series has been tremendously better than expectations of a Saturday night entertainment."

After *Out of This World* came to an end, its slot was taken over by producer Leonard White's second season of *The Avengers*, with Ian Hendry having left the cast, Honor Blackman joining it and one-time Karloff co-performer on *The Veil* Patrick Macnee taking center stage as Steed. In December 1962, Sydney Newman left ATV, having been poached by the BBC, with whom he would soon embark on new science fiction adventures with *Doctor Who*. Irene Shubik also went over to the BBC in 1964 and fairly transparently revived the format of *Out of This World*, albeit no longer with a host, in the shape of the science fiction anthology series *Out of the Unknown*, which ran for two seasons in black and white from October 1965 and then returned for two further seasons in color beginning in January 1969. The eleventh and twelfth episodes of the 1969 color season were indeed new versions of Clifford D. Simak's "Target Generation" and Rog Phillips' "The Yellow Pill," previously adapted as the twelfth and debut episodes of *Out of This World*.

As for Karloff, there was to be a posthumous coda to his career as drama anthology series host: Fans were caught off-guard at the end of the 1970s by the unheralded arrival on television of three features assembled from episodes of *The Veil*. In a February 2017 discussion at the *Classic Horror Film Board* online, retired theater actor Rick Pruitt – a lifelong genre devotee and completist – remarked, "The sudden, unexplained appearance of a new Karloff 'movie' on a cable station almost sent me spinning into madness." The Sleepy Hollow-based "host" of the book you hold in your hands, Tom Weaver, responded: "I too was agape at the idea of seeing Karloff movies never mentioned in any of the Karloff books."[136]

The return of the never-before-seen show from "behind the Veil" was good not merely for a quick surprise, though; it also ensured that we (*whatever we are*) have the enduring opportunity to watch and experience Karloff-as-host in something other than the ubiquitous *Thriller*. Without *The Veil*, our only resource for doing that would be the lone surviving episode of *Out of This World*.

Appendix 4
"I Wish He Were My Grandfather"
"Thriller"'s Jo Swerling Jr. Remembers Boris Karloff
By Tom Weaver

Ask a fan of the *Thriller* TV series to name the best thing about it, and a good-sized percentage will say the spooky introductions by host Boris Karloff. And it's a safe guess that most of the show's fans would probably assume that each intro was written by that particular episode's writer and directed by its director. Early in the series' run, that *was* how it worked. But fairly quickly, the responsibility of writing *and* directing those shuddersome lead-ins fell to one person—someone whose name was never once seen in the on-screen credits.

Jo Swerling Jr. grew up in the movie colony as his playwright-screenwriter dad Jo Swerling labored on the scripts of scores of movies, including *Blood and Sand* (1941), *Lifeboat* (1944) and *It's a Wonderful Life* (1946)—not to mention *The Pride of the Yankees* (1942), for which he was Oscar-nominated. In the fall of 1957, Swerling Jr. got a job at Revue Productions, the television film subsidiary of MCA, and worked behind the scenes on a variety of series. Alongside William Frye (*Thriller*'s producer) and Doug Benton (its associate producer), Swerling Jr. had the "very gratifying" experience of doing some of his first writing and directing on *Thriller* and collaborating with his favorite of all the actors he's ever worked with, Boris Karloff.

What was your first job at Revue?

For some reason, I skipped the mailroom; I guess it was nepotistic pull or something like that, that got me "in" at one level above the mailroom [*laughs*]. The job was called "coordinator," and it was nothing like the production coordinators we have today, that's a whole other, different job category. Of course I wasn't made a coordinator right away, because I didn't know anything about it: I was put together with a coordinator who had been working there for quite a while and I was taught the job by him. A coordinator at Revue Productions...today he'd probably be called an assistant to the

Three decades before Jo Swerling Jr. wrote Boris Karloff's *Thriller* intros, his dad Jo Swerling scripted the macabre crime drama *Behind the Mask* (1932), one of Karloff's first post-*Frankenstein* films.

producer. The job was part business affairs: The coordinators would make the deals for writers and directors on the various TV series. The coordinators would *not* make deals for producers, those deals were made on a much higher level at Universal. But once a show was sold and a coordinator assigned to it, he would make the deals for the episode writers and directors.

Jo Swerling Jr.'s TV career advanced from "coordinator" (a job he often hated) to producer chores on such series as *Run for Your Life, Baretta, Captains and the Kings* and *Wiseguys* – to name four for which he was Emmy-nominated.

Select the writers and directors, you mean?

Oh, no, no. On *Thriller*, for instance, Bill Frye and Doug Benton would choose the writers and directors and then they would hand over to me, the coordinator, the responsibility of negotiating the deals with the agents and then making sure that contracts were drawn up accordingly and sent to them and returned signed. Scut work. I had to have a tickler file to remind me to follow up, to make sure we got the signed contracts back. The rule at Universal was, you had to have the signed contract in your hand prior to the artist starting to work. We would get yelled at if a director started shooting and we didn't have a signed contract. Incidentally, when Revue Productions started, they were not even at Universal. At Republic Studios they had a Revue building and a Mark VII building, twin buildings. [Mark VII, Jack Webb's company, was a joint venture with Revue.] We moved over to Universal after I'd been there a couple of years.

Did you like that coordinator job?

I used to *hate* that job [*laughs*], because I hate to negotiate. I can tell you an anecdote about that, that doesn't have to do with *Thriller* but with Revue-Universal. When I first went to work there, my boss was the head of TV business affairs, Manning O'Connor, a sweetheart. He was this soft-spoken Irishman, charming. I was this guy off the street, I came in to work there, $75 a week, a know-nothing, they gave me a small office that I shared with another guy, and I remember Manning coming into the office and welcoming me aboard and saying, "If there's anything I can do to help..."—he was so nice, this guy. And he was *so tough* a negotiator, it was hard to believe that it was the same person! To give you an example: I was trying to make a deal for a story and script for the series *Markham* [1959-60] with Ray Milland, a half-hour detective thing. The producers always seemed to be behind on the material, they were always hurting for scripts, and so getting a script out in time was always a crisis. A writer came in, I don't remember who he was, and he pitched a story to them, and they really liked it and they really wanted to make it. I now had to make the deal. I of course knew what he was paid the last time he worked there, $500, and our edict from O'Connor was: "You don't give anybody a raise. You pay 'em what they got the last time. That's *it*. No exceptions." So I entered into these discussions with that in mind. The writer's agent said, "He has an established price that's higher than that now, because at Metro-Goldwyn-Mayer last month they paid him $700." I said, "No, no. *You* know how it works here. We don't give raises. It's $500." The agent said, "Well, we're gonna have to pass. He's established that price at MGM." And we had a standard line in response to that: "Well, if Metro-Goldwyn-Mayer wants to go bankrupt, that's their problem, not ours. We're not giving any raises." But I *had* to make this deal, we really needed this story for *Markham*. I called up Manning and I told him what was going on, "This guy is stonewalling me," and he said, "Here's what I want you to do: I want you to stonewall him back. You call this agent again and tell him that you're gonna make the offer one more time, that it's take-it-or-leave-it and then it's off the table." I said, "You sure you want me to—" He said, "Just...*listen* to me. That's what I want you to do." So I did it. And the agent told me, "Okay, you got a deal."

I went to Manning's office and I filled him in, and he said, "I knew that's what would happen." I said,

"Well, how the fuck did you know that was gonna happen? *Teach* me this. What kind of a mind reader are you? How did you *know*?" And Manning said, "Well, I happen to know that the writer's wife has cancer, and medical bills are killing him, and he's about to lose his house." Can you *imagine*? These guys like Manning, they *knew* stuff like that and would *use* it to their advantage in negotiations. Here's this man who was such a sweet guy to talk to, and would do anything for you—apart from pay you a raise [*laughs*]! He'd probably jump into a river full of crocodiles to get you a lemonade, but he wouldn't give you a dime more. It was amazing.

Did you have any other responsibilities as a coordinator?
Yes, to kind of monitor the set, be the eyes and ears of the head of the studio on the set, supervise the dubbing of the episodes—those kinds of things. The great part about that job was that, on every show I knew about, the door was open to the coordinator to monitor or to audit *every*thing that went on. In other words, coordinators were able to go to cutting sessions, we were able to go to casting sessions and throw in our two cents, and the producers would always listen to us. If we came up with a workable idea, they would incorporate it, and if it was not a good idea, they'd say, "That's a shitty idea." [*Laughs*] So it was a great kind of training position.

What was your first series as coordinator?
Once I became a coordinator on my own, without being on the coattails of someone else, the first show I worked on was called *The Restless Gun* [1957-59], a half-hour black-and-white cowboy show starring John Payne, a level-two leading man in Hollywood for many years. The producer that I worked for on the show was a fellow by the name of David Dortort, who went on to create and produce *Bonanza*, a very, very nice man. It was funny, when I was doing *Restless Gun* they also put me on *M Squad* with Lee Marvin, which created a "problem." I went to the next higher authority in the administrative part of the company and I said, "I'm in an awkward position here. It's not that I don't want to do both shows, but John Payne thinks I work exclusively for him and he's made this clear to me on any number of occasions. Now the studio has me *not* working exclusively for him. What should I do?" He looked at me and he said, "Well, *that's* a stupid question. The simple answer to that question is, make him *think* you're working for him exclusively!" [*Laughs*] So I tried to do that, and I guess I got away with it.

Then the next show was *Markham*. The problem I had on *Markham* was the executive who was supervising it. In those days, MCA company policy was to not give screen credit of any kind to MCA executives who had authority over shows. So this fellow *didn't* get credit on *Markham*, but he was a vice-president of Universal, his name was Richard Lewis, and he was *not* my favorite guy. He was very demanding...the sort of person who was very willing to criticize but *un*willing to praise. All I ever got from him was criticism. He made my life pretty miserable. One time he went off to Europe on a vacation, and while he was gone, on my own initiative I took a script that had been shelved and I rewrote it to the producer's satisfaction, to the point where they felt it was shootable. *Another* thing that they liked us to do: We had three-day shooting schedules on the half-hour shows, but every once in a while they wanted us to put two scripts together and shoot both in five days—two and a half days each. It was just a way to get some money back to offset overages and so on, and it was not a bad plan at all. Well, when Lewis came back from Europe, I ran into him in the hall, and there was no "Hello, how are you?"; he said, "You didn't do a five-day schedule while I was gone." No acknowledgment of the fact that I had saved a sick script and kept them in production. If I hadn't saved that script, they wouldn't have had a script to shoot that week. I was pretty proud of myself for that, but he never mentioned it. This individual had me in a frame of mind where I was wondering whether I was in the right business, whether I should think about doing something else.

Speaking of Markham, *the Internet Movie Database says your dad wrote an episode, "Woman of Arles." Is that a mistake? Was it* you *who wrote that episode?*
No, my dad actually wrote it, as a favor to me and to the producers, Joe Sistrom and Warren Duff. As usual, Dick Lewis was eager to tell me he was disappointed in the script ... that it lacked the charm he expected. His first name was truly eponymous.

Around that same time I also did a couple of short stints on *Wagon Train*, and then I was put on *Thriller*. Before I came along, when they made the *Thriller* pilot, there was another coordinator on the show, Jerry Adler was his name, and for whatever reason, I never found out, they decided to put him somewhere else and I took over from him on *Thriller*. *Thriller* was a Hubbell Robinson Production, and Hubbell Robinson had been head of programming for CBS, he was a big name in television—*Playhouse 90* was developed under his aegis. He was quite a well-respected network executive, and thought to be kind of a visionary guy. When his tenure ended at CBS, he came over into a joint venture with

REVIEW
THRILLER (TV)

You can say one thing for *Thriller*, a new hour-long suspense series now on exhibition Tuesday nights at NBC, and that's that it *is* more thrilling than a brownie picnic. But not much.

Thriller stars Boris Karloff, who used to be so sinister that one look at him would turn you to salt before you could say, "Lot's wife." But as the genial host on *Thriller*, Karloff is as frightening as Grandma Moses.

It was the whim of Hubbell Robinson, from whom one has come to expect better things, to package *Thriller*, and the caprice of Fletcher Markle

Thriller got off to a shaky start and ran right into the critical buzzsaw. Fortunately, important changes were soon made to the series.

Universal to produce whatever shows that he could come up with, and the first one he came up with was *Thriller*. There was an excellent pilot, and the show sold.

Initially Fletcher Markle and James Cavanagh were producing on the show, working for Hubbell. They produced six or seven episodes. At the time I came in on the show, there'd been a couple of episodes produced, and both the studio and NBC were *extremely* unhappy with the show. In fact, they hated everything about it. For one thing, they felt it was a big mistake to have Boris Karloff *not* be Boris Karloff, to instead be acting like a professorial kind of nice chap, English country gentleman. If you're gonna hire Boris Karloff, you should *use* him like Boris Karloff and not like a professor! *That* was one of the problems. Another problem was that they thought that the demographics of the casting was *way* too old, they were too many old gray-haired ladies and old men limping around [*laughs*], and not younger characters. And then a variety of smaller reasons where they just didn't like the episodes because of this or that. Markle also got in trouble because he kept re-using sets without re-dressing them enough to disguise them, and that drove [Universal honcho] Lew Wasserman crazy. Markle thought he was doing the right thing because he was saving money. Wasserman didn't agree.

When I was brought aboard, I was kinda briefed on all of this stuff, and I was supposed to keep an eye on what was going on; and if I thought things were going awry, I was to report to Alan Miller, the head of the studio,. But before I had much of a chance to get into that, the whole thing blew up: Another episode came out with a bunch of old actors and a set that was very

TV: Bad Omen for '60-61

Premiere of N. B. C.'s 'Thriller' Series Is Preposterous Mystery Long on Violence

By JACK GOULD

A PREPOSTEROUS hour-long mystery—silly in its narrative construction, unpleasant in its tone and cumbersome in its production—served last night to introduce a series entitled "Thriller," which was billed as a major fall entrant of the National Broadcasting Company.

If viewers thought that last season's post-quiz uproar might have had some beneficial consequences, "Thriller" should put a stop to such incipient naïveté. A gruesome, choking child kidnapping,

recognizably used in the previous episode, and Wasserman just said, "That's *it*!" and he fired Fletcher Markle.

The "damage control" that then went on was pretty impressive, 'cause NBC was threatening to cancel the show before it went on the air. Wasserman had to take dramatic action to show that something serious was being done to change the tone of the show. and so he brought in two producers, Maxwell Shane was one and Bill Frye was the other. As I recall it, Maxwell's job was to jump on the six or seven episodes that had been shot and re-work them completely. In other words, cut out scenes, re-shoot scenes, write new material and so on. It was quite a big job, and Max Shane did a splendid job of taking these six or seven "sick" episodes and making them reasonably presentable. He handled that with great skill and speed. I had a great deal of admiration for the manner in which he was like a doctor on these episodes: They had cancer and he cured them. That was sort of the first onslaught of his effort, following which he would produce an occasional new episode. His forte was more in the suspense genre than in the horror genre.

Allstate Chills On NBC 'Thriller'; 'Where's Quality?'

Chicago, Sept. 20.

Problem of buying a show without benefit of a pilot is being experienced now by the Leo Burnett Agency and client Allstate with NBC-TV's new Tuesday night "Thriller."

Seeking continuation of its "tradition" as underwriter of quality shows (based on its association with "Playhouse 90"), insurance company had bought into the Boris Karloff-hosted series out of confidence in packager Hubbell Robinson and off a verbal presentation. It had believed the show would be in a quality league with "Twilight Zone" and "Alfred Hitchcock Presents." Even before the premiere last week, Allstate was disillusioned with the program concept and with proposed scripts and let NBC-TV know it in no uncertain terms.

Sponsor has been appeased for time being by the network's as-

Now, Bill Frye, his mission was to start from scratch—new episodes. Bill very much thought that the show should be more of a horror show, and the impact of that was that the look of Boris Karloff changed quite drastically: We darkened his hair and made him behave much more ominously. Act more like Boris Karloff. Not to the extent of being Frankenstein's Monster [*laughs*], but Karloff in some of his later films. That big change was mostly executed by Bill.

Did you work with both of them, Frye and Shane?
Yes I did. Max didn't stay around past the first season. I think one of the reasons he left was that the studio felt they didn't need him any more, because Bill Frye was doing such a good job with new episodes, new episodes that were exactly what they were looking for. So they phased out Max and he went on to do other things, and Bill took over the show completely. And Doug Benton came along to work with Bill as associate producer. That was basically the staff: Bill Frye, Doug and myself. I had known Doug for a couple of years before the *Thriller* experience, I just knew him from being on the same lot. We got to be much better friends once we were doing *Thriller* because we were working so closely together. Doug Benton was one of the nicest guys that I've ever known in my life, and another was Bill Frye. Earlier in our conversation I mentioned this whole story about developing an inferiority complex while working for Dick Lewis, where I thought that I couldn't do anything right; well, it was Bill Frye who turned my life around completely. When I got with Bill, Bill appreciated my efforts and he had confidence in me, God knows why [*laughs*], and was very helpful as a mentor and let me be by his side during meetings with every department, wardrobe, hair, sets, casting, editing, the whole megillah.

So I began on *Thriller* as the coordinator, making deals with the writers and directors and watching the budget. If the budget started getting out of control, I had to raise flags.

What was *the budget of an "average" Thriller episode?*
The pattern budget for each *Thriller* episode was $100,000. I believe it was the first Revue-Universal show to break the hundred grand threshold. I didn't know enough then to really know what to *do* [if the budget got out of control], but I would be the watchdog. And I'd be at the beck and call of the producer and do anything he wanted. For example, if he wanted me to go to a wardrobe session because he couldn't make it, I would do that.

And as you mentioned earlier, you were the "eyes and ears" for the higher-ups at the studio.
You just reminded me of an incident with Lew Wasserman. Before I tell it to you, first let me say that Wasserman was like Manning O'Connor insofar as knowing everything, the way Manning knew about the writer's wife having cancer. Wasserman was the all-seeing eye. He never asked a question he didn't already know the answer to. He scared a lot of people. And he would use any means whatsoever to make the best deal he could make for the company. But once he said the magic words "We've got a deal" and shook your hand, you could take that to the bank. The word "renege" was not in his vocabulary. If he had an agent like me, or one of his other minions, working for him, who ever reneged on a deal, that'd be the end of the guy's career at that company. You could be as ruthless in *making* the deal as you could possibly imagine, but once it was agreed to, then that was *it*. Interesting place.

Now here's the anecdote, which goes back to the beginning of the *Thriller* series and has to do with what I just told you about the network being unhappy with the elderly casting and the repetition of sets. Bill Frye was brought in and he got his first episode to the soundstage, I don't remember which one it was. I went to the dailies with Bill and whoever else went, and we watched the dailies, and I thought they were pretty good. And Bill Frye was tickled pink. You gotta understand, Bill Frye was the hottest fair-haired-boy producer on that lot; he'd done *The General Electric Theater* for years, a big prestige TV series. Bill had relationships with every movie star that you've ever heard of from that era, he was best friends with Cary Grant and Jimmy Stewart and all the old leading ladies, Bette Davis, Rosalind Russell, Olivia de Havilland...! All those people adored him and he was best friends with all of them, he really was, it wasn't an act or a bullshit, it was for real. Lew and Bill had a major mutual admiration society going, and Bill was happy with the dailies, so I figured, "They must be all right" 'cause I didn't know anything, I hadn't been watching dailies for years.

Well, after the dailies had been seen, I was summoned to the office of Alan Miller, who was the head of Revue Productions on into Universal Television when it morphed into that title. I got called into Alan's office and there was Alan sitting behind his desk, and there was Lew, and there was a fellow named Jerry Gershwin, who was like Lew's right-hand man. They were sittin' there kind of glowering at me as I walked into the office. I was invited to sit down, which I did, and Lew asked, "Have you seen the dailies?" I said, "Yes, sir."

At the start of *Thriller's* run, host Karloff played it benign – and rather dull. Once Swerling started writing and directing the intros, Karloff got into the spirit of fearsome fun.

"What did you think of them?" he asked me, quietly. He never raised his voice to me. Lew used to adjust his style of raking you over the coals depending on how he felt and who you were and what the circumstances were. He was capable of throwing things and yelling and screaming, but with me he was speaking in this very low, calm voice. When he asked me what I thought of the dailies, I said, "I thought they were okay, they were fine." He asked, "It didn't *bother* you that every actor was over the age of 65? The mansion set...it didn't *bother* you that I've seen that *fucking* black-and-white-checkered foyer floor *15 times*? That didn't bother you?"

Now I was beginning to sweat. Then Lew asked, "What do you *do* here, Jo?" This went through me like an arrow in the heart. I didn't know how to answer it, so I started stammering, "I—I—I make the deals for writers and directors, and I do the dubbing sometimes, and I watch the budget—"

He said, "*I* know all that shit! But what's the most important thing you do?" and I said, "I really don't know how to answer that." He said, "You are the eyes and ears on the set. This man..." — and he pointed to Alan Miller — "...has 18 shows on the air right now, in production simultaneously. He cannot be everywhere at once. And so we have guys like you who are supposed to be his eyes and ears on the set. When you see somethin' going south, you're supposed to *tell* him. And you didn't."

I had the angel on one shoulder and the devil on the other, and the devil was saying to me, "Well... tell him that Bill Frye liked the dailies. And then ask him, 'What am I supposed to say when the best producer on the lot liked the dailies? Am I supposed to go running and tell people the dailies are no good?' And the angel on my other shoulder said, "*Don't say that*. Own up to it. it's your fault, own up to it." 'Cause I realized that I had been in meetings that Bill Frye had not been in, and he might well not have been privy to some of those discussions. So I said, "Lew, I'm terribly sorry, I fucked up, and it'll never happen again." And he said, "You know, Swerling, sometimes I wonder how much of *my* money goes down the fucking drain because some guy like *you* fucks up." Again I said, "Well, I'm really sorry, and I promise you it won't happen again," and Lew went, "Goodbye!" And I walked out of the room not knowing if "Goodbye!" meant I'm fired or not [*laughs*]! It turned out that I wasn't. I worked there for 24 years and never had another meeting like that with him. And the angel was right: If I had tried to pass the buck to Bill Frye, I would have been fired instantly. I know that as surely as I know my name, that that would have been the end of me if I'd done that.

In a mid-1960s interview, Karloff is asked about Thriller, *and the only thing he said about it was what a very good friend Frye was to him, that he had great respect for Frye, that Frye was a wonderful producer, that Frye had gone to Columbia to make movies and that was "a great loss to television"—ai yi yi! What was it about Frye that brought out such loyalty in the old stars?*

Bill was a just plain wonderful, talented guy. He knew his job, he had superb taste, and they just don't come more charming and likable. He was a great host, a great storyteller—a better word would be *raconteur*. He was fun to be with, very entertaining, and with a heart as big as North America. He was gentle with his criticisms and utterly generous with his praise. He was just blessed with all those qualities which made people want to be his best friend. I visited him a couple of months ago at his home in Palm Desert. He's over 90 now and not in the best of shape, but all his marbles are intact and it's still a hoot to hang out with him. He definitely *had*, and still *has*..."*it*."

Karloff—talk about writing and directing his intros.

They needed somebody to sort of be in charge of Boris Karloff, and that "somebody" turned out to be me. Under Hubbell Robinson, whoever wrote the script, wrote the introductions, that was just part of writing the script. When Bill took over, he decided that somebody needed to write all of the introductions, the same procedure as Alfred Hitchcock [the on-camera host of Universal's *Alfred Hitchcock Presents*] used with his guy James Allardice who, for those years, got paid big money to write Hitchcock's lead-ins and lead-outs. I think Allardice got paid more to write those intros than some of the writers got to write scripts! I just read a biography of Hitchcock, and it emphasized how important a guy Allardice was to Hitchcock: Allardice wrote speeches for him and all kinds of things. He could write with that Hitchcock twinkle-in-the-eye kind of wry humor.

Anyway, Bill felt that somebody should be writing the *Thriller* intros à la James Allardice instead of having the individual teleplay writers write them. He really wanted more of a consistency with them, and not have them be written by a different person every week. They needed somebody to do it, and I was handy, and Bill entrusted me with that. That's the kind of thing that made me love Bill Frye.

So I took a whack at a couple of them, and Bill was pleased with the results, and then I became kind of Boris Karloff's overall "concierge" when he was in town. He lived on the outskirts of London, and he would come here X-number of times a year, I believe it may have been three or four times a year. Each time he would come for about two weeks, and during the two weeks he was in town, we would shoot as many lead-ins and lead-outs as we could while he was here. I would write intros for scripts that were in production, for scripts that were already shot and for scripts that had come out at least in first draft; and when Karloff was here for two weeks we would shoot the intros, as many as possible. We could shoot three or so a day. And when he was in town, we always tried to have a script available for him to do a guest star shot in. I don't think we did this every time, but we did on many occasions.

And you were "in charge" of him away from the soundstages also.

I would pick Boris up at the airport, I would make sure that he was comfortable at the Chateau Marmont which is where he and his wife Evie stayed when they were in town, and I would drive him around to all of his appointments on the lot, take him to the stage when we were shooting his intros, take him to the looping stage to do voiceovers and so on and so forth. I was responsible for Boris as well as the introductions [*laughs*]!

What can you remember about directing the Karloff intros?

I was the *de facto* director. I directed them because I had done all the preparation, but I was "illegal" because I wasn't a member of the Directors Guild. So I had to have a member of the Directors Guild on the set. My wife's father was a producer-director who worked on the lot; in fact, that's how I met his daughter. His name was Richard Bartlett, he had a partner named Norman Jolley and they had a little company called Bartlett-Jolley Productions and they did *Wagon Train*s — Jolley was a writer and Dick was the director. They did quite a few shows there at Universal. So...if you can't help your family, who *can* you help? I threw that bone to my father-in-law, whose career was a little bit on the wane at the time, and he would get two days' pay, one day of prep and one day of shooting. But my understanding with him was that he wouldn't have to come down and prepare, he just had to be there on the day of shooting and say "Action!" and "Cut!" And he would always look at me before he said "Cut!" [*Laughs*]

I would tell Boris what I wanted him to do, and tell the crew guys what I wanted the camera setup to be, and what props were needed, and all that kind of stuff. So Dick got the dough and I got the practice. It wasn't difficult. It *starts* getting difficult when you add characters to a scene. If you've got one character in a scene, the extent to which you can get "fancy" with the shooting is somewhat limited. So it was pretty easy to direct those intros.

Do you remember what Thriller *intro was your first?*

I do not. I don't think it was the first Bill Frye episode because it *had* to take a little time for me to phase into that. But it was early on.

Did Karloff memorize those intros or did he have cue cards?

He had cue cards. By the way, his catchphrases "This is a *Thriller*!" and "As sure as my name is Boris Karloff..." were left over from his professional host days — that dialogue was in the pilot ["The Twisted Image," aired in September 1960]. I continued to use it because it had been established ... and it was good!

Did Karloff enjoy himself doing these macabre and sometimes hokey intros?

I think he enjoyed himself enormously.

Karloff regularly commuted 12,000 miles (London to Universal City, California) to work on *Thriller*, a series that, like the legendary *Shock!* movie packages of the 1950s, mixed horror and crime stories. In this series of publicity shots, Karloff appears to be prowling the studio's back lot.

Arthur Hiller directed three Thrillers *in the early days when the episode director directed Karloff's intro, and he told me Karloff was "insecure ... always worried about, 'Was that okay? Was I all right?'"*

I remember Boris being the way Arthur described him, but I doubt it was insecurity he was projecting. I'd be more inclined to think it was just his humble and polite demeanor at play. He'd been around too long and was too much of a professional to actually be insecure in his role as host. I do think he was much more comfortable playing pure Karloff than he was in the early shows when they wanted him to play it more like an English professor.

Was he usually good for one take?

Pretty much so. When Boris did more than one take, it was usually for technical reasons, rather than his performance, which was always spot on.

How much directing of Karloff would you actually do? Or did you just set him loose?

In terms of directing his performance? Nahhh, he directed him*self*. Basically what I did was conceive what the setting was, decide what props we were going to use, etc. We tried to be clever when we would show each cast members as Boris mentioned each name; we'd have their faces appear in a mirror, in a thousand dollar bill in place of the president, and stuff like that, that I would come up with. But as far as Boris' performance, he needed no direction. There might have been a few rare instances where he transposed some words or something like that, and had to do it over; but as far as telling him how to shape a performance, it was unnecessary. He knew better than anybody else in the world how to *do* that.

How large a crew did you have?

Oh, boy, I could probably re-construct it. I had a cameraman and a camera operator; I had a gaffer; I had an electrician; an assistant director; wardrobe person, makeup person; a sound mixer and boom man; and that was probably *it*.

And your father-in-law saying "action" and "cut"!

[*Laughs*] Yes! Oh, and there may have been a special effects guy there, if we were doing smoke or something like that. Not more than about ten people.

When you conceived a setting for an intro, would you place it in a set that you knew already existed, or have a set built?

All of the above. One of the standard things we did in shooting the episodes as a whole was seeing what sets were available on the lot. Of course, Universal was a huge studio with 32 soundstages or something like that, so "stealing" sets and redressing them was the norm, and building sets was the unusual. Whenever we needed a particular kind of set, I would take a tour of the stages and find out from the production office which ones were not going to be in use on the day that *I* was going to shoot. I'd go look at those stages and see

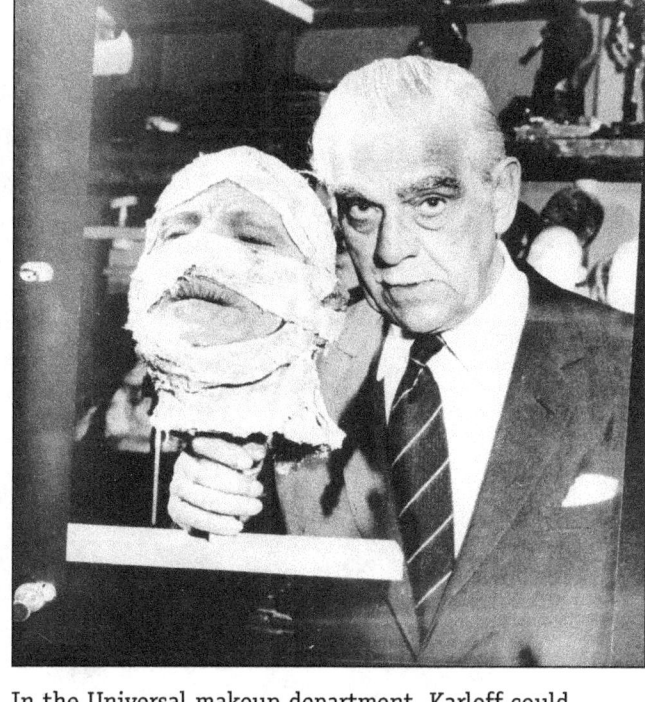

In the Universal makeup department, Karloff could always count on finding a few familiar faces.

if there was anything that I could redress into whatever it was I needed. Failing that, we would try to put together something that was more of an illusion than a set, with a black scrim and some bee smoke and a couple of props and/or set dec [set decoration]. Like in "Pigeons from Hell," Boris is out in some woods, with the fog and all of that. I'm sure that that was something I found on the back lot, or that was already standing.

Here's an interesting little thing about Karloff that's indicative of the kind of person he was: We were in my car one day and I was taking him to a soundstage or somewhere like that, and he was muttering to himself about how lucky he was. I asked, "Why do you say that, Boris?" and he said, "Jo," he said, "how many actors do you know, who have made as many bad movies as I have, and are still working?" [*Laughs*] And it was true — his movies *didn't* tend to be Academy Award material! But that [self-effacing response]: that's who he *was*. And of course, everybody who ever interviewed him in his entire career post-*Frankenstein* would ask, "How do you feel about being typecast? Does it bother you that when people say 'Boris Karloff,' they immediately think of the Frankenstein Monster?" All interviewers asked him that question, and his stock answer was, "The Frankenstein Monster was my best friend. Where would I be without him? It doesn't bother me when people associate me with him."

Was his wife on the set all the time?

No, she wasn't, but I met Evie on numerous occasions. Lovely, lovely lady…wonderful lady. A perfect wife for him. He was the English country gentleman and she was the English country lady.

Most of the spooky shows back then had a host: Rod Serling on Twilight Zone, *John Newland on* One Step Beyond, *and of course Hitchcock. In writing and directing your intros, did you derive any inspiration from the way those folks did theirs?*

I think if I got any inspiration, it was from Hitchcock. Even though we were doing them in a macabre way, when possible I tried to get a little bit of humor into those intros — which I don't recall Rod Serling or John Newland doing, they were always pretty serious. So I was definitely inspired by Hitchcock. I don't think that our intros on *Thriller* were in the same ballpark with the Hitchcock intros. His intros were *spectacularly* good and ours were good … they did their job for our show. I think if there was a contest, Hitchcock would be the winner [*laughs*]!

Throughout the Thriller *run, did you see much of Hubbell Robinson?*

I saw quite a bit of Hubbell before the takeover, but that was only over a period of a few weeks. Once

In addition to hosting, Karloff also acted in several *Thrillers*, none better than "The Incredible Doktor Markesan." In the first photo, he poses with director Robert Florey; in the second, he and his fellow ghouls (Basil Howes, Richard Hale, Billy Beck) look like they're waiting for one more member of "The Crypt-Kicker Five"!

Bill and Doug took over the show, I never saw Hubbell again. I liked him, he was very cordial to me, but I had a feeling he was seriously out of his element. I remember one amusing thing he said to me: I got married shortly after being assigned to the show, and he said, "Congratulations. You've just cut your usefulness to me by 50 percent."

Your Thriller *job was to alert your bosses if things started going south on the set. Did you ever have to "blow the whistle" on a director?*
No. I never did have to blow the whistle on a director. Once Bill and Doug arrived, there were no more problems of that kind.

But were there Thriller *directors you knew you had to keep an eye on?*
I had to keep an eye on all of them, but there were some whom I considered bulletproof. One was Herschel Daugherty. Another was Doug Heyes. Mitch Leisen, Ida Lupino and John Brahm were also very reliable. Basically these choices were made by Bill and Doug, and I don't recall ever having any problems with any of them. John Brahm was a very nice, gentle man. I visited him at his home in Malibu on many occasions. I have no idea what it was about him that suited him so fully to the world of the macabre.

Talk about the other people involved behind the scenes on Thriller, *starting with some of the writers, like Donald Sanford.*
Donald Sanford probably wrote more *Thrillers* than anybody else. He was a very good writer and a hard-working guy. I was over to his house a few times for dinner and he and his wife made and served great cassoulet, and it was my introduction to that particular dish. He was a very nice guy, not an egomaniac or a prima donna of any kind. He was a very down-to-earth, decent guy and wrote more than anybody else...but other than his cassoulet, I can't think of any anecdotes!
Robert Bloch, personally, was kind of a quiet fellow that I didn't get to know real well. I admired his work tremendously and I thought he had a wonderful knack for writing this type of material. His scripts were always almost entirely shootable when he would turn them in.
Doug Heyes is a guy I knew *very*, very well. I guess I met him on *Thriller*. A couple of years after *Thriller*, I was sort of taken out from under the wing of Bill Frye—

about which I was not too thrilled—and I ended up under the wing of Roy Huggins, who was another big shaker and maker in television. *The Fugitive* and *77 Sunset Strip* and on and on and on, up to *The Rockford Files* and *Hunter*. I was with Roy for about 18 years, until he retired. Doug and Roy were very close friends, so Roy employed Doug Heyes many many many times through all the shows that Roy and I worked on together. It started with *Kraft Suspense Theatre* and then went on to *Run for Your Life* and *Alias Smith and Jones, Cool Million, City of Angels* and *The Rockford Files*. Doug was the sort of guy that Roy could depend on. Doug was a very talented artist, he could draw, he could paint, and he used to be able to do storyboards for himself. I think he worked for Hallmark at one time, doing greeting cards [*laughs*]! He was a very good writer and I *loved* Doug Heyes. Had an ego as big as North America, but he was one of those guys whose big ego didn't turn him into any kind of a monster. Stephen Cannell was also like that, and there wasn't a nicer man in the world than Steve. His big ego didn't corrupt his *soul*. Doug used to talk about himself in the third person: "They wanted a Doug Heyes script," he would say, instead of saying, "They wanted a script from me." Nevertheless, he was a very, very nice guy and a hard worker and always delivered quality material. And was quite a good director because he was so talented visually, because he had the eye of an artist. I would attribute his skill at picking interesting camera angles to the fact that he was a talented artist.

Richard Matheson, who just passed away, was a giant in the business. I lived in a community called Hidden Hills out here for a number of years, and Dick Matheson was a neighbor of mine. I knew him quite well and we would have dinner at each other's houses and things of that nature. He was very droll and funny...not the guy that you cast as a master of horror and suspense! He was just a kind of a "regular guy." His son Richard Jr. used to work for us at Cannell. He's a lovely young man.

You mentioned once saving a "sick" Markham script. On Thriller *did you ever do any re-writing?*

No, I never did any writing on *Thriller* scripts, other than lead-ins and lead-outs.

Karloff once called himself "lucky," prompting Swerling to ask him to explain himself. "Jo," Karloff said, "how many actors do you know, who have made as many bad movies as I have, and are still working?"

Good question!

Once Universal and NBC and everybody decided "This crime stuff isn't what we want on Thriller,*" why did crime episodes continue to appear throughout the whole two years?*

Once Bill Frye took over, it seems to me there were only a *few* episodes that Max Shane did, that were strictly suspense episodes. Under Bill, there may have been a couple that slipped by, just because we were short of material, but I think Bill [mostly stuck to horror stories]. Doug Benton read every *Weird Tales* story that was ever written, and there must have been thousands of them. That "library" that came out of *Weird Tales* magazine was our principal source. So the show was definitely meant to be more of a horror show than a crime or suspense show and that's what seemed to work best, that's what made the studio happy, and that's what Bill Frye liked to do best. If there were crime episodes that snuck in for all two years, there may have been a couple of Max Shanes that were held back for some reason or another. I really don't recall.

In the late 1950s, new monster movies were popular in theaters and the oldies were getting great ratings on TV, and yet there were no horror TV series and I always wondered why. But recently I found articles from those days saying that horror TV series would violate the Television Code, be the target of TV "policing" groups, etc. How'd you get away with Thriller? *How much of a pain were the TV censors?*

The network censors were a constant pain in the ass. Way too much time was spent negotiating trade-offs with them. Incidentally, I once actually saw a guy with a vanity license plate on his car that read **TVCENSR**. Can you imagine anyone in that job wanting to advertise it that way to the whole world? Oh my God!

Early in Thriller's *run, the sponsor Allstate Insurance was a bit squeamish about gruesome murder in a TV series sponsored by an insurance company—it could hurt their image.*

I really don't recall the problem with Allstate but it certainly rings true. It's logical that there would be some wariness on the part of Standards and Practices and/or squeamish food companies where horror series were concerned. Once Bill Frye and Doug took over the show, I don't think we had any serious problems either with the network or the sponsors.

The Weird Tales *writers — what kind of money did they get for allowing their stories to be used on* Thriller?

As I recall, we paid not more than $500 for a story. Maybe sometimes less. There was a guy named Forrest something [Forrest J Ackerman] who was our conduit to the authors when and if needed.

Were you a fan of horror or science fiction movies as a kid growing up in Hollywood?

On the contrary. I recall being scared by *The Wizard of Oz* [1939]. The Wicked Witch in *The Wizard of Oz* scared the shit out of me, and I didn't get a night's sleep for a month after seeing it. I'm going back to when I was five or six years old. And then there was a movie called *The Return of Doctor X* [1939], which was a horror picture starring Humphrey Bogart. The synopsis is that a surgeon develops a means of bringing a dead person back to life, and after a fellow scientist, Doctor X, played by Humphrey Bogart, dies in the electric chair, this surgeon is able to claim the body and bring it back to his lab and revive the man. The hitch is that Doctor X can't regenerate his blood supply, so in order to stay alive he has to get transfused all the time. The bulk of the movie is about Doctor X finding out somehow who has the same rare blood type that he does, and killing these people and draining them of their blood. They gave Bogart this pasty white makeup and a white stripe through his hair where allegedly the electrode was, and he would be peering into windows and things like that. *It scared the shit out of me*, and again I couldn't turn the lights out in my bedroom for months! I recently ran across the movie on Turner Classic Movies and watched it, and I thought it was just as tame as could be [*laughs*]. That's a lengthy answer to your question, but I really was susceptible to being scared as a little kid by that type of movie, and I avoided seeing them.

Doug Benton got to do some socializing with Karloff, on and even off the lot. Did you also get to do so?

Yeah. There were times, I think, that we were going to have a dinner up at Bill Frye's house that I would be included in, and Boris and Evie would be there. It was not a regular, everyday kind of thing, but occasional.

A goofy question that only a goofy fan would ask: Was it fun to hear your words coming out of Boris Karloff's mouth?

Absolutely. I loved it. It was not a monumentally large challenge, nothing I will go down in history for, but it was really nice, particularly because I hadn't *done* anything like that before. To see something take shape out of an idea, onto the paper and then on film, was quite gratifying, and good for my ego. Particularly after my experience with Mr. Lewis, where I couldn't hit my ass with both hands as far as *he* was concerned. I wouldn't compare it to Steven Spielberg directing a hundred million dollar movie, but in its own little way, it was very gratifying.

Did you ever get any idea whether Karloff actually watched his own series, Thriller?

That's a great question...and I don't know the answer [*laughs*]! I have no idea.

*Did you ever see him again post-*Thriller?

I remember only one instance: He was at Universal working in some show, I don't remember what it was, it was some series that was being done on the lot [possibly Karloff's 1968 episode of *The Name of the Game*]. He let Doug and me know that he was there, and we went down to visit him in his dressing room. I remember being pleased that we were able to do that, because he died not long after. And he did not look good when we saw him there, he had these bad knees and he looked like he had aged quite a bit since we'd seen him last. It was really a golden opportunity to see him once more, before he passed away.

It's sort of astonishing that on one series, *Thriller*, there could be three people that I interfaced with, who were among the nicest people that I've ever known in my lifetime: That's Bill and Doug and Boris. People ask me all the time, "Who was your favorite actor that you've worked with?" and without blinking, the answer is Boris Karloff. I've worked with Jim Garner and Joe

Jo Swerling Jr. in 2017 with a prized possession, the signed Karloff portrait visible in the background.

Campanella and a lot of guys who were really, really nice guys, but Boris was the champ of all of them. He was just a sweet English country gentleman who was a *thousand* percent professional. He wanted to do things that, because of his age and physical condition, we didn't want him to do. We'd have a thing where he'd have to go up a flight of stairs rapidly, and we would hire a double and put the wardrobe on him and all of that. We'd get the double ready to shoot, and Boris would spot the guy and ask, "What's *he* doin' here?" "We don't want you to run up the stairs." "Why *not*? *I'll* run up the stairs." Bad knee and all. What a wonderful, professional guy he was. In the '80s I worked with an actor in a show called *Hunter*, Fred Dryer, who was an all-pro defensive end for the L.A. Rams, and he wouldn't even get *wet*. This guy was a physical specimen like you can't believe, he ate rabbit food all day, and he wouldn't get wet. Whereas one night on a *Thriller* where Boris was guest starring ["The Prediction"], we had the rain towers out on the back lot for a scene where his character gets hit by a car on a dirt road. We had a double hired for that shot, and of course when Karloff's character is hit by the car and falls, it *was* the double; but we needed Boris to roll into the next shot, in a closeup. It required that he get down in six inches of mud with rain falling on him, and he did it without batting an eyelash. Now, Fred Dryer would have refused to do that shot. Boris would want to do things that we absolutely didn't want him to do, because he was a professional.

He was so unlike the characters he played, it was mind-boggling. I have a picture of him on my office wall, and the inscription that he wrote to me was, "As long as Jo is my shepherd, I shall not want. Regards, Boris Karloff." I *treasure* it, it's one of my favorite possessions. I wish he were my grandfather.

Appendix 5
Karloff and the Kritters

In 1961, while hosting the *Thriller* series, Karloff dropped in at the ranch of Jim Dannaldson, who provided animals (and reptiles and insects, and and and) to movie and TV companies. This visit became a cute newspaper story with several photos, which surely was the whole reason Karloff was there in the first place.

The newspaper story appears on the next two pages. On subsequent pages, you'll find additional, perhaps never-before-published shots of Karloff at the Dannaldson ranch. All these photos are from …

Left, Boris Karloff examines raven held by Jim Dannaldson. After much thought, Karloff didn't buy since raven was stubborn, wouldn't quoth "Nevermore."

Right, Amazon parrot, American cat have talk as Karloff chuckles over casual conversation. Karloff wanted parrot to hold key to plot.

Prop shopping with

by ERIC BARNES

Karloff chats with a marmosa opossum who seems to be getting best of argument. Discussion centered on why women fear small, scurrying animals.

Capuchin monkey, above, didn't make list since Karloff won't change diapers.

Boris Karloff

• When shopping for a script idea, Boris Karloff, host and sometime star of NBC's Monday night Thriller, chooses his items with care. A while ago, he browsed around Jim Dannaldson's Tarzana, Cal., ranch, where the film industry can rent such dainty dishes as rats, cockroaches, grasshoppers, rare birds, lizards and other oddball delicacies. Being a typical shopper, Karloff was extremely choosy about his selection. He began by gently poking some items, but gave this up when he almost lost a finger to a Mexican beaded lizard. "Surly chap," said Karloff. Unfortunately, sample tasting is not allowed in this market since the merchandise often bites back. "And their little teeth are so sharp," said Karloff, wrapping a handkerchief tightly about a wound. Noticing that prices were high, Karloff attempted a little shoplifting, but encountered difficulty in getting an 8-ft. boa constrictor to lie quietly in his pocket. Finally satisfied, Karloff left with his bag filled. But he's still nervously trying to find the tarantula he bought. Maybe you've seen it, hmmnm?

Right, wary Karloff checks over an item from afar. "They look so hungry—for me."

Appendix 6

YOU'VE THRILLED TO THE BRIDE
YOU'VE CHILLED TO THE SON
NOW MEET THE...
NIECE OF FRANKENSTEIN!

In December 1958, while *The Veil* was on hiatus, Boris Karloff's niece Diana Bromley murdered her own sons, 10 and 13 – "acts rivaling those in her uncle's horror films," as one UPI story put it. Eerily, her m.o. almost exactly matched that of Karloff's character in the still-in-theaters *The Haunted Strangler* (1958), with Karloff as a killer who chokes his victims and then polishes them off with a scalpel.

You'll find more on this tragedy on page 45 of this book; in the books *Women of the World: The Rise of the Female Diplomat* by Helen McCarthy and *Foul Deeds & Suspicious Deaths in Guildford* by Caroline Maxton; and in the 1958-59 newspaper stories on the pages that follow.

SONS SLAIN—Mrs. Diana Bromley (above), niece of actor Boris Karloff, is being held in Haslemere, England, in connection with the slash-slaying of her two son. She is now in a hospital after being found wandering about with a throat wound. The boys' bodies were found a few hours after they arrived home from school.

2 Relatives Of Karloff Knife Victims

HASLEMERE, England (AP)—Two grandnephews of Actor Boris Karloff, the sons of a British cabinet official, were found dead with their throats cut in their country home Thursday night.

Their mother, Mrs. Diana Bromley, Karloff's niece, lay in a hospital with throat wounds apparently caused by a razor. Police waited at her bedside to hear her story of how the stabbings took place. Police said she is expected to live.

THE BOYS' father, Thomas Bromley, found his sons dead when he drove home with Christmas gifts Thursday night to his mansion in Surrey.

Martin, 13, was dead in the garage.

Stephen, 10, lay dead in a bathroom.

Both were in their pajamas.

The boys recently returned home from boarding school for their Christmas holidays.

In a nearby woods Bromley found his dark, attractive wife walking among the pines and holly. She was taken to a hospital.

MRS. BROMLEY, 39, is the former Diana Marion Pratt, daughter of Sir John Pratt, British diplomat, authority on Far Eastern affairs, and brother of the screen and stage star who dropped his family name and assumed a stage name of Karloff.

She married Bromley in 1944. He is 48.

He was British consul in Washington 1946-49, then became first secretary of the British Embassy at Baghdad. He is attached to the cabinet secretariat and the ministry of defense now.

12/20/58

Karloff's Niece Held as Slayer of Her Son

HASLEMERE, England—(AP)—Mrs. Diana Bromley, 39-year-old wife of a British cabinet official, was charged at a Guildford court today with murdering her elder son, Martin, 13.

The bodies of Martin and his brother, Stephen, 10, were found with their throats cut at their country home Thursday.

★ ★ ★ ★

Mrs. Bromley, niece of horror actor Boris Karloff, was found wandering in woods nearby with wounds on her throat. She was taken to a hospital, and physicians decided she was fit today to make a court appearance.

Thomas Bromley, British consul in Washington 1946-49 and now attached to the prime minister's cabinet secretariat and the ministry of defense, found his sons dead Thursday night when he arrived with Christmas gifts at his mansion in Surrey.

Martin, 13, was in the garage and Stephen, 10, was in a bedroom.

Mrs. Bromley, 39, was found walking in nearby woods and was taken to a hospital.

She is the former Diana Marion Pratt, daughter of Sir John Pratt, British diplomat and brother of the actor who dropped his family name and took the stage name of Karloff.

AP Wirephoto by radio from London
MRS. DIANA BROMLEY
Held in deaths

Spain Moves to Clean Up Money Scandal

12/20/58

Two Sons Murdered
Police Arrest Karloff's Kin

BASLEMERE, England (UPI) A niece of horror movie actor Boris Karloff was arrested yesterday on a charge of murder in the death of her two sons whose throats were slashed in the family home where they had returned from school for the Christmas holidays.

Thomas Bromley, a civil service of-

Mrs. Diana Bromley

ficial attached to the Defense Ministry, found the bodies of his sons, Martin, 13, and Stephen, 10, Thursday night. He also found his wife, Diana, unconscious with a throat wound.

MRS. BROMLEY, 39, was taken to a hospital but was released yesterday and brought before a magistrate in nearby Guildford where she was formally charged with murdering Martin. This is in line with normal English legal practice of charging a suspect with one slaying in multiple murders.

Detective Inspector George Cornish told the court that his investigation had "satisfied" him that Mrs. Bromley "had caused his [Martin's] death."

An inquest is expected to be held here Tuesday into the deaths of the boys who had come home from boarding school for the holidays.

Bromley told police the first thing he saw on his arrival home was a bloodstained cricket bat and the boy's football boots and clothing in the hall of his six bedroom home.

12/21/58

Decision on Murder Trial Of Karloff's Niece Delayed

GUILDFORD, England. (AP)—The prosecution has been given until Jan. 14 to decide whether to bring Mrs. Diana Bromley, a niece of actor Boris Karloff, to trial on a charge of murdering her 13-year-old son.

The magistrate's court in Guildford granted the additional week yesterday and ordered the 39-year-old woman held without bail.

She is the wife of Thomas Bromley, 43, who was British consul in Washington in 1946-49. He is now attached to the cabinet secretariat and the ministry of defense. Mrs. Bromley is the daughter of Sir John Pratt, British diplomat and brother of the stage and screen star.

Bromley found their two sons, Martin, 13, and Stephen, 10, dead with their throats cut when he returned from Christmas shopping Dec. 18.

Mrs. Bromley was found wandering in the woods near their Surrey mansion with throat wounds.

Physicians say she is now fit to appear in court.

Radio Grant Affirmed

WASHINGTON. (AP) — The Federal Communications Commission yesterday affirmed its grant of last September giving radio station KNAF, Fredericksburg, Texas, permission to change from 1340 kilocycles to 50 watts, unlimited time, to 910 kilocycles, 1 kilowatt, daytime. The grant was protested by Sherman, Texas, station KRRV.

1/8/59

WOMAN ACCUSED IN STRANGLING

GUILDFORD, England, Feb. 19 —(AP) Mrs. Diana Bromley, 39-year-old niece of actor Boris Karloff, has been ordered to trial on charges of strangling one of her small sons and drowning the other.

Mrs. Bromley was charged in magistrate's court yesterday in a preliminary hearing. No date was set for the trial.

The woman is the wife of Thomas E. Bromley, a Foreign Office official attached to the British cabinet who was British consul in Washington, 1946-49. Her father is Sir John Pratt, British diplomat, authority on the Far East, and brother of the stage and screen star, who dropped the family name and took the stage name of Karloff.

At the preliminary hearing, prosecuting attorney M. J. Jardine told the court Mrs. Bromley drugged the two — Martin, 13, and Stephen, 10 — after they came home from school last Dec. 18 for the Christmas holidays.

He said she laid the unconscious children on a bed in the garage, backed in a car and started the motor to pump out carbon monoxide fumes, and lay down with them.

After a while she realized they were still alive, said Jardine, and "she then killed Martin by strangling him with a belt. She carried Stephen upstairs to the bathroom and drowned him."

The attorney said Mrs. Bromley hacked at the boys' throats after they were dead, then cut her own throat and tried to drown herself in a lily pond.

Bromley, returning home that night with Christmas gifts, found the bodies of the children and then found his dark, attractive wife wandering in the woods. She has been in a London hospital since.

2/19/59

Mother 'Insane,' Slay Trial Ends

Reuters News Agency

LONDON, Feb. 25 — Mrs. Diana Bromley, 40, wife of a senior government official and niece of actor Boris Karloff, was judged insane Wednesday and released from trial on charges of slaying her two young sons. The court ordered her to be kept in strict custody indefinitely.

A prison official said Mrs. Bromley had attempted to kill herself since her arrest in December.

Mrs. Bromley, a slim dark-haired woman, sat quietly in court between two women police during Wednesday's 10-minute hearing. She had been accused of drugging her sons Martin, 13, and Stephen, 10, and then strangling Martin with a belt and drowning Stephen in a bathtub.

2/26/59

Appendix 7

"The Vestris"

By Robert Dale Owen

> This story, taken from Robert Dale Owen's 19th-century book *Footfalls on the Boundary of Another World*, provided the basis for the *Telephone Time* episode "The Vestris" (February 25, 1958) with Boris Karloff. "The Vestris" also served as the *Veil* pilot. My write-up on "The Vestris" appears on pages 17 and 18.

The following narrative, drawn from nautical life, exhibits coincidences unmistakably produced by some agency other than chance.

Mr. Robert Bruce, originally descended from some branch of the Scottish family of that name, was born, in humble circumstances, about the close of the last century, at Torbay, in the south of England, and there bred up to a seafaring life.

When about 30 years of age, to wit, in the year 1828, he was first mate on a bark trading between Liverpool and St. John's, New Brunswick.

On one of her voyages bound westward, being then some five or six weeks out and having neared the eastern portion of the Banks of Newfoundland, the captain and mate had been on deck at noon, taking an observation of the sun; after which they both descended to calculate their day's work.

The cabin, a small one, was immediately at the stern of the vessel, and the short stairway descending to it ran athwart-ships. Immediately opposite to this stairway, just beyond a small square landing, was the mate's stateroom; and from that landing there were two doors, close to each other, the one opening aft into the cabin, the other, fronting the stairway, into the stateroom. The desk in the stateroom was in the forward part of it, close to the door; so that anyone sitting at it and looking over his shoulder could see into the cabin.

The mate, absorbed in his calculation, which did not result as he expected, varying considerably from the dead-reckoning, had not noticed the captain's motions. When he had completed his calculations, he called out, without looking round, "I make our latitude and longitude so and so. Can that be right? How is yours?"

Receiving no reply, he repeated his question, glancing over his shoulder and perceiving, as he thought, the captain busy writing on his slate. Still no answer. Thereupon he rose; and, as he fronted the cabin door, the figure he had mistaken for the captain raised his head and disclosed to the astonished mate the features of an entire stranger.

Bruce was no coward; but, as he met that fixed gaze looking directly at him in grave silence, and became assured that it was no one whom he had ever seen before, it was too much for him; and, instead of stopping to question the seeming intruder, he rushed upon deck in such evident alarm that it instantly attracted the captain's attention. "Why, Mr. Bruce," said the latter, "what in the world is the matter with you?"

"The matter, sir? Who is that at your desk?"

"No one that I know of."

"But there *is*, sir: there's a stranger there."

"A stranger! Why, man, you must be dreaming. You must have seen the steward there, or the second mate. Who else would venture down without orders?"

"But, sir, he was sitting in your armchair, fronting the door, writing on your slate. Then he looked up full in my face; and, if ever I saw a man plainly and distinctly in this world, I saw him."

"Him! Whom?"

"God knows, sir: I don't. I saw a man, and a man I had never seen in my life before."

"You must be going crazy, Mr. Bruce. A stranger, and we nearly six weeks out!"

"I know, sir; but then I saw him."

"Go down and see who it is."

Bruce hesitated. "I never was a believer in ghosts," he said; "but, if the truth must be told, sir, I'd rather not face it alone."

"Come, come, man. Go down at once, and don't make a fool of yourself before the crew."

"I hope you've always found me willing to do what's reasonable," Bruce replied, changing color; "but if it's all the same to you, sir, I'd rather we should both go down together."

The captain descended the stairs, and the mate followed him. Nobody in the cabin! They examined the staterooms. Not a soul to be found!

"Well, Mr. Bruce," said the captain, "did not I tell you you had been dreaming?"

"It's all very well to say so, sir; but if I didn't see that man writing on your slate, may I never see my home and family again!"

"Ah! writing on the slate! Then it should be there still." And the captain took it up.

"By God," he exclaimed, "here's something, sure enough! Is that your writing, Mr. Bruce?"

The mate took the slate; and there, in plain, legible characters, stood the words, "STEER TO THE NOR'WEST."

"Have you been trifling with me, sir?" added the captain, in a stern manner.

"On my word as a man and as a sailor, sir," replied Bruce, "I know no more of this matter than you do. I have told you the exact truth."

The captain sat down at his desk, the slate before him, in deep thought. At last, turning the slate over and pushing it toward Bruce, he said, "Write down, 'Steer to the nor'west.'"

The mate complied; and the captain, after narrowly comparing the two handwritings, said, "Mr. Bruce, go and tell the second mate to come down here."

He came; and, at the captain's request, he also wrote the same words. So did the steward. So, in succession, did every man of the crew who could write at all. But not one of the various hands resembled, in any degree, the mysterious writing.

When the crew retired, the captain sat deep in thought. "Could anyone have been stowed away?" at last he said. "The ship must be searched; and if I don't find the fellow he must be a good hand at hide-and-seek. Order up all hands."

Every nook and corner of the vessel, from stem to stern, was thoroughly searched, and that with all the eagerness of excited curiosity, for the report had gone out that a stranger had shown himself on board; but not a living soul beyond the crew and the officers was found.

Returning to the cabin after their fruitless search, "Mr. Bruce," said the captain, "what the devil do you make of all this?"

"Can't tell, sir. *I* saw the man write; you see the writing. There must be something in it."

"Well, it would seem so. We have the wind free, and I have a great mind to keep her away and see what will come of it."

"I surely would, sir, if I were in your place. It's only a few hours lost, at the worst."

"Well, we'll see. Go on deck and give the course nor'west. And, Mr. Bruce," he added, as the mate rose to go, "have a look-out aloft, and let it be a hand you can depend on."

His orders were obeyed. About three o'clock the look-out reported an iceberg nearly ahead, and, shortly after, what he thought was a vessel of some kind close to it.

As they approached, the captain's glass disclosed the fact that it was a dismantled ship, apparently frozen to the ice, and with a good many human beings on it. Shortly after, they hove to, and sent out the boats to the relief of the sufferers.

It proved to be a vessel from Quebec, bound to Liverpool, with passengers on board. She had got entangled in the ice, and finally frozen fast, and had passed several weeks in a most critical situation. She was stove, her decks swept, – in fact, a mere wreck; all her provisions and almost all her water gone. Her crew and passengers had lost all hopes of being saved, and their gratitude for the unexpected rescue was proportionately great.

As one of the men who had been brought away in the third boat that had reached the wreck was ascending the ship's side, the mate, catching a glimpse of his face, started back in consternation. It was the very face he had seen, three or four hours before, looking up at him from the captain's desk.

At first he tried to persuade himself it might be fancy; but the more he examined the man the more sure he became that he was right. Not only the face, but the person and the dress, exactly corresponded.

As soon as the exhausted crew and famished passengers were cared for, and the bark on her course again, the mate called the captain aside. "It seems that was not a ghost I saw to-day, sir: the man's alive."

"What do you mean? Who's alive?"

"Why, sir, one of the passengers we have just saved is the same man I saw writing on your slate at noon. I would swear to it in a court of justice."

"Upon my word, Mr. Bruce," replied the captain, "this gets more and more singular. Let us go and see this man."

They found him in conversation with the captain of the rescued ship. They both came forward, and expressed, in the warmest terms, their gratitude for deliverance from a horrible fate – slow-coming death by exposure and starvation.

The captain replied that he had but done what he was certain they would have done for him under the same circumstances, and asked them both to step down into the cabin. Then, turning to the passenger, he said, "I hope, sir, you will not think I am trifling with you; but I would be much obliged to you if you would write a few words on this slate." And he handed him the slate, with that side up on which the mysterious writing was not. "I will do anything you ask," replied the passenger; "but what shall I write?"

"A few words are all I want. Suppose you write, 'Steer to the nor'west.'"

The passenger, evidently puzzled to make out the motive for such a request, complied, however, with a smile. The captain took up the slate and examined it closely; then, stepping aside so as to conceal the slate from the passenger, he turned it over, and gave it to him again with the other side up.

"You say that is your handwriting?" said he.

"I need not say so," rejoined the other, looking at it, "for you saw me write it."

"And this?" said the captain, turning the slate over.

The man looked first at one writing, then at the other, quite confounded. At last, "What is the meaning of this?" said he. "I only wrote one of these. Who wrote the other?"

"That's more than I can tell you, sir. My mate here says you wrote it, sitting at this desk, at noon today."

The captain of the wreck and the passenger looked at each other, exchanging glances of intelligence and surprise; and the former asked the latter, "Did you dream that you wrote on this slate?"

"No, sir, not that I remember."

"You speak of dreaming," said the captain of the bark. "What was this gentleman about at noon today?"

"Captain," rejoined the other, "the whole thing is most mysterious and extraordinary; and I had intended to speak to you about it as soon as we got a little quiet. This gentleman," pointing to the passenger, "being much exhausted, fell into a heavy sleep, or what seemed such, some time before noon. After an hour or more, he awoke, and said to me, 'Captain, we shall be relieved this very day.' When I asked him what reason he had for saying so, he replied that he had dreamed that he was on board a bark, and that she was coming to our rescue. He described her appearance and rig; and, to our utter astonishment, when your vessel hove in sight she corresponded exactly to his description of her. We had not put much faith in what he said; yet still we hoped there might be something in it, for drowning men, you know, will catch at straws. As it has turned out I cannot doubt that it was all arranged, in some incomprehensible way, by an overruling Providence, so that we might be saved. To him be all thanks for his goodness to us."

"There is not a doubt," rejoined the other captain, "that the writing on the slate, let it have come there as it may, saved all your lives. I was steering at the time considerably south of west, and I altered my course to nor'west, and had a look-out aloft, to see what would come of it. But you say," he added, turning to the passenger, "that you did not dream of writing on a slate?"

"No, sir. I have no recollection whatever of doing so. I got the impression that the bark I saw in my dream was coming to rescue us; but how that impression came I cannot tell. There is another very strange thing about it," he added. "Everything here on board seems to me quite familiar; yet I am very sure I never was in your vessel before. It is all a puzzle to me. What did your mate see?"

Thereupon Mr. Bruce related to them all the circumstances above detailed. The conclusion they finally arrived at was, that it was a special interposition of Providence to save them from what seemed a hopeless fate.

The above narrative was communicated to me by Capt. J.S. Clarke, of the schooner *Julia Hallock*, who had it directly from Mr. Bruce himself. They sailed together for 17 months, in the years 1836 and '37; so that Capt. Clarke had the story from the mate about eight years after the occurrence. He has since lost sight of him, and does not know whether he is yet alive. All he has heard of him since they were shipmates is, that he continued to trade to New Brunswick, that he became the master of the brig Comet, and that she was lost.

I asked Capt. Clarke if he knew Bruce well, and what sort of a man he was.

"As truthful and straightforward a man," he replied, "as ever I met in all my life. "We were as intimate as brothers; and two men can't be together, shut up for 17 months in the same ship, without getting to know whether they can trust one another's word or not. He always spoke of the circumstance in terms of reverence, as of an incident that seemed to bring him nearer to God and to another world. I'd stake my life upon it that he told me no lie."

Appendix 8
A Karloff Kavalcade

A roundup of rare photos of Dear Boris from the mid-1950s up to 1968, the year before he died. Also a few newspaper interviews that may be of interest to the committed Karloffians among you. All the photos are from…

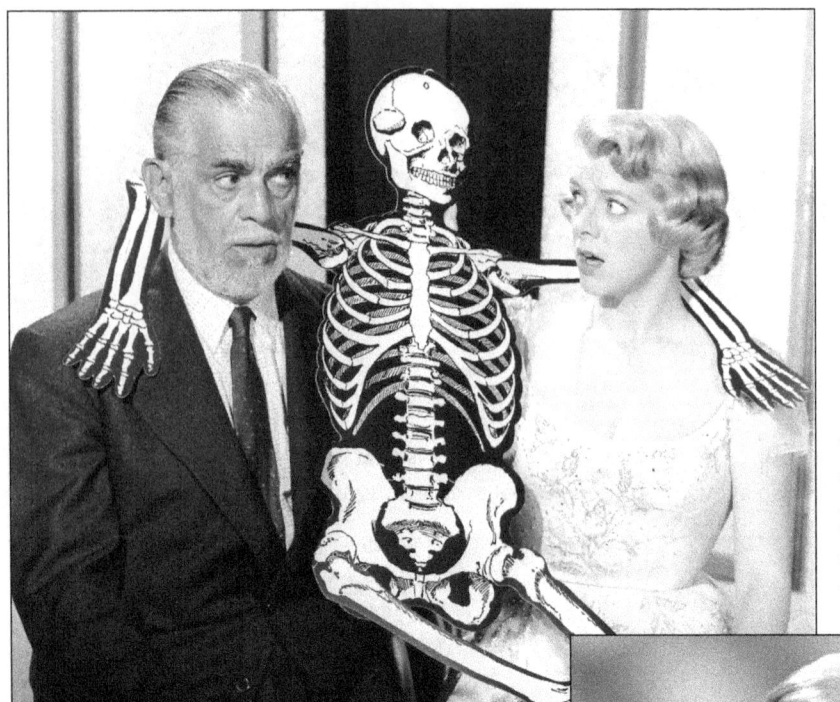

The movie fiend turned silver-haired TV singer-farceur also guested on Rosemary Clooney's teleseries. And I guess for some ... but I can't imagine who ... hilarity ensued.

For better or worse, TV allowed Karloff to let audiences see more of his comic side and hear more of his singing voice. *Variety* panned the February 1955 *Donald O'Connor Show* in which he appeared and pinned the rap on star-producer-director O'Connor. Pictured right to left, Karloff, O'Connor, Jeanne Mahoney.

Karloff set aside all his British reserve when he cavorted on a 1957 *Dinah Shore Chevy Show*. A bat replaced the peacock in the NBC logo, the episode was sponsored by "Shiverolet" and an exuberant Boris helped make it a "gay, snappy and showmanly" good time (*Variety*). Left to right, singing "Little Darlin'": Betty Hutton, Karloff, Dinah Shore and Art Carney.

For NBC-TV in 1957, Karloff and Julie Harris reprised their roles from the Broadway play *The Lark* (1955-56). (The Hallmark Hall of Fame presentation featured Basil Rathbone, also pictured in the photo below.) In 2008, Greg Mank reviewed Karloff's remaining belongings and found his *Lark* play script, marked with many annotations and including some rehearsal snapshots. It was unique in the archive as it appeared to be the only script the actor had saved. Possibly this was because Karloff considered the play his high point as a serious actor: He was Tony-nominated for Best Actor.

Karloff Wants a Gentle Role

★ ★ ★
After 50 Years, He'd Bury Frankenstein

By JAMES BACON

HOLLYWOOD—(AP)—Boris Karloff celebrates his 50th anniversary as an actor in 1959—and his greatest ambition is to portray a charming, poised, articulate, soft-spoken gentleman.

It's a role that the master of the horror films says he never has played on stage or screen. Although he didn't say it, such a portrayal would be tantamount to Boris Karloff playing the off-screen Boris Karloff.

At 71, he is one of the busiest actors in the business. He recently made a movie in England called "The Doctor From Seven Dials," in which he enacts the discoverer of modern medical anesthesia.

So far, he says, it is his favorite all-time film role.

What about Frankenstein? Has that role been a monster for him?

"Of course not," he answers. "I have no regrets ever for having played the monster. It changed my whole life. I was just another actor until I played that. It made me a personality."

Just 3 Times

There have been a dozen or so monsters portrayed on the screen since Karloff's first in 1931. He has appeared in the role only three times. Yet, the monster label has always dogged him.

Unlike the late Bela Lugosi, whose portrayal of "Dracula" made it hard to get other roles, Karloff is one of the most versatile actors in the business.

Karloff in some of the roles he made famous
As "The Mummy"   As "Frankenstein"

He currently is starring in a new television series for Hal Roach Jr., called "The Veil." It's that studio's answer to the saturation of TV Westerns. In the series, Karloff plays an entirely different character in each episode. Theme of the series is extra-sensory perception.

It's a chiller, but as Karloff says, "in an intellectual way."

Groucho Marx tells of the time back in 1931 when he was alone in his big house except for a maid. The Frankenstein monster had not yet been seen on the screen but Groucho reports that Karloff phoned him that he was coming over from Universal to see him.

"I was in a back room playing my guitar," recalls Groucho, "when the doorbell rang. The maid opened it. I heard her scream. She later fainted.

"Then I heard these heavy footsteps coming down the hall to my room. The door opened and there stood this monster. It was Karloff in his get-up."

Groucho said Karloff, an old friend, thought it would be a great rib if he came over to see Groucho the first time he put on the makeup.

"He came over in a cab," recalls Groucho. "I've always wondered how many people stopped drinking after pulling up to a stop light and glancing over to the back seat of that cab with Karloff sitting there."

Karloff pooh poohs the story.

"Groucho exaggerates," says Karloff. "I didn't intend it as a rib. He just happened to have his house for sale and I had a few hours off from the set so I went over to look at the house. It was a perfectly normal thing to do."

This Associated Press article commemorated Karloff's 50th year as an actor and plugged *The Veil*.

IT'S GOOD TO GO HOME
by BORIS KARLOFF

ALL PRODIGAL SONS go home sooner or later. Even if it's 50 years later.

I suppose when you're 72, you're bound to wake up one morning and say, "I've got to go home."

That's what happened to me. That's why I'm living in London again, half a century after I sailed away from England feeling very much the black sheep.

I was the youngest of eight sons, you see, and a lazy little devil. I never knew my father; he died when I was an infant. He was in the diplomatic service, and he thought of government service as the only logical career for all his eight sons.

My brothers obeyed—most of them spent their lives in India and China—but you had to pass a stiff examination, and I wasn't keen on study. Not since the day, when I was 11, that I performed in a parish play. From then on I was determined to be an actor.

This amused my family when I was a boy, but not when I grew up. My brothers were horrified. I was obstinate. And in those days there was only one decent thing for the disobedient son to do—"go to the colonies." So I flipped a coin for Canada or Australia—and it came up Canada.

My brothers were delighted to get rid of me. It was "Here's half a crown, my boy, and never let us see your face again." It took me years to realize that they were giving me the best possible help merely by allowing me to make my own way in the world. Each of my brothers made his own success, and I am quite sure I never would have succeeded as an actor if they had continued supporting me indefinitely.

But there I was 50 years ago, 22-year-old William Henry Pratt of Enfield, England, sitting in western Canada without a penny but full of determination to "sink or swim" as an actor. Well, for 20 years I floundered. My good fortune didn't come till I was in my forties, by which time I had learned that while there's no particular advantage in going hungry occasionally, at least it doesn't kill you.

My fortune was of course *Frankenstein*, and it was a great relief to my brothers as well as to me. Though I remember my oldest brother Ted, Judge Edward Pratt, telling me:

"I hope you're saving every farthing you can lay your hands on, my boy, because obviously this can't go on much longer."

It has gone on though, much longer than I had any right to expect. America has been good to me, and even now that I'm home, I can't give up the United States. I commute from London to Los Angeles every eight weeks to film my NBC television series, *Thriller*. A long way to go for a job, perhaps, but it gives me both things I want: the work for which I played the prodigal 50 years ago, and . . . home. ∎

London's famed "Big Ben," unchanged in 50 years, is one of Boris Karloff's homecoming thrills.

After a decade as a Manhattanite, Karloff went back to the warm bosom (well, the rainy, cold bosom) of Mother England. He described his final relo in this 1960 article.

Boris and Evie Karloff during the making of the *Route 66* episode "Lizard's Leg and Owlet's Wing." "I'm sorry *Route 66* even took a shot at the Frankenstein makeup — pitiful," said *Cult Movies* magazine writer Rich Scrivani. "I hated it right from the first time I saw it in 1962. 'We've got all this extra cookie dough, Mr. Karloff, so if you don't mind…'"

After years of stage success with *Arsenic and Old Lace*, Karloff did it three times on TV, including this 1962 Hallmark Hall of Fame production. Sitting: Mildred Natwick and Dorothy Stickney as Martha and Abby Brewster and Tom Bosley as Teddy. Standing: George Voskovec as Dr. Einstein, Boris as Jonathan and Tony Randall as Mortimer.

By 1962, Karloff had his fill of appearing in his own weekly TV series. He told an interviewer that while making *The Raven*, he and Peter Lorre were propositioned by a promoter to star in a series, and they chased him from the set. "Who wants to go back to stock? I want to take time out to live. I spent the summer watching the cricket matches in England, and now rugby is in full cry. I can hardly wait to get back. What does one work for, if not to enjoy the fruits of his labor?".

The grand old man of horror flicks looks grandly happy to pose with devoted wife Evie.

For the animated TV special (and instant classic) Dr. Seuss' *How the Grinch Stole Christmas!* (1966), narrator Karloff won the one award of his life, a Grammy. Pictured: producer-director Chuck Jones and Karloff.

Endnotes

Endnote for "Behind The Veil"

1 Here is that website's write-up on Dad's documentary *Project Hope*: On September 22, 1960, the SS *Hope* set sail on its maiden voyage from San Francisco bound for Indonesia. During that time, the hospital ship's volunteer personnel managed to train hundreds of doctors and nurses, open an orthopedic rehabilitation center in Indonesia and treat thousands of people suffering from cancer, leprosy, infections and malnutrition. A documentary film entitled *Project Hope* captured this first mission, and director Frank P. Bibas won the 1961 Academy Award for Best Documentary Short Subject.

[Bibas] accompanied medical volunteers serving onboard the SS *Hope* for three months on its maiden voyage to Indonesia. While oversees and midway through film production, Bibas and his film crew learned the ad agency that contracted the film, cancelled the project and informed him that he should cut production and return to the U.S. Instead of doing so, he negotiated a deal which allowed him to keep the film footage in lieu of payment, because he knew there "was an important story to tell."

The film aimed to show that America was a good friend to the world, helping those in need. It also served as an effective fundraising tool. The film was translated into 23 languages which helped expand Project Hope's reach to secure additional missions to Vietnam, Peru, Ecuador, Guinea, Nicaragua, Colombia, Ceylon (Sri Lanka), Tunisia, Jamaica and Brazil.

Although the SS *Hope* was retired in 1974, the spirit of those first missions lives on in the film Bibas believed in.

Endnotes for "The Veil" Production History and Episode Guide

1 Roach paperwork reveals that Tudor Owen was originally cast as the Scotsman, but in the episode the role is played by Kendrick Huxham. It ended up as a non-speaking part, so Owen missed out on nothing but a paycheck. Owen later appeared in *The Veil*'s "No Food on the Table."

2 Ruth Burch had a long and interesting career which started in the 1930s when she and her husband moved to L.A. and Ruth got a job as Hal Roach's secretary. By the end of the decade, she was his casting director. (She "discovered" Victor Mature when he was at the Pasadena Playhouse, washing dishes for enough to eat, and sleeping in a tent.) In the 1940s, Burch – Hollywood's only woman casting director – went from Roach to David O. Selznick, helping to cast *Since You Went Away*, *Duel in the Sun* and Hitchcock's *Spellbound* and *Notorious*. She then became an agent.

After that, Burch worked as an independent casting director, filling supporting roles on such classic TV series as *My Little Margie*, *I Love Lucy*, *Our Miss Brooks*, *Make Room for Daddy*, *The Dick Van Dyke Show* and *The Andy Griffith Show*. In 1955, United Press' Aline Mosby quoted an unnamed actor as saying, "If you don't know Ruth Burch, you don't work in TV," and there may be some truth in that: In a 1956 article, Burch wrote, "Each year I cast more than 5000 players for 15 television programs" and that she set aside every Tuesday "as casting day for new faces. With the help of Kerwin Coughlin, my assistant, I interview 80, 90,100 hopefuls, all sizes, shapes and ages, in a six-hour span." She was still at it in the 1990s, when she was in her 90s. Burch was 100 when she died at the Motion Picture and Television Hospital in 2000.

3 From King Features Syndicate writer Harrison Carroll's column "Behind the Scenes in Hollywood," mid-September 1940: "In spite of all that's happening in England [the Blitz], BK's niece, Diana Pratt, is returning home to enter a famous university this fall. She has been staying with the star for several months now. Boris said that he has advised strongly against the trip but his niece won't be dissuaded. She made her application three years ago to enter the school and she says that German bombs are not going to stop her. She already has booked passage and sails within the next two weeks."

Endnotes for Appendix 3

1 British audiences had the chance to see six episodes of *Inspector Morley of Scotland Yard*, though only in re-edited form, by way of the theatrical features *King of the Underworld* and *Murder at Scotland Yard* (both 1952).

2 *Broadcasting•Telecasting*, March 7, 1949, 18.

3 "Two on the TV Aisle," *Radio and Television Mirror*, March 1949, 78.

4 Ronald L. Smith, *Horror Stars on Radio: The Broadcast Histories of 29 Chilling Hollywood Voices*, Jefferson NC: McFarland, 2010, 19-23.

5 "Expert Opinion" would be adapted for television again as the August 1, 1949, episode of NBC's *Colgate Theatre* with Richard Hart in the lead role. The same cast and crew restaged the production a week later to serve as the August 8, 1949 episode of the network's *The Clock*.

6 "A Passenger to Bali" had previously been adapted for radio by Orson Welles in an hour-long version for *The Mercury Theatre on the Air* (November 13, 1938) and in a half-hour version for *The Mercury Summer Theatre on the Air* (July 5, 1946). Another television adaptation would follow as the March 27, 1950, episode of CBS's *Studio One* with Berry Kroeger playing Ralph Walkes.

7 Collier's 1938 story would be memorably adapted for CBS-TV as the September 30, 1956, opening episode of the second season of *Alfred Hitchcock Presents*, starring Sir Cedric Hardwicke.

8 See for example "Teen-agers Like Mysteries," *Sponsor*, April 1948, 29, 52.

9 "Drama Gaining in Viewers' Preferences," *Broadcasting•Telecasting*, November 14, 1949, 48. Two further mystery-suspense television drama anthology shows originating from radio featured in the results, with NBC's *The Clock* in seventh place, watched by 28.8 percent of interviewees, and the same network's *Lights Out* in ninth place, watched by 26.8 percent.

10 "Boris Karloff Stars in First of Series on WGN-TV April 11," *Chicago* (IL) *Sunday Tribune*, April 3, 1949, Part 3, 17SW.

11 "ABC Signs Karloff for Fall TV Series," *The Billboard*, July 16, 1949, 11. This news item incorrectly maintains that Karloff "had a brief TV run a couple seasons ago, but his show was yanked because it was considered too horror-laden." In fact, the show referred to was a *radio* revival of *Lights Out* by ABC which had been scheduled as the summer replacement for *The Henry Morgan Show* and intended to run from July 16 through September 3, 1947. Reviewers found the revival to be disconcertingly strong meat. Even though *Variety* averred that the opening July 16 episode ("Death Robbery," co-starring Lurene Tuttle as a housewife returned to life by a doctor [Karloff], only no longer in possession of her soul) was "well tailored and effectively presented," it further commented, "Mystery, detective and crime shows seem like good clean fun alongside this horror of horrors. Why anyone without a barely latent thirst for blood would care to inflict these ghoulish goings-on on themselves of a hot summer night is hard to understand." Two further episodes, "The Undead" and "The Ring," were broadcast on July 23 and 30, before a *Billboard* news item dated August 2 revealed that Karloff had stepped down from the show, stating "his dissatisfaction with the scripting, which he claims is too much on the gruesome and frightening side." The program was canceled with immediate effect. It's possible that Henry Morgan had jinxed the entire enterprise by declaring at the end of his departing July 9 show that he hoped nobody would buy any of sponsor Eversharp-Schick's razors while he was away on his eight-week vacation! See also *The Billboard*, August 9, 1947, 5; *The Billboard*, August 16, 1947, 10; and *Variety*, July 23, 1947, 32.

12 Larry Wolters, "Radio's Tiptop Shows Arrange Double in TV," *Chicago* (IL) *Daily Tribune*, September 21, 1949, Part 2, 5. Wolters explicitly mentions "the Boris Karloff mystery series on ABC" in this discussion of "dual format" shows.

13 Boris Karloff, letter to Sir John Pratt, November 6, 1949, quoted in Stephen Jacobs, *Boris Karloff – More Than a Monster: The Authorised Biography*, Sheffield (UK): Tomahawk Press, 2011, 335.

14 Sonia Stein, "Karloff Likes to Scare People," *The Washington* (DC) *Post*, December 11, 1949, quoted in Jacobs, 333.

15 *Ibid.*

16 "Karloff to Star in *Conflict*," *Olean* (NY) *Times Herald*, September 9, 1949, 9; *Des Moines* (IA) *Register*, September 21, 1949, 11; Charlene Brown, "The Open Mike," *Kokomo* (IN) *Tribune*, September 20, 1949, 10; *The Battle Creek* (MI) *Enquirer and News*, September 21, 1949, 22; and *The Anniston* (AL) *Star*, September 21, 1949, 8.

17 "Block Drama Programming Increases on Web Schedules," *Radio Daily*, October 3, 1949, 5.

18 *Burlington* (VT) *Free Press*, September 28, 1949, 15.

19 *The Long Beach* (CA) *Independent*, October 27, 1949, 10B.

20 *The Billboard*, October 1, 1949, 11.

21 *Ibid.*

22 *Ibid.* Robert Stephen Brode's previous forays into screenwriting included RKO's *Dick Tracy's Dilemma* (1947) and several 1948 episodes of NBC's television crime series *Public Prosecutor* with John Howard and Anne Gwynne.

23 See for example the front-page article "Gold Chaplet Crowns Early Peruvian Mummy," *Los Angeles Times*, September 21, 1949, Part 1, 1.

24 In reality the mummy was placed on public exhibition at the American Museum of Natural History from September 30 through October 17, 1949. See for example "Mummy on Display," *Brooklyn* (NY) *Eagle*, September 30, 1949, 4; and Robert C. Ruark, "Lethal Art Changes But Results Always the Same," *El Paso* (TX) *Herald-Post*, October 3, 1949, 8.

25 *The Cincinnati* (OH) *Enquirer*, October 13, 1949, 16.

26 *Long Beach* (CA) *Press-Telegram*, November 16, 1949, A12.

27 *Pittsburgh Post-Gazette Daily Magazine* (supplement to the *Pittsburgh* [PA] *Post-Gazette*), October 26, 1949, 3.

28 *The Cincinnati* (OH) *Enquirer*, October 6, 1949, 18.

29 See especially "Suggestion for Death Is Theme of Oboler's Drama," *The Shreveport* (LA) *Times*, October 27, 1942, 12. Another television adaptation of "Munghara" was produced as the March 28, 1952, episode of MCA-TV/Revue Productions' filmed anthology series *Chevron Theatre* starring John Hoyt and Gar Moore, and also featuring George Zucco's daughter Frances. The episode was subsequently rebroadcast as the August 15, 1954, installment of ABC's *The Pepsi-Cola Playhouse*, in which form it would continue to play in syndication until as late as 1965.

30 Jacobs, 329.

31 Kermit Bloomgarden's Broadway production of *The Lark* at the Longacre Theatre ran for 229 performances from November 17, 1955, to June 2, 1956. At the 1956 Tony Awards, Julie Harris won in the "Best Performance by an Actress in a Leading Role in a Play" category (in which she was up against Barbara Bel Geddes, Gladys Cooper, Ruth Gordon, Siobhán McKenna and Susan Strasberg), while Karloff was nominated in the "Best Performance by an Actor in a Leading Role in a Play" category (which was won by Paul Muni for *Inherit the Wind*). *The Lark* picked up further nominations for Best Direction (by Joseph Anthony), Best Costume Design (by Alvin Colt) and Best Scenic Design (by Jo Mielziner). In addition to Karloff and Harris, original Broadway cast members Michael Higgins (as Ladvenu), Bruce Gordon (as La Hire) and Ralph Roberts (as the executioner) reprised their roles in the *Hallmark Hall of Fame* rendition.

32 *Sponsor*, October 5, 1953, 44.

33 The first two episodes of *Colonel March of Scotland Yard* aired on KTTV prior to the station dissolving its affiliation with the DuMont Network.

34 *Brooklyn* (NY) *Eagle*, December 4, 1953, 29.

35 See for example "SG Sells 'Horror' Package to Nine Stations in Week," *Broadcasting•Telecasting*, August 26, 1957, 66.

36 "Second 'Horror' Package Offered," *Broadcasting•Telecasting*, September 2, 1957, 79.

37 Much of this ethos had already been communicated by Karloff back in 1949 when he discussed *Starring Boris Karloff* with Sonia Stein of *The Washington* (DC) *Post*: "An actor should be constantly working at his trade…. I must have developed myself as an actor during this series." Quoted in Jacobs, 334.

38 Terence Fisher had, incidentally, directed the episode "The Invisible Knife" from Karloff's filmed television series *Colonel March of Scotland Yard*.

39 *Television Digest*, October 26, 1957, 10.

40 Tom Weaver, *The Horror Hits of Richard Gordon*, Duncan (OK): BearManor Media, 2011, 84.

41 Many newspapers published shortened versions of Bacon's syndicated column that did not include this statement by Karloff. One source that published the unexpurgated text, in which *Corridors of Blood* is referred to under its working title *Doctor of Seven Dials*, was the *Raleigh Register* (Beckley, WV), January 6, 1959, 8. When MGM belatedly released the feature in the U.S. in 1963, it was reviewed in *Film Bulletin*, June 10, 1963, 24, as a "[w]ell-made drama of doctor's research in drugs" and "really not a true horror picture. Realism and integrity are sustained throughout... The literate script by Jean Scott Rogers is rooted in fact, and the setting of London, 1840, is authentically reproduced... Karloff virtually monopolizes the film as an idealistic surgeon dedicated to developing an anesthetic to relieve the tortures of patients undergoing operations."

42 *The Independent* (Pasadena, CA), September 21, 1957, 7; and *Sponsor*, September 28, 1957, 46.

43 Ann Wardell Saunders, "Looking 'n Listening," *San Bernardino* (CA) *Sun-Telegram*, September 29, 1957, 23; "After Westerns Maybe Horror," *The Billboard*, September 25, 1957, 8; and *Broadcasting•Telecasting*, September 30, 1957, 99.

44 "Start Production on Frankenstein Horror Series," *Sandusky* (OH) *Register*, October 28, 1957, 20.

45 Glen Davies, *The Unfilmed Hammer – Unmade, Unseen, Rewritten and Beyond. The Definitive Edition, 1936-2010*. Self-published in .pdf format, 2011, 32.

46 "Start Production on Frankenstein Horror Series," 20.

47 Harry Harris, "Screening TV," *The Philadelphia* (PA) *Inquirer*, December 19, 1957, 22.

48 *Ibid.* Harris evidently acted like a magnet for agitated readers wishing to compare Karloff with Roland. In his October 27, 1960, column, he published a letter from one "Miss M.L.M. of Havertown" berating the first season of *Thriller*: "These so-called *Thriller* shows are a joke. Old-fashioned, stilted, Victorian-type, ridiculous stories that would scare nobody!... Why Boris Karloff as a host? Even Roland was better!" Harry Harris, "Screening TV," *The Philadelphia* (PA) *Inquirer*, October 27, 1960, 32.

49 See for example "Film-Scope," *Sponsor*, April 5, 1958, 49; and "How Fall TV Programing Shapes Up," *Sponsor*, April 12, 1958, 35.

50 Almost a year after the last substantial reports about the show, "M.G. of Miami, Florida" sent a question to Steven H. Scheuer's "TV Key" column: "Last summer, I recall hearing about a 39-week series starring Boris Karloff, entitled *Tales of Frankenstein*. Can you tell me what has come of this?" The published reply read: "The pilot film for a *Tales of Frankenstein* series was produced, but it did not feature Karloff. ABC-TV was supposed to telecast it on Saturday nights, but couldn't find a sponsor." *The Troy* (NY) *Record*, April 4, 1959, 23.

51 Davies, 32-33.

52 *Television Digest*, April 20, 1957, 7.

53 This does not, of course, imply that the stories being approached in this manner were necessarily anything other than the creations of writers.

54 Obviously it's possible that Karloff had been approached concerning yet a third "series having to do with psychic phenomena," perhaps even ABC's extremely short-lived quiz show *E.S.P.*, which would ultimately employ Vincent Price as its moderator.

55 Jacobs, 427.

56 Karloff's stand-in column appeared on November 25, 1958, east of the Mississippi.

57 *Sponsor*, May 3, 1958, 63.

58 G.H. Kennedy and Vance King (editors), *Production Encyclopedia: 1952 Edition*, Hollywood (CA): The Hollywood Reporter, 1952, 677.

59 *Television Digest*, March 28, 1959, 17.

60 NBC also ditched Milton Berle's *Jackpot Bowling* to make way for the second season of *Thriller*, although this decision was surely predicated on the fact that its bizarre and unfocused bowling-celebrity-comedy-variety set-up had left viewers feeling bamboozled and turning off in droves.

61 *Sponsor*, September 28, 1957, 46. A nationwide survey of teenagers in the summer of 1959 reached comparable conclusions, as reported in Eugene Gilbert, 'Horror Addicts? No, Spook Films are Just Big Fun to Young,' *Lincoln Evening Journal and Nebraska State Journal*, July 11, 1959, 2.

62 "The new quiz show has turned into a series of psychological films dealing with the 'sixth sense.' Vincent Price remains as host, and the home viewers' prize offer is retained," read the vexed description in *The Salt Lake Tribune Home Magazine* (supplement to *The Salt Lake* [UT] *Tribune*), August 17, 1958, 13.

63 *Sponsor*, June 6, 1959, 71; and *Broadcasting*, March 16, 1959, 115.

64 *Report of the Trustees of the U.S. District Court for the Middle District of Pennsylvania in the Matter of Hal Roach Studios and Rabco TV Productions, Debtors, May 26, 1961*, 19, cited in Richard Lewis Ward, *A History of the Hal Roach Studios*, Carbondale (IL): Southern Illinois University Press, 2005, 153.

65 *Ukiah* (CA) *Daily Journal*, May 13, 1959, B4. Many other publications first carried the undated news item days later.

66 Representative of the uncertainty that surrounded the release dates of all and any Hal Roach Studios product during the dying days of the brand, Hedda Hopper had been informed ahead of her October 17, 1958, column that the episode would air for New Year 1959, while Erskine Johnson in his syndicated "Hollywood Today" column of December 22, 1958, believed that it would be broadcast on February 17, 1959.

67 "Boris Raises Flowers – and Goose Bumps: He Discusses New Show," *Detroit* (MI) *Free Press*, August 21, 1960, 8TV. This advance publicity piece for *Thriller* was published in many tens of newspapers and supplements.

68 Gay had been jointly nominated, with Terence Rattigan, for an Academy Award in the "Best Writing, Screenplay Based on Material from Another Medium" category for *Separate Tables* (1958). Wendy Hiller and David Niven indeed won Academy Awards for the movie, in the "Best Actress in a Leading Role" and "Best Actor in a Leading Role" categories.

69 Win Fanning, "Boris Karloff at 73 Still as Busy as Ever," *Post-Gazette Daily Magazine* (supplement to the *Pittsburgh* [PA] *Post-Gazette*), February 22, 1960, 3. Karloff would not actually

turn 73 until November 23, 1960.

70 See for example "Winter Book on the Fall Lineup," *Broadcasting*, February 15, 1960, 31; and "Hitchcock Switch," *Broadcasting*, February 22, 1960, 68.

71 Jacobs, 434.

72 "In Review: *Alfred Hitchcock Presents*," *Broadcasting•Telecasting*, October 10, 1955, 12.

73 Pinky Herman, "Television – Radio," *Motion Picture Daily*, August 10, 1955, 7; and "Shows on the Mark," *Motion Picture Daily*, August 15, 1955, 11.

74 "*TV Radio Mirror* Award Winners, 1956-57," *TV Radio Mirror*, May 1957, 31.

75 Charlotte Barclay, "The Horror 'Kick,'" *TV Radio Mirror*, May 1959, 50-53, 81-82.

76 This does not, of course, preclude the possibility that, prior to hosting *Alfred Hitchcock Presents*, Hitchcock might have seen or potentially been influenced by the press attention-grabbing *The Vampira Show* while it aired in Los Angeles from April to August 1954.

77 *Orlando* (FL) *Sentinel*, August 1, 1960, 8B.

78 *The Daily Herald Weekly TV and Amusements Guide* (supplement to *The Daily Herald* [Provo, UT]), August 29, 1960, 1.

79 Cecil Smith, "Nation Braces for Tuesday Jitters," *Los Angeles* (CA) *Times*, September 13, 1960, Part II, 8.

80 Win Fanning, "A Promising Three for Next Season," *Pittsburgh* (PA) *Post-Gazette and Sun-Telegraph*, June 19, 1960, Section 5, 4.

81 Aleene Barnes, "Karloff Runs *Thriller* Biz," *Los Angeles Times TV Times* (supplement to the *Los Angeles* [CA] *Times*), September 11, 1960, 11.

82 An earlier description of the show furnished by Robinson referred to it as "a combination of mystery and adventure, with special accent on stories of normal people who find themselves – because of emotion, greed or circumstances – involved in or threatened by crime." "Stars Signed for 'The Twisted Image,'" *Entertainment in the Reno Area* (supplement to the *Reno* [NV] *Evening Gazette*), March 11, 1960, 11.

83 See especially Alan Warren, *This Is a "Thriller": An Episode Guide, History and Analysis of the Classic 1960s Television Series*, Jefferson NC: McFarland, 2004, 9-11. Hubbell Robinson Productions' so-called "entertainment anthology series" *Startime* for NBC the previous year had likewise suffered from directionlessness, with its content alternating unpredictably from week to week between musical performance, earnest drama, variety and so forth. Although individual episodes were highly acclaimed, including its October 20, 1959, adaptation of Henry James' "The Turn of the Screw" starring Ingrid Bergman, the show as a whole shifted around too haphazardly to engender much audience loyalty and was canceled after a single season.

84 *Orlando* (FL) *Sentinel*, September 13, 1960, 8B.

85 *Los Angeles Times TV Times* (supplement to the *Los Angeles* [CA] *Times*), September 11, 1960, 1.

86 Samuel L. Singer, "Boris Karloff to Host, Act in Thrill Series," *The Philadelphia* (PA) *Inquirer*, September 12, 1960, 26.

87 Dick Shippy, "Audio and Visual," *Akron* (OH) *Beacon Journal*, September 14, 1960, 64.

88 Fred Danzig, "New TV *Thriller* Routine and Shabby," *The New Mexican* (Santa Fe, NM), September 14, 1960, 17.

89 *San Mateo* (CA) *Times*, September 14, 1960, 23.

90 Win Fanning, "*Thriller* Wasn't; Colonialism on 13," *Pittsburgh* (PA) *Post-Gazette*, September 15, 1960, 47.

91 Harry Harris, "Karloff Wrong on *Thriller*," *The Philadelphia* (PA) *Inquirer*, September 14, 1960, 38.

92 Ogden Dwight, "On Television," *Des Moines* (IA) *Register*, September 19, 1960, 22; Charlie Wadsworth, "Mr. Robinson Goes to Bat with NBC's *Thriller*," *Orlando* (FL) *Sentinel*, September 14, 1960, 5B; Danzig, 17; and Fred Remington, "*Thriller*'s Opener Was Anything But: First of the New Hour Shows Was Shabby, Tedious, Implausible," *Pittsburgh* (PA) *Press*, September 14, 1960, 74.

93 Shippy, 64.

94 Amid all the negative reviews of "The Twisted Image," Fanning's stood out for going singularly gentle on his regular interviewee Karloff: "This accomplished actor, this truly gentle man, deserves better. Much better." Fanning, "*Thriller* Wasn't; Colonialism on 13," 47.

95 Like Win Fanning before her, Hopper was wrong about Karloff having already turned 73, which wouldn't happen until November 23, 1960.

96 Hopper's math is again off, since Karloff had entered pictures in 1919.

97 Fanning, "*Thriller* Wasn't; Colonialism on 13," 47.

98 A detailed account of these changes can be found in Warren, 11-19.

99 *Film Bulletin*, October 3, 1960, 23.

100 *Broadcasting*, February 19, 1962, 44.

101 Harold A. Nichols, "*Thriller* Didn't," *Rochester* (NY) *Democrat and Chronicle*, September 14, 1960, 15.

102 Singer, 26.

103 See for example Fred Danzig's syndicated United Press International "Television in Review" column of October 19, 1960.

104 Warren, 19.

105 Warren, 20.

106 *The Daily Herald* (Provo UT), November 7, 1960, 6.

107 Harry Harris, "Screening TV," *The Philadelphia* (PA) *Inquirer*, January 5, 1961, 8.

108 Eunice Field, "What's New on the West Coast," *TV Radio Mirror*, January 1961, 6.

109 Cecil Smith, "The TV Scene," *Los Angeles* (CA) *Times*, February 21, 1961, Part II, 10.

110 Cecil Smith at the time described this line-up as "one of those superb casts that only producer-director George Schaefer seems able to assemble." Cecil Smith, "The TV Scene: Karloff – Arsenic, Very Old Lace," *Los Angeles* (CA) *Times*, February 5, 1962, Part IV, 12.

111 *The Philadelphia* (PA) *Inquirer*, January 24, 1962, 14.

112 Vernon Scott, "Not Like Old Days: Film Monsters Now Fun-

ny, Says Karloff," *The Evening Press* (Binghamton, NY), March 7, 1961, 8. Karloff adds, "I feel sure that if a truly good terror script came along with a believable monster, it would find great success. But it would have to be reasonable and believable."

113 See for example the *Orlando* (FL) *Sentinel*, February 26, 1962, 8B.

114 "Let's You and Him Fight – Off Screen: Now TV Violence is Falling on the Cutting Room Floor," *Broadcasting*, August 28, 1961, 74-76. On page 10 of the same issue, an anonymous contributor referencing the forthcoming *Thriller* episode "Masquerade" suggests under the heading "Grim humor": "Perhaps one approach to counteracting charges of violence leveled at network tv programs is to inject humor."

115 *Television Digest*, February 27, 1961, 5.

116 Warren, 23.

117 "Hubbell's Homecoming," *Television Digest*, March 12, 1962, 4.

118 "Three New MCA TV Series," *Broadcasting*, March 12, 1962, 5.

119 Rick Du Brow, "Hitchcock Air Time Will Be Extended Next Season," *The Times Record* (Troy, NY), May 16, 1962, 21.

120 All three are included on the Region 2 DVD *Out of This World: "Little Lost Robot*," London (UK): British Film Institute, 2014. The audio recording of "Impostor" is lacking approximately five minutes of the episode.

121 When first published in *Galaxy Science Fiction*, July 1952, 49-74, "Dumb Martian" was presented as a 'novelet.'

122 "An Empty Face in Space," *TV Times*, June 22, 1962, 13.

123 Quoted from the original script in Leonard White, *Armchair Theatre: The Lost Years*, London (UK): Kelly Publications, 2003, 72.

124 Hendry subsequently headlined such genre fare as *Children of the Damned* (1964), *Journey to the Far Side of the Sun* (1969) and *Tales from the Crypt* (1972), and portrayed Price and Rigg's archnemesis Peregrine Devlin, head of the Critics' Circle, in *Theatre of Blood*.

125 Born to Jewish émigré parents in London, the ten-year-old Shubik had been evacuated to Canada together with 13-year-old brother Martin following the declaration of war in Europe in 1939. The siblings maintained a transatlantic outlook thereafter with Martin studying at the University of Toronto and Princeton University prior to joining the faculty of Yale University in 1963; he rose to become one of the nation's foremost economists. The pair's elder brother Philippe had been educated at Oxford University and served as a medical doctor in World War II. Moving to Chicago in 1947, he established himself as a leading cancer specialist, employed as director of the Institute of Medical Research at Chicago Medical School from 1957 to 1967 and as expert advisor to the World Health Organization from 1960. See in particular Irene Shubik, *Play for Today: The Evolution of Television Drama*, 2nd ed., Manchester (UK): Manchester University Press, 2001, ix-xii.

126 Carnell (known to many, including Shubik, by his middle name John although family members and childhood friends called him Ted) initially served as the magazine's editor in 1946 and occupied the position anew from 1949 to 1963.

127 Boris Karloff, "Stand By for Shocks," *TV Times*, June 22, 1962, 13.

128 Raymond E. Palmer, "Karloff to Play Himself, an Ordinary Englishman," *Fort Myers* (FL) *News-Press*, August 29, 1962, 7A. The undated story was carried without Palmer's byline in other U.S. newspapers as early as August 24.

129 White, 72. In the 2014 audio commentary for the DVD *Out of This World: "Little Lost Robot*," White further remarks: "It wasn't inappropriate to ask Boris Karloff…to introduce the series, because he played so many peculiar – I might say 'out of this world' – characters."

130 White, 79.

131 A limited number of British television shows had been produced in color prior to 1967 for the purpose of overseas sales, in particular to the U.S. Such a consideration clearly wouldn't have applied to a live series intended solely for domestic consumption such as *Out of This World*.

132 White, 72.

133 H.F. Hall, *Yorkshire Evening Post*, July 25, 1962; and Tony Gruner, *Kinematograph Weekly*, August 9, 1962, both quoted in White, 78.

134 U.S. distributors may have been happy to release the movies but they surely didn't like their titles. To wit: *The Quatermass Xperiment* (1955, U.S.: *The Creeping Unknown*), *Quatermass 2* (1957, U.S.: *Enemy from Space*), *The Strange World of Planet X* (1958, U.S.: *Cosmic Monsters*), *The Trollenberg Terror* (1958, U.S.: *The Crawling Eye*) and *Quatermass and the Pit* (1967, U.S.: *Five Million Years to Earth*).

135 *Sponsor*, January 1, 1962, 37.

136 "From Our Special Correspondent," *The Times*, August 4, 1962; and Peter Black, *Daily Mail*, September 17, 1962, both quoted in White, 79.

137 http://monsterkidclassichorrorforum.yuku.com/reply/1237994/SCRIPTS-FROM-THE-CRYPT-7-Boris-Karloffs-The-Veil#reply-1237994   Retrieved May 3, 2017.

Other Books from the "Scripts from the Crypt" Collection available from BearManor Media

ISBN 9781593937003
$24.95

ISBN 9781593937010
$24.95

ISBN 1593938233
$24.95

ISBN 9781593938574
$24.95

ISBN 1593939205
$29.95

ISBN 1629331163
$24.95